WRITING ACROSS LANGUAGES AND CULTURES

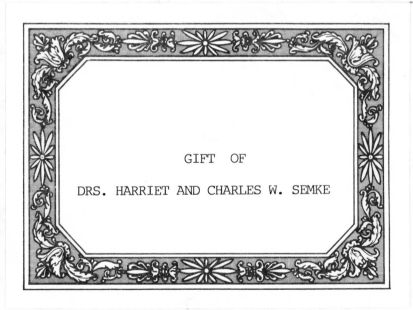

WRITTEN COMMUNICATION ANNUAL

An International Survey of Research and Theory

Series Editors

Charles R. Cooper, *University of California, San Diego*
Sidney Greenbaum, *University College, London*

Written Communication Annual provides an international forum for cross-disciplinary research on written language. The **Annual** presents the best of current research and at the same time seeks to define new research possibilities. Its purpose is to increase understanding of written language and the processes of its production and comprehension. Each volume of the **Annual** focuses on a single topic and includes specially commissioned papers from several countries.

Volumes in This Series

Volume 1   STUDYING WRITING: Linguistic Approaches
           Charles R. Cooper and Sidney Greenbaum
Volume 2   WRITING ACROSS LANGUAGES
           AND CULTURES: Issues in Contrastive Rhetoric
           Alan C. Purves

WRITING ACROSS LANGUAGES AND CULTURES
Issues in Contrastive Rhetoric

edited by

ALAN C. PURVES,
State University of New York, Albany

WRITTEN COMMUNICATION ANNUAL
An International Survey of
Research and Theory

Volume 2

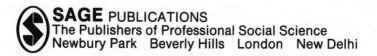

SAGE PUBLICATIONS
The Publishers of Professional Social Science
Newbury Park   Beverly Hills   London   New Delhi

For information address:

SAGE Publications, Inc.
2111 West Hillcrest Drive
Newbury Park, California 91320

SAGE Publications Inc.
275 South Beverly Drive
Beverly Hills
California 90212

SAGE Publications Ltd.
28 Banner Street
London EC1Y 8QE
England

SAGE PUBLICATIONS India Pvt. Ltd.
M-32 Market
Greater Kailash I
New Delhi 110 048 India

Printed in the United States of America

International Standard Book Number 0-8039-2686-3 (c)

International Standard Book Number 0-8039-2687-1 (p)

International Standard Series Number 0883-9298

Library of Congress Catalog Card No. 88-80974

FIRST PRINTING 1988

Contents

Preface

Children learn to speak through frequent exposure to samples of their language, and through interaction in speech with their peers and with adults. In contrast, they learn to write through formal instruction, normally in a school setting. Children have little need to write outside school, but they are called upon to write frequently as students. Many are later required to write frequently as members of a society that is advancing technologically. Both the content and the form of various functions of writing are culturally determined. To be effective, writers have to learn what is expected of them within their own culture.

Differences in cultural expectations are an obstacle for those who are learning to write in a foreign language. Under the influence of the norms within their own culture, they may deviate from the norms of the foreign culture in what kinds of material are to be included in a particular variety of writen discourse, what style is appropriate, and how the discourse is to be organized. In quite another domain, differences in cultural expectations also confront scholars who want to compare across cultures the standards of student writing and the criteria used for evaluating student writing. What may be valued in one culture may be disregarded or even stigmatized in another.

Such issues are addressed in this volume on contrastive rhetoric. It brings together contributions from scholars of several countries, who present contrastive studies in the rhetoric of writing in a large number of countries. This is the second volume of the *Written Communication Annual: An International Survey of Research and Theory*, which is part of Sage Publications' publishing program in composition studies, a program that includes the quarterly journal, *Written Communication*. This second volume has an obvious interest for teachers of composition, particularly those who teach foreign learners of English. But we also expect it to appeal to many teachers and researchers in rhetoric, linguistics, anthropology, and psychology.

> —*Charles R. Cooper and*
> *Sidney Greenbaum*
> Series Editors

Introduction

ALAN C. PURVES

In the 1960s, when the first large influx of international students in the colleges and universities of Western Europe and the United States was at a flood, teachers of the language of instruction and particularly of English, noted that these students did not write in the way that was expected. What the students wrote was not necessarily wrong, but it was different. Among the first people to examine this phenomenon was Robert Kaplan, who coined the term *contrastive rhetoric* to describe these differences (Kaplan, 1966). We might define rhetoric as the choice of linguistic and structural aspects of discourse—chosen to produce an effect on an audience. Rhetoric, therefore, is a matter of choice with respect to the uses of languages as opposed to those used that are determined by lexical and grammatical strictures. By the term, Kaplan implied that the international students had learned ways of organizing and presenting what they wrote that did not match the standards of the target language and he sought to determine the nature of those differences. He examined the texts that students wrote in the foreign language, in his case, English. This volume expands that approach, to which Kaplan refers in the final essay in the volume, and it explores the differences among student compositions written in the native language, compositions written in a second language (English), and the criteria that monocultural raters use in judging compositions by students from other cultures. This volume focuses on two studies, the International Association for the Evaluation of Educational Achievement (IEA) Study of Written Composition, and the Educational Testing Service Study of the Graduate Record Examination (GRE) and Test of English as a Foreign Language (TOEFL) Study of Composition by international students. The first concentrates on students writing in their mother tongue (or the language of instruction), and the second concentrates on students writing in a foreign language. The first focuses on the actual texts produced by the students, and the second on the criteria used by native speakers of the target language in judging the approximations to appropriate style produced by nonnative speakers.

Three adjunct studies are also included: one by Yamuna Kachru on professional writers of English and Hindi, the second and third by Anna Söter and Chantanee Indrasuta, both on student writing in first and second languages (both of which follow from the IEA study). In this introduction, we will focus on theoretical and methodological issues involved in studying contrastive rhetoric, whether it be viewed from the perspective of textual analysis or analysis of the criteria for judgment of good writing.

CULTURE AND WRITTEN DISCOURSE

Two recent comparative studies of writing, Scribner and Cole's *The Psychology of Literacy* (1981), and Heath's *Ways with Words* (1983), examine the relation of culture to discourse and particularly to written discourse. Scribner and Cole study the Vai of Liberia, among whom there are three types of literates (in the indigenous Vai, in Arabic, and in English) as well as nonliterates. Heath examines two groups of poor Appalachians, one black and one white, and contrasts them with the urbanized middle-class black and white. Both studies point to the fact that written texts, and the ways in which they are used and perceived, vary according to the cultural group to which an individual belongs.

Both studies point to two aspects of that variation: the content or what is written, and the forms or structures or the shape used to encode that content. Together, the two aspects constitute the surface manifestations of cultural differences. In Heath's study, the two Appalachian groups differ as to what should be included in a story. For one group the story must contain only "true" events and it should not have direct speech; for the other, embellishment and fantasy are permitted and dialogue is a staple. The two groups differ, as well, as to the nature of the formulae that are used to open and close a tale. Scribner and Cole show the formulaic nature of Vai letters and how those letters differ from the formulae used by the English writers. The variations in content and form have been studied by many researchers in the areas of comparative literature and contrastive rhetoric.

Behind these surface manifestations of cultural difference lie three other aspects of discourse, and particularly written language, that Heath and Scribner and Cole also suggest. The first of these aspects is the relative stress given to the functions of discourse. If we adopt

Jakobson's listing of functions: expressive, referential, cognitive, metalingual, poetic, and phatic, we see that in both of Heath's groups writing is seen as primarily referential, as it is among the Vai literates in Liberia. There is also some metalingual use of written language. In the Qu'ranic writers, the use of literacy is primarily phatic. In Heath's Black Appalachian group, much oral discourse is poetic, but there is little poetic discourse among the white group. To a certain extent, these functional demands of discourse dictate both the content and the forms it will take. This seems to be particularly true of written discourse.

Closely connected with function, however, and perhaps influencing it, there exist two other aspects of written discourse that seem to vary according to culture and that seem to affect the content and form of texts. One of these aspects we may think of as the cognitive demand of the discourse, as Vähäpassi observes in her chapter in this volume; in other words, the degree to which the writer must "invent" either the content of the written text or the form of the text. Much writing is transcription, in which the writer has both the content and the form and has simply to transcribe them. This is done in copying from oral or written discourse or filling in forms, and much of the writing in all of the cultures these authors study is transcription. Another large segment of the writing involves the organization or reorganization of material that is known to the writer—shopping lists and brief reports, such as directions and the like. The form into which the material is to be placed may also be well known to the writer but the writer has to select it from among a variety of forms; the demand, then, is to select an appropriate form and put the material into the proper places. A third kind of writing involves the generation of both the content and, in many cases, the form or structure—although that may be a conventional form, such as the story, or the rhyme, or the proposal. Such generation appears to play little part in the lives of any of the groups of writers studied by Heath or Scribner and Cole, although Heath's Black Americans do engage in creative generation in their talk. It seems clear that the townspeople are encouraged in school to generate to a limited extent in their writing.

The last area in which cultural variation plays a part might be defined as the pragmatics of discourse. Written discourse, like oral discourse, occurs in a social setting, and there exists rules of behavior with respect to writing. In Heath's White Appalachian community, a child should write a thank-you note for a present; in the Black community, such an obligation does not exist. In the Vai community, it was hard for the Vai language writers even to conceive of engaging in some of the tasks that Scribner and Cole asked them to do. Because they had difficulty conceiving of it, they did not know what to write or how to write it.

We may represent the interaction of these aspects of cultural variation as in the following diagram.

Sociocognitive Influences	Textual Effects
perceived function	type of information
pragmatics of discourse	formal characteristics
cognitive demand	

It is clear that the three cultural variables interact with each other and that the particular situation in which a writer writes may also determine the pragmatics and the function, which may, in turn, affect the text produced. That is to say that writing in a business setting may become a different sort of activity from writing at home or in a community.

This depiction of cultural variation suggests that written language and the activities involved in composing or reading and responding are highly conventional. Convention and need dictate the occasions for writing or reading and the functions of discourse appropriate to those occasions. From these two sources, the writer or the reader then applies his knowledge of both the content and form appropriate to a function on an occasion and conducts the appropriate search of his long-term memory. At that point, the writer goes on to certain text-producing, or what we might think of as enscribing activities, as well as discourse-producing, or meaning-making activities (Takala, 1983). The text-producing activities include the more mechanical or physical; the discourse-producing activities include those related to the selection and arrangement of content. The reader goes on to certain decoding activities and certain types of response to the text material. Again these activities are bounded by convention (Purves, 1987).

WRITING, SCHOOL, AND CONTRASTIVE RHETORIC

Heath clearly establishes that children learn many of the occasions and functions of oral discourse in the home, and may also learn some of the occasions and functions of written discourse as well. For the most part, however, people learn to write in schools or through some sort of instruction (this even appears to be the case of the Vai literates in Scribner and Cole's study). It is in schools that students learn to write according to certain conventions, many of which have little to do with the structure of the language and more to do with the literary and cultural heritage of the society. Bloom (1981) has resurrected the idea of linguistic determinism as expressed in the Whorf-Sapir hypothesis, arguing from the fact that Chinese does not contain the condition contrary to fact. His argument is subtle, but he fails to suggest that some people at some time determined that the structure was unnecessary, and therefore the grammatical form did not become nascent, or was allowed to atrophy. It appears that many aspects of texts are not bound by the morphology and grammar of a particular language in and of themselves, but by custom and convention, which may, in fact, have earlier shaped the morphology and syntax of the language. The relationship between language, thought, and discourse will remain problematic, but the role of the school in promulgating rhetorical styles remains clear, as Kádár-Fülop shows. It serves as a primary agent in the transmission of cultural, and thereby rhetorical and stylisticm, norms.

It is certainly demonstrable at the upper reaches of formal writing, that when writing in many academic disciplines, as well as in certain professions that demand a great deal of writing, individuals learn to write according to certain explicit and implicit conventions that affect patterns of organization, syntax, and phrasing, and even the selection from the lexicon. It is apparent that the scholarly article in a given academic discipline has properties demanded by the history of that discipline. In the humanities, references to previous research on the topic comes at the beginning of an article, or they are sprinkled throughout the text where needed; in psychology they always occupy the second of five sections of the article; and in the biological sciences they occur in separate articles from the report of a particular piece of research. In addition to structural conventions, disciplines differ in the degree to which they allow the writer to use the first person, the degree to which the passive is tolerated, and the degree to which interpretation or inference is permitted, to name but three instances. If such differences divide academic disciplines and even permeate these disciplines to the extent that the conventions obtain regardless of the language in which the article is written, it would seem reasonable to expect that similar kinds of differences separate ethnolinguistic or geographically distant cultures and societies. Such is the emergent line of reasoning behind contrastive rhetoric.

Early studies in the field of contrastive rhetoric concentrated primarily on people writing in a common second language or on literary styles as they change across linguistic or temporal boundaries. More recently, scholars have begun to look at people writing in their native language. This is the focus of Kachru's chapter, which examines the structures used by professional writers in two fields— criticism and science writing in Hindi. They have, like Kachru, sought to examine writing that would appear to have the same discursive function and perhaps even the same genre. In order for contrastive rhetoric to have a secure basis for study, there at least must be agreement on the possibility of similar setting or similar function across the groups of writers. Some of the studies, in fact, suggest that in some cultures the function itself may indeed vary more than one might at first suspect. The current International Association for the Evaluation of Educational Achievement (IEA) Study of Written Composition is a case in point. The IEA study intends to provide a way of examining a systematically drawn sample of writing in a number of rhetorical modes by an average school population writing in the language of instruction. It also examines the criteria of "good" writing used by teachers of writing in each of the countries in order to see if there are systematic differences that might help define rhetorical communities. This approach is exemplified in the studies by Carlson and Park, which examine how monocultural raters judge writing from other cultures. They show how important it is for raters to define their criteria and the effects of their biases. A part of the problem, as the studies reported by Takala and Degenhart and by Indrasuta suggest, is that for cultural reasons, students in some countries interpreted a set of task directions differently from those in another, in part because they see that the function of discourse varies not according to the task, but according to the setting (a narrative might have a differing functions in different societies). One of the tasks called for the students to write a note to the head of the school apologizing for and explaining the reasons for a missed appointment. In some cultures the apology dominated the text, in others the explanation dominated it. Such variation may be explained, in part, by the fact that the conventions of discourse are related to the perceived hierarchies in the society (Hofstede, 1982).

THE METHODOLOGY OF
CONTRASTIVE RHETORIC

The methodology of contrastive rhetoric is still in its formative stages. In part, this formative nature of the field constitutes a part of its charm. Although contrastive rhetoric is not yet a rhetorically based methodology, it is beginning to forge one, as the essays in this volume attest. The practitioners come from diverse backgrounds including linguistics, anthropology, psychology, and rhetoric. As Barry (1979, p. 208) observed, cross-cultural studies necessitate a hybrid approach. He suggests that cross-cultural or contrastive studies seek to overcome the limitations of both psychology and anthropology, which he sets forth as follows:

	Psychology	Anthropology
Topic	individual behavior	exotic culture
Technique	quantitative analysis	fieldwork
Principal Contribution	statistical inference	comprehensive observation
Principal Limitation	single variable and culture	lack of analysis or comparisons

Barry suggests an approach that brings together the best combination of the two approaches. That fusion is what seems to be emerging in contrastive rhetoric, as the chapters in this volume demonstrate. Clearly, the studies described here deal with language as used in written texts by people who are members of either separate cultures or of hybridized cultures (immigrants or second language users). The studies tend to observe groups of individuals as they represent cultures; they tend to combine fieldwork and observation with quantitative analysis and statistical inference, and they tend to aim at providing comparisons. They thus seek to avoid the limitations of making judgments based on a single variable as do many of the monocultural case studies, such as those that have permeated writing research in England and the United States.

The basic premise of contrastive rhetoric studies is that one must deal with at least two groups of writers; therefore the contrast. The problem is that one must deal with a number of sources of variation in order to see what indeed emerges from the contrast and to avoid making overgeneralizations. Heath and Scribner and Cole point to a number of these sources as does the task analysis work of the IEA study (Purves, Söter, Takala, & Vähäpassi, 1984). Vähäpässi's chapter discusses this issue in some detail. These writings and others suggest that the following five rules need to be followed in a study of contrastive rhetoric:

(1) *The settings in which the writing occurs should be as similar as possible.* In many of the studies described in this volume, the texts are produced in examination settings that, although artificial, do standardize the constraints place upon the writers. Some of the other studies describe texts that are produced in other situations, which, although not rigidly standardized, can be sufficiently described so the reader can assent to their comparability.

(2) *The writing task should be consistently set in its function and cognitive demand as well as in the specific subject matter.* Plainly it is inappropriate to compare business letters written in one culture with detective fiction written in another. Since many of the studies refer to school-based writing, the writing assignment may be invariant even though the students' familiarity with the kind of task or topic may vary. In her chapter, Vahapassi discusses the complexities of creating tasks for use in cross-cultural assessment and the problems in determining the comparability of tasks.

(3) *The language (i.e. native or foreign) in which the writers are writing must be defined.* In a study that would contrast Nigerian and Australian writers writing in English, it would be important to note that for the Nigerian writers, as well as for a specified proportion of the Australian ones, English is a second language. Soter clearly shows that it is important to distinguish among the Vietnamese and the Lebanese students in Australian schools; they should not be lumped merely as second-language learners.

(4) *The occupation of the writers should be similar or, if not, should be defined and accounted for as a variable.* In her chapter, Yamuna Kachru examines the writing of people in two professional fields. To the extent that it is possible the fields across cultures should be similar or the variations should be specified. One might assume that the "house style" of a particular corporation in any culture would dictate some of the rhetorical features of the texts, and the house style of a chemical company may very well differ greatly from that of an advertising agency. Again it may be that the style in the chemical company will vary according to whether it is produced by people on the engineering staff or people in the personnel section. Sybil Carlson's study of applicants to U.S. graduate schools must account for the individuals' prospective fields, as Park's reanalysis of the data indicates.

(5) *The education of the writers should be similarly defined and described.* As one looks at the writing of people outside of educational institutions, one should take note of their background, for it might be the education and training that makes the rhetoric of the personnel manager differ from that of the chemist. So in a school-based study, one should be sure that the variations in program are taken into consideration. These variations are discussed in the studies looking at the IEA data.

We may say that these five conditions set the controls over the functions and processes by which the texts are produced, and thus enable the analyst of the textual artifacts to be able to make the comparisons and contrasts with greater authority.

THE TREATMENT OF TEXT
IN CONTRASTIVE RHETORIC

What does contrastive rhetoric look at? Clearly, the objects of study are written texts, but there is some variation on the aspects of texts that form the particular focus of study. Some would look at larger patterns of organization, at the movement of the text from paragraph to paragraph; this was the initial approach used by Robert Kaplan in the 1960s. More recently researchers have been looking at linguistic aspects of the texts using such techniques as analysis of cohesive ties or analysis of propositional movement. Some of the authors in this volume take the more microscopic view, and some take the view that it is the broader structures of organization that are most important.

These two groups agree that what one observes are textual phenomena, that is to say, verifiable aspects of the text. In a sense, however, the choice between aspects of a text is, in part, a choice betweeen two methodologies that may be employed, which methodologies tend to dictate the textual features studied. One is a methodology that isolates verifiable linguistic features, usually syntactic features, although semantic and morphological features may also be considered. The sum of these features in a given text may point to a rhetorical attribute. That approach is discussed in the chapter by Carlson, in which she describes her use of The Writer's Workbench to examine text features. Connor and Lauer also use this method without the aid of the computer, as do Söter and Indrasuta.

The complementary approach is to see the text through the eyes of expert readers who have been trained to observe the presence or absence of particular features. As Robert Kaplan states in a recent article (Kaplan, 1986), his initial work was based on his "sense" of the structure and movement of ideas in the texts. This method is paralleled in the work of Glenn and Glenn (1981), in which they distinguish between abstractive and associative texts. Such an initial "hunch" can be followed in a number of ways. One method follows the format of the descriptive scale, following from the work of Carroll (1958) and his use of adjectival rating scales and trained raters. The differences that might emerge between groups of texts, then, are differences agreed upon by the raters, even though there may be no specific textual backing for the perceived dimensions.

When the methodology was applied in the initial stages of the IEA study, it confirmed the Kaplan and Glenn and Glenn distinctions, but added to it additional dimensions as Degenhart and Takala indicate in their chapter. They suggest that there are semantic aspects of rhetorical differences such as the degree to which the writer's personal thoughts may appear in the text, the amount of figurative language, and the amount of concrete reference as opposed to abstract reference. In addition, there seemed to be systematic variation in the amount of information that was included about the subject, and whether the writer explicitly addressed a reader or addressed the subject. When one examines narrative, as Soter does in her chapter, one finds that there may be systematic differences between groups in their focus on action, on character and setting, and on dialogue.

Still another way to examine raters is as Carlson and Park do in their chapters, which show how different evaluative rating styles appear to uncover the presence of contrastive features that then need to be described. Park's Chinese scientists are obviously writing in some fashion that lowers the quality of their compositions in the eyes of U.S. academic raters, and he and Carlson seek to uncover what sorts of lenses those raters have.

As with the perceptions of trained raters, so it is with those who pursue more traditional linguistic approaches. Here the most promising features appear to lie in the relative frequency of certain cohesive ties, in the patterns of subordination and coordination, and in the placement of modifiers. There may also be some possibility in the study of modes of topical progression, but that area of inquiry does not have as clear-cut a methodology as have some of the other approaches (Noh, 1985). In many studies reported in this volume, the researchers are using both a linguistic approach and a rating approach to the text. At times the two approaches confirm each other and what emerges forms some of the dimensions by which the models of text are delimited in certain cultures (Purves and Purves, 1986). It is, after all, the model of text that the student of contrastive rhetoric is seeking to establish, and subsequently explain in terms of the cultural and cognitive influences on those models.

Once those tasks have been accomplished and once one can establish which models appear to interfere with cross-cultural communication, appropriate pedagogical strategies can be developed. One pedagogical implication has been ever present throughout the body of study in contrastive rhetoric: The differences among rhetorical patterns do not represent differences in cognitive ability, but differences in cognitive style. When students, taught to write in one culture, enter another and do not write as do the members of the second culture, they should not be thought stupid or lacking in "higher mental processes," as some composition teachers have stated. They lack knowledge of the appropriate structures of the new culture, and often they can learn these quite quickly, usually as quickly as a native speaker learns the conventions of a new discipline.

THE ORGANIZATION OF THIS VOLUME

This volume will begin with the more theoretical and methodological approaches to the issues of contrastive rhetoric and its relation to curriculum and instruction, as described by Kádár-Fülop, Degenhart and Takala, and Vähäpassi. Each of these papers deals with issues that arose from the IEA Study of Written Composition. The second section contains articles that focus on the contrasts between writers who are writing in their presumed first language: first professional writers in Kachru's paper, and then student writers in the papers by Bickner and Connor and Lauer, each of whom use data from the IEA Study. The third section examines the issue of transfer of cultural patterns in second language writing. Söter uses a sample of students who are immigrants to Australia, and therefore all writing in a second language. Indrasuta relates second language writing directly to the first language by using a sample of students who are writing in foreign language classes at the same time that they are studying their mother tongue. The fourth section approaches the issue of the criteria applied by monolinguals to the writing of nonnative speakers. Carlson sets forth the basis issues of the GRE-TOEFL study, and Park provides an important addition by showing that the criteria may be applied both against different language nationals and against different disciplines. In the concluding article, Robert Kaplan sums up the field of contrastive rhetoric and opens up issues of pedagogy, thereby providing an appropriate finale to the volume.

REFERENCES

Barry, H. (1979). Forecasts on the evolution of cross-cultural psychology and anthropology. In L. H. Eckensberger, W. J. Lonner, & Y. H. Poortinga (Eds.), *Cross-cultural contributions to psychology* (pp. 207-218). Lisse: Swets and Zeitlinger.

Bereiter, C., & Scardamalia, M. (1981). *Information processing demand of text production*. Paper presented at the Deutsches Institut fur Fernstudien an der Universitat Tubingen.

Bloom, A. (1981). *The linguistic shaping of thought: A study in the impact of language on thinking in China and the West*. Hillsdale NJ: Lawrence Erlbaum.

Carroll, J. A. (1960). Vectors of prose style. In T. A. Sebeok (Ed.), *Style in language*. Cambridge, MA and New York: Technology Press/John Wiley.

Glenn, E. S., with Glenn, C. G. (1981). *Man and mankind: Conflict and communication between cultures*. Norwood, NJ: ABLEX.

Heath, S. B. (1983). *Ways with words*: New York: Cambridge University Press.

Hofstede, G. (1982). *Culture's consequences*. Beverly Hills, CA: Sage.

Kaplan, R. (1966). Cultural thought patterns in intercultural education. *Language Learning, 16*, 1-20.

Kaplan, R. (Ed.). (1983). *Annual review of applied linguistics* (Vol. 3).

Kaplan, R. (1986). Cultural thought patterns revisited. In U. Connor & R. Kaplan (Eds.), *Writing across languages: Analyzing L2 texts* (pp. 9-22). Boston: Addison Wesley.

Noh, M. W. (1985). *Topical progression and the writing of summaries*. Unpublished doctoral dissertation, University of Illinois at Urbana-Champaign.

Purves, R. (1986). On the nature and formation of interpretive and rhetorical communities. In T. N. Postlethwaite, (Ed.), *International educational research: Papers in honor of Torsten Husen* (pp. 45-64). Oxford: Pergamon.

Purves, A, & Purves, W. (1986). Culture, text models, and the activity of writing. *Research in the Teaching of English*, pp. 174-197.

Purves, A. (1987). Literacy, culture, and community. In D. A. Wagner (Ed.), *The future of literacy in a changing world*. Oxford: Pergamon.

Purves, A., Söter, A., Takala, S., & Vähäpassi, A. (1984) Towards a domain-referenced system for classifying composition assignments. *Research in the Teaching of English*, pp. 385-416.

Scribner, S., & Cole, M. (1981). *The psychology of literacy*. Cambridge, MA: Harvard University Press.

Takala, S. (1983). *On the nature of achievement in writing*. (Available from IEA International Study of Written Composition, Urbana, IL.)

Takala, S., Purves, A. C., & Buckmaster, A. (1982). On the interrelationships between language, perception, thought and culture, and their relevance to the assessment of written composition. In T. N. Postlethwaite & B. Choppin (Eds.), *Evaluation in education: An international review series, 5*, 317-342.

PART I
Theoretical Considerations

1

Culture, Writing, and Curriculum

JUDIT KÁDÁR-FÜLOP

Writing is a recent invention. The fundamental changes it has brought about in the life of man and society, and in language and usage are probably inestimable. So are its benefits and problems as far as education is concerned.

The student of the history of European education learns that the first public schools were established in Athens in the fourth century B.C. It was a period of intellectual harvesting: Plato and Aristotle systematized the knowledge accumulated in earlier centuries and summarized it in a language refined by public orators. Writing became a prime factor in preserving and transmitting this knowledge, for the oral culture of ancient Greece was already doomed to decay. What writing rescued of Greek culture is, even in torso, an impressive and memorable example of the interdependence of political democracy, morals, and communicative competence.

Literacy education was a two-stage process from its beginnings. The acquisition of basic reading and writing skills was only the first stage. Longer and more painstaking efforts were necessary for acquiring skill in the effective use of the highly elaborate and formalized linguistic code of *public* communication both oral and written. This second aim was pursued in the rhetorical schools, which, in later centuries, gained ill repute for treating communicative skills as a technique that could be used to any end, and the orator a specialist who could serve any cause.

The conception that formal language education (beyond the teaching of basic literacy skills) is a necessary part of encyclopedic (or general) education originates from republican Rome. McKeon (1964) notes that the Romans provided us with the influential model of *humanitas,* arguing that "To be a human a man must understand what has been accomplished and what can be accomplished by the arts of men" (p. 159). The "liberal arts"—canonized studies or, as we would call them, subjects—were considered instrumental in reaching the goal of *humanitas*. They constituted a balanced whole of the arts of word (grammar, logic, and rhetoric) and the arts of things (geometry, arithmetic, astronomy, and music among them). McKeon points out that the Romans "did not conceive of the liberal arts as methods of systematizing philosophy or organizing erudition but as preprofessional education and as compendia of information" (p. 163) for a man who wishes to become a professional (lawyer, orator, and architect).

In those early days of schooling, written knowledge and written communication had a modest role in the world of daily work: in farming, industry, and business. It served primarily the maintenance of social order, and the accumulation and communication of knowledge from generation to generation. Since the liberal arts were disciplines by which knowledge could be applied to *statement* in contrast to the mechanical or vulgar arts—disciplines by which knowledge could be applied to *action*—encyclopedic education, which was primarily verbal education, was the duty and privilege of those who served and ruled society by the power of the word.

We find that 2000 years later, in countries of advanced technology, hardly any kind of mechanical skill is needed any more. At the same time, there is a growing demand for educated minds: people who can use the elaborate language of public communication (e.g., who can learn from text, or do things according to written instruction). With some exaggeration, it seems as if the nature of wealth-producing work had undergone a fundamental change. Instead of *doing* things ourselves, it seems as if our task were to *teach* machines how to do those things for us and, meanwhile, *learn* how to teach them new "skills." Teaching and verbal learning are communication skills. It has become clear from a number of international educational studies (e.g., Passow, Noah, Eckstein, & Mallea, 1976) that a state's gross national product correlates with the general level of literacy of its subjects. The establishment of nationwide school systems, even in the poorest countries, is a recognition of this fact.

The general level of education varies over a wide range in the countries of the world today (Thorndike, 1973). Correspondingly, written communication has penetrated daily life to varying degrees in different countries. In very poor countries, few people depend on their reading skills, while there are countries in the world, though few, where reading has been considered a basic survival skill for decades. In these latter, telecommunication through computers may soon make writing an omnipresent activity as well, and the acquisition of composing skills a condition of normal functioning in society.

It is no paradox that in the countries where technological advancement is the greatest, dysfunctions of the school as the institution of literacy education are more apparent than is the case in less developed countries. Countries like the United States or Germany, which, because of their expanding economies, have attracted masses of immigrants from very different—often not even literate—cultures in recent decades, experience a chaotic situation in their educational systems: The gap between the literacy and language skills desired and those attained through schooling appears to grow rather than diminish, in spite of enormous national investments in education.

The problems of communication education and literacy that were once the problems of a city (the "polis") have become crucial international issues. Awareness of these makes researchers look beyond the borders of their own countries and sense the worldwide educational crisis brought about by the situation that Margaret Mead (1978) described as "the airport of the 20th century," where societies from the nineteenth century as well as from the stone age land simultaneously. In 1980, the IEA Written Composition Study, a large-scale international assessment study of students' writing performance, undertook the task of analyzing and comparing writing curricula (stated and hidden) in 14 countries on five continents, including countries with very long and very short literacy traditions, simple and pluralistic societies, and Oriental and Western cultures. The conceptual analysis of the relationships of culture, writing, and the curriculum presented in this paper evolved from that study.

Understanding and interpreting written documents and statements of educational policymakers and teachers about the means and ends of literacy education is difficult within any one educational system. First of all, it is difficult to identify the reading and writing curriculum across school subjects, all of which contribute to the development of literacy-based communicative skills. Second, the stated educational aims are often more misleading than informing about the real curriculum of literacy education. Third, the mother tongue as a subject—to which most of the responsibility for literacy education is erroneously assigned in our day—is a battlefield of diverse political interests and educational philosophies, and therefore communication about its goals and objectives is often hindered by unconscious presumptions and claims underlying discussions. The task becomes formidable in a cross-cultural setting, in which a shared understanding of the meaning of culture, writing, education, and curriculum must be arrived at by mother-tongue educators in various countries, before the question can even be asked: What is the writing curriculum (or the writing curricula) in the educational systems under study?

In an attempt to clarify the basic notions we have to deal with an analyzing curricula, I shall, in the following pages, seek answers to the following questions:

(1) What is the *function of literacy* in society?
(2) What is the *function of literacy education* for society and for the individual?
(3) What is the *domain of literacy in the school*?

Since my knowledge of oriental educational philosophies and practices is very limited, I shall confine discussion to the European concepts of literacy education, which have been highly influential in shaping modern civilization.

THE FUNCTIONS OF LITERACY
IN SOCIETY

Writing has extended man's intellectual and interactional capacities in three directions. In its *documenting* function, writing has extended man's rote memory (see, for example, encyclopedias, dictionaries, directories). In its *transactional* function, writing has extended man's possibilities to cooperate with others irrespective of distance and time (see, for example, the effect of written law on civic life, or the effect of banking on economy). In its *epistemic* or interpretive function, writing has extended man's ideational or concept forming capacity (consider Wann's 1939 argument that the essay developed as a linguistic response to the needs of interpretative verbal reasoning).

Writing was invented in the struggle against forgetting. This is especially clear if we examine writing systems older than alphabetic writing. Quippu, the Peruvian knot-string "writing" system, like the knots on our handkerchiefs, could serve only record-keeping purposes. Similarly, the clay tokens used by Mesopotamian merchants to document their agreements were actually reminders. However, the Mesopotamian writing system, which developed from a method of using the print of these tokens as language symbols, also provides an example of how writing can serve transactional functions as complex as legal systems (Nystrand, 1982). Chinese ideographic writing, which developed from drawing, is a pure example of the epistemic function of writing: The ideograms are graphic representations of concepts and conceptual relationships.

The invention of writing was by no means the only attempt to extend memory and cognitive capacity in society. Oral literary tradition, as Suhor (1984) points out, shows many examples of how verbal memory was aided by poetic techniques. Rigor in the use of narrative structures, rhythm, rhyme, and refrain have long been known to aid verbatim recall of information. Aristotle's *Poetica* and *Rhetorica* prove that an impressive body of practical knowledge had been accumulated in oral tradition about the use of language and persuasion and in the transmission of knowledge and experiences.

The invention of alphabetic writing was a major advance in popularizing writing as a mode of communication and learning. The genuine novelty of the alphabetic writing system was the idea of recording living speech by distinguishing a finite number of functionally equivalent speech sounds, or phonemes. The method of phonemic transcription ignores the relationships of the semantic and morphemic units of speech. For this reason, the alphabetic system could conveniently be applied to any oral language. It also made the study of spoken language possible.

The linguistic history of Europe enables us to analyze the important effects of alphabetic writing on communication. First of all, this speech coding system had a stabilizing effect on oral languages through the 'codification' of language use. Codification was spelled out in orthographic conventions, etymological, unilingual, and bilingual dictionaries, and in standard grammars. The spelling anarchy of the first period of the print age made scholars aware of an inherent problem of phonemic writing: that it is sensitive to the changes of pronunciation. Furthermore, it became clear that the changes of the semantic distribution of words is an inevitable evil from the point of view of intergenerational communication. The necessity of "language maintenance" created national academies of scholars who undertook the responsibilities of keeping records of the state of the language and of controlling change. As a side-effect, the code systems of written languages could more easily be made objects of formal study, both for communicative and for scientific purposes. As can be expected, this intervention in language development created distance between oral dialects and the written language, yet the benefit of preserving the code for communication between generations, between speech communities of different dialects and languages, balanced this disadvantage in the long run. Many historical and current examples can illustrate this point. One example is the survival of written Latin. In its written form, Latin remained a language of common reference in multilingual Europe. In oral usage, its dialects became mutually unintelligible as the offspring languages: French, Italian, Spanish, and Portuguese show. For the same reason, English can function as a "lingua franca" today, because its written form keeps equal distance from all its main dialects, and thus serves as a common reference for its literate speakers. When spoken by illiterate speakers, English is largely unintelligible for foreigners who have not lived in the speaker's speech community. From another aspect, literacy helps small languages survive. Ethnic groups with their own literacy traditions can, sometimes, successfully protect their linguistic and cultural identity under the pressure of dominant written cultures around them. In Hungary and Finland, in the eighteenth and nineteenth centuries, for example, national literacy played an important role in defending ethnic integrity when confronted by dominant political powers like Austria and Sweden.

The literary history of Europe is a rich source for study of the effects of alphabetic writing on culture. We find, for example, that from medieval times, poetry drew both on the metric forms of ancient literature and the rhyming traditions of oral dialects, and the two versification methods merged into a common European literary tradition of novel flexibility and sophistication. This happened in spite of the fact that a number of different new written languages emerged at the same time, very much as a result of the efforts of poets with different vernaculars like Dante or Chaucer who were also Latin scholars. It should be noted that the main influential factor in forming common poetic traditions was Christianity in the Middle Ages. Common faith motivated the development of European prose traditions as well. The authors of early vernacular homilies and sermons as well as the Bible translators had a major influence on the development of modern literate languages. Owing to the lively interconnections of the literatures of multilingual Europe motivated by common faith and supported by common Greek-Latin scholarship, classical culture and the oral cultures of numerous ethnic groups began to flow forth to form one unified river of literature as soon as the dark centuries of migrations were over.

In succeeding centuries *Humanitas* was enriched by the individual contributions of outstanding authors like Cervantes, Shakespeare, Voltaire, Goethe, Tolstoy, Thomas Mann, Franklin, Newton, Freud, and Einstein, to name only a few. The pertaining practice of translating the best pieces of national literatures into the other European languages has been a sign of awareness of the community of European literary traditions. Each translated book has reinforced this commonality by contributing to the adjustment of national rhetorical development to the mainstreams of European rhetorical traditions. Translation activity has thus proved influential in maintaining the "polyphonic" character of European literature, in which national languages of smaller ethnic groups like Hungarian, Finnish, Danish, or Czech can retain their distinct yet harmonizing voices. On examining the extension of this verbal culture, one finds that only the languages that adopted phonemic writing systems could join the orchestra of Western verbal culture.

Summarizing the above arguments, I would like to suggest that the societal value of writing must be seen in its integrative role on communication and culture, both within and across language communities. It is also worth noting that this integrative effect asserts itself through the combined efforts of members of the literate community.

THE SOCIETAL FUNCTIONS
OF LITERACY EDUCATION

Literacy education is a societal effort to teach individuals to use the standard language both in oral and written communication. Literacy education has three interrelated functions following from the societal values of writing. The first is to *diminish language distance* between the members of society by developing communicative competence in at least one standard written language: the language of national literacy. The second is to *develop language loyalty* toward the language of literacy. The third is to *develop individuality* through education in the language of literacy. These three functions of literacy education are discussed below.

Function 1: Diminishing Language Distance

The term *language distance,* as used by Weinreich (1963), denotes the total of code and subcode differences within society. In Weinreich's terminology, the equivalent of code is language; dialects, sociolects, argots are termed subcodes. Gumperz (1962) distinguished several sources of code and subcode differences. He pointed out that frequent and intensive communication *within* groups of code users favors the development of specific versions (subcodes) of the code: dialects, sociolects, and professional argots. However, frequency, intensity, and variety of communicative acts *between* groups, and rigidity or flexibility of the group structure of society (the role matrix) determine whether subcodes develop in isolation or maintain a closer relationship with each other and the code from which they originate. Flexibility of the role matrix (i.e., social and cultural conditions that allow the individual to choose his roles and reference groups) and the existence of a common standard language favor decreasing language distance, whereas both the rigidity of the role matrix (a characteristic of cast societies) and the lack of a standard language have the effect of increasing language distance.

State school systems were established in many countries in the hope that instruction and education in the standard written language would diminish language barriers between communicants. The history of nations and languages shows that these were not unrealistic expectations: Compared with the oral languages of the past and the present, written languages are few, stable, and efficient in accumulating and communicating information both within and across societies. Yet, the sociocultural conditions, the social and political "contracts and conflicts" between the ethnic and social groups concerned, often make these hopes illusory. School systems today are expected to neutralize the negative effects of the rapid changes of economy, lifestyle, and ethnic composition on the communication matrix and the code matrix.

The problems of language distance are varied both in nature and intensity in the countries of the IEA writing study. In Hungary, for example, where the distance of dialects from the standard language is negligible and language minorities constitute a very small proportion of the population, the source of language distance is, almost exclusively, the differences in sociolects. The situation is similar in Finland. A far greater problem is faced in countries where, as in the United States and Germany, large populations with a vernacular other than the language of the state are to be schooled in one common language, and where the situation is often aggravated by the fact that the language background of some immigrant groups is not another standard written language, but a low-prestige sociolect of it.

Apart from these differences, there are common elements in the conflicts and difficulties of the school systems in question. The two problems briefly discussed here are: (a) the inequality of entry conditions; and, (b) the inequality of the outcome demands.

It has been clear to educators for the past 30 years that scholastic failure is, to a great extent, a result of the student's inadequate knowledge of the standard written code: the language of the school. Solutions to the problem were sought in two directions. On the one hand, efforts were made to *make reading easy* by providing textbooks that impart knowledge with less reliance on text-grammatical information and more reliance on pictorial and situational information. On the other hand, efforts were made to organize compensatory programs for children whose home language differed from the standard language too much to allow for a simple transition from the oral to the written code.

Both strategies have been shown to have serious limitations. The strategy of "making reading easy" is an illusion that follows from the alphabetic character of our writing system (neither Hebrew nor Chinese writing allows such illusions). It misleads the learner by obliterating important learning objectives, such as the study of literature and the study of written style, vocabulary, and spelling conventions—text-grammatical features of well-formed texts (for example, workbooks and textbooks that adopt the communicative strategies of comics and questionnaires).

The compensatory strategy has also proved largely unsuccessful. It has become clear that even the best pedagogical efforts can be shipwrecked by the lack of motivation of the learners and that this perplexing problem cannot be solved by purely pedagogical means (Passow 1974). If the individual has little hope for social integration and mobility through schooling, the basic motives of language learning are missing. The desire of acceptance as a member of the community, as Lambert has shown (1968), speeds and facilitates the acquisition of the code, whereas the lack of such motives impedes code learning.

A systematic analysis of the problem is offered by Skutnabb-Kangas and Toukamaa (1976), who studied the chances of educational success in language-minority children. They propose that agreement between the majority and the minority groups over the goals of the minority group, with respect to social integration (or, as they call it, structural incorporation), is a determinant of success in cultural assimilation—at least to the extent that it is desired by the minority group. Thus, a desire for structural incorporation and cultural assimilation on the part of the minority group, and agreement over these goals on the part of the majority group, provide the best hope for success. In the case in which structural incorporation (equal economic and social rights and chances) are denied to the minority by the dominant group, cultural assimilation is impeded through lack of economic incentives. In the case in which the minority itself keeps a distance from the dominant group (as is the case of groups with strong cultural cohesion), the limits of cultural assimilation through schooling are set by the minority group itself. Highly educated biliterates as well as semilingual illiterates may grow up in such a situation, depending on the economic means and the educational offerings of the minority group.

The second problem related to the school's function of diminishing language distance is the inequality of society's demands for reading and writing literacy. More precisely, whereas the school is expected to diminish language distance, at the same time it is also expected to provide young people with communicative skills sufficient in their adult roles so they can successfully participate in the societal division of labor. *Sufficient*, however, is a relative concept. Sufficient reading and writing competence in the role of a park caretaker is certainly different from the reading and writing competence sufficient for the role of professor of English even if the person in the latter role may need the same literary skills for *household purposes* as would the former.

Natural and economic limitations force societies to compromise with respect to the relative amount of time and effort spent on teaching communicative skills and other skills. Since the development of advanced communicative competence is a time-consuming educational process, the question arises as to when and how selection and specific education for linguistically demanding roles should take place in the school system without violating the principle of diminishing language distance through schooling.

The answer to this question for educational systems has been the branching of the system at some point beyond the common elementary level into academic and nonacademic tracks, with more language education in the former and less in the latter. The answer determines to what extent members of the next generation are offered the possibility to be *equal* in the use of the language of literacy, and to what extent language education is considered *role specific*.

As technology required advanced literacy skills from an increasing proportion of the labor force, the cutoff point for branching into separate tracks was moved upward, in some countries up to late puberty. Yet uniform mother-tongue education for eight or more years has appeared to have pedagogical disadvantages, too. Tasks that are found trivial for one part of the population seem to bear relevance for the other, whereas relevant tasks for more advanced students appear too demanding for the poor students. Motivation problems arise which cannot be solved in the classroom, and it is often argued that valuable learning time of fast learners is wasted because of students of poor language background. The dilemma of how much *general* or *basic* literacy and how much *role specific* language competence should be provided by the school is less sharp in societies that, as part of their national tradition, have a strong emphasis on developing language loyalty in their members.

Function 2: Developing Language Loyalty

The second function of literacy education is to develop language loyalty. Language loyalty is a positive attitude toward a language, "a state of mind, in which the language as an intact entity, and, in contrast to other languages, assumes a high position in a scale of values, a position in need of being 'defended'" (Weinreich 1963, p. 99).

Becoming literate in a language means not only the acquisition of the elaborate written code with its complicated orthographic conventions, lexicon, and grammar, but also the acquisition of *values* attached to the written code, for language can be appreciated as a treasury of information on the life and communication experiences of previous generations. Much of this information is contained in the spelling conventions and grammatical standards of written communication. Spelling, for example, often makes the morphemic structure or the etymology of the word visible, thus informing about semantic and historical bonds between concepts. For the understanding reader, dictionaries reveal the life of language as a history of negotiations for meaning. Furthermore, well-formed texts—the literature of a language—embody the models of written communication in that language. They define rhetorical patterns to be followed, stylistic conventions and standards, organizational modes, and areas of content that are acceptable to be communicated in writing. Although these models change over time, the changes are relatively slow compared with the degree of a language existing only in a spoken form.

It is an important aim of mother-tongue education to educate pupils to appreciate the communicative and cultural value of the written language and to develop willingness to preserve it: to develop language loyalty. Language loyalty has the function of stabilizing the code across generations through the common effort of its users. It is a form of cultural loyalty, and also of national loyalty, in societies were language is held to be the major cohesive force among its members.

Both diminishing language distance and the transmission of cultural values accumulated in language are important socializing functions of literacy education. They may come into conflict, however, at times of rapid changes in the communication matrix. Such are the periods of explosive social mobility, mass immigration, or the quick spread of writing in areas of life in which, formerly, oral communication was exclusive. In such emergency situations, pragmatic reasons may force society to upset the balance between goals of diminishing language distance among contemporaries and of developing loyalty to the language of previous generations. The reduction of literacy education to a minimum of a given generation may, however, undermine the verbal culture of society.

Function 3: Developing Individuality

The third function of literacy education is to help students become independent communicants. What does this mean?

It has been pointed out that our written culture has a polyphonic and orchestral character. It is multilingual and we know by name most of the individuals who have enriched it by their writings. Instead of an anonymous canonized literary tradition, we have a huge trust of texts written by known authors of different nationalities and different professions. These texts can be classified by excellence of content, by languages, by areas of experience and/or knowledge, by relation of text and context (for example, fictional versus nonfictional texts), and by formal textual features.

Since the total of written culture is unattainable for any one person, each of us drawing on this resource has to select texts and, consequently, authors to rely upon for information. Each of us can also contribute to the trust of texts individually. Selection of texts (or informants) requires judgment, which is based upon personal values, knowledge, analytic skills, and communicative competence. The expected outcome of literacy education is that each individual be able to draw upon the common verbal culture for developing his or her own "individual culture" (Kiss, 1969)—*humanitas*—as defined at the beginning of this paper. More specifically, this means that we hope to develop in students awareness of foregone and contemporary communicants, awareness of the communicative and cultural value and resources of language(s), and awareness of his or her personal responsibility as a recipient (reader) and as a producer (writer) of texts.

Developing individuality, unlike socialization, is not a generally acknowledged function of literacy education. Although "communication with ourselves," (i.e., learning and thinking by reading and writing) has always been a primary source of creating culture, individuality and individual responsibility are issues in which educational philosophies and, for that matter, learners' aims, differ most, both across and within cultures. First, we must consider that the creative, critical, and responsible mind—the classic ideal of *humanitas*—is a concept of Western educational philosophy. In some Oriental cultures, such as Chinese, individuality seems to be a far less emphasized educational value. It is an intriguing question how far this is attributable to the written culture of Chinese based on ideographic writing. But even in Western education, verbal thinking, which "liberates us from the constraints by culture" (Stenhouse 1967, p. 58), is an oft stated and rarely realized educational ideal because the constraints are harnesses manufactured by economic and social reality. Further, the independent creative mind is the product of a very long educational and self-educating process and the final results of this process are out of the vision of the ordinary teacher.

THE DOMAIN OF LITERACY
IN THE SCHOOL

Communicative competence is acquired in interactions between the child and the adult, who have complementary and interdependent roles in the learning process, and who share responsibility for its success. On the basis of empirical evidence from the Bristol child language study, Wells (1985) argues that "responsibility for what is learned and for the order in which learning takes place rests almost entirely with the child." At the same time, the adult is responsible for "the provision of the primary linguistic data" from which the child can "construct both a repertoire of linguistic resources and procedures for drawing upon them in interaction with others" (pp. 395-396). The role of the school in literacy education is very similar to the role of adults in the child's family. The main difference, however, is that the school's primary function is to guide and support learning the language of *written communication*. It must, therefore, provide socially relevant situations for written communication, texts that represent the pragmatic and linguistic features of written communication, and, finally, interactions with supportive adults who can guide learning. In this section we shall examine how all this is organized in the institutional framework of the school.

The Societal Functions of
Writing in the School

How is the school organized to function as a "literate society?" First of all, its teachers—scholars of different subjects—have the common feature of being literate communicants who can learn from text and who can express themselves in the standard language. Second, the students enter this "literate society" with the expectation (on both sides) of becoming literate communicants themselves. Third, the communication system of the school represents and confirms the three basic societal functions of writing: the documenting, the transactional, and the epistemic functions.

The documenting function of writing appears both in the informational material used for learning purposes and in the communication about the teacher-learning process. Most of the knowledge to be taught is documented in writing: in reference books and textbooks. The students are expected to give account of their knowledge in examinations, of which the most important ones are written examinations. The school's appraisal of the students' knowledge is documented in the form of qualifications, such as certificates of graduation.

Abuses can make the validity of the documenting function doubtful for the student. Bad, inadequate, irrelevant textbooks undermine the authority of the knowledge accumulated in writing, and the authority of text as a source of learning. Certificates that do not give a truthful account of the students' knowledge, and thus misguide the parties relying on them, undermine the authority of the written document for long term cooperation.

The transactional function of writing is represented in the pragmatic use of written communication between the student and the school (teachers) about what should be learned, how it should be learned, and what has been learned. Tasks, instructions in school books, workbooks, and tests, are examples of texts that have a transactional function in the teaching-learning context. Other examples are teachers' notes, comments on the students' work, and students' answers to test questions.

The main abuses of the transactional function of written communication are poor (ill-formulated, irrelevant, ambiguous) test questions and illegitimate testing. The latter occurs when testing knowledge outweighs teaching, that is, more is tested than is taught, or when too much student time is spent on test writing.

The epistemic function of literacy is represented in the school in the texts students study for their content and form. It is also manifest in the students' writing tasks: notes taken and made, outlines, summaries, and compositions written for the language teacher or for other subject-matter teachers as homework or schoolwork.

It may be concluded that the societal functions of writing are present in the school. Whether they appear as a *valid* representation of these societal functions in any particular school system or in any particular school is a different question. If they do, students and parents sense that the school has high professional standards.

The Domain of Written
Texts in the School

In the practice of education, goals are translated into curricula. Throughout the history of schooling, two fundamentally different approaches toward education, namely the pragmatist approach and the formal approach, have been competing. In periods of rapid growth of scientific knowledge, growing pressure on the school to teach more facts favored the pragmatic approach. Yet there are pedagogical limits to teaching facts, therefore, these periods were always followed by periods in which emphasis shifted from teaching facts to developing learning skills, and students could fill in the gaps of their knowledge independently. It seems that the formal approach in education is the sensible pedagogical answer when an increased amount of knowledge is "banging on the gates" of the school. Current debates about "permanent learning," "computer literacy," "numeracy," "basic literacy," and "musical literacy" are symptoms that educational pragmatism in our days is recognized as failing.

In the area of verbal literacy, the difference between the pragmatic and the formal approach can best be seen in the relative emphasis on the content and form of communication in school, more specifically, in the relationship of the facts and concepts taught and the texts (if any) in which these are described and explained.

The pragmatist approach induces the curriculum planner to give the child texts and reading and writing tasks similar to the ones he can expect to read and write in his adult life. Such a demand implies several assumptions. One is that "life" is outside the school and that the communication situations in life are fundamentally different from those appearing in school life (which may well be the case in individual instances, but does not follow from the institutional characteristics of the school). The second assumption is that "similarity to real life" should necessarily mean similarity both in topic and form, that is, the text forms introduced in school should carry the same information as they currently carry in adult rhetorical communities where they are most frequently used. An example may illustrate this point. The formal logical rules of scientific argumentation have parallel text form rules that conventionalize the verbal expression of scientific argumentation. But the topic treated in such a text form can range from the simplest proof in Euclidian geometry to the most complex proofs in modern physics. The claim that teaching scientific argumentation on texts of the latter content is more practical than teaching it on the former, is based on the pragmatist argument that those who will most need scientific argumentation as a verbal skill can and will learn the complex and abstract factual knowledge contained in such texts, whereas those who need to know only the basic concepts of Euclidian geometry need not be burdened with reading such a complicated text form.

The formal approach to literacy education, by contrast, considers school a real life situation for both the teacher and the child, a situation in which the common aim is to develop intellectual faculties and language competence on topics that are most appropriate for learning purposes. It ignores the question whether a certain text or text-related exercise (e.g., summarizing) has any immediate practical value outside the school. It assumes that the cognitive and communicative competence which is instrumental in independent learning and cooperation with others can be acquired by studying a few subjects that represent commonalities and specifics of the problem areas of life. Pragmatism in the formal approach is related to life inside the school rather than life outside the school. Pedagogical pragmatics requires that topic and form of educational communication—learning goal and learning activity—be harmonized with a view to the child's age characteristics, society's cultural traditions, and education values, rather than with a view to immediate social or environmental impulses—though, clearly, these too must be reckoned with.

In the formal approach, effort is made to acquaint the student with the representative text forms of literature (fictional and nonfictional) within the context of subject matters. If these are defined with due care (like the seven liberal arts of the Middle Ages), it can be hoped that, while studying them, the student will also learn to recognize the relevant aspects of reading and writing situations and he or she will

learn to respond to them. It is the independent text ("an extended
structure of syntactic units such as words, groups, and clauses and
textual units that is marked by both *coherence* and *completion*,"
Werlich, 1976, p. 23) that takes over some of the adult's role in the
formal approach to literacy education.

Is it possible to select a sample of texts that exemplify the most
important aspects of the written communication situation? It is
certainly not possible within the curriculum of one subject (i.e., the
mother tongue) or one school (grade) level, but it is possible if the
total range of subject matters and all succeeding grade levels are taken
into account.

If we map the relevant text forms on a hypothetical school
curriculum, we can examine which of them fit into the communicative context of various subjects taught in the school and whether the
important text forms can all find a place in the curriculum. Total or
nearly total coverage of educationally relevant text forms is the
criterion by which one can adopt a formal approach to literacy
education.

At this point, the question arises whether we can find a method of
classifying communication situations, and, what is equally important, text types and text forms that are worth studying if one wishes to
become an "independent communicant." In analyzing the parameters
that influence the produced text, Takala (1982) found that an
enormous variety of writing situations and, consequently, text forms,
appear in modern literate societies. Obviously, not all of them are
relevant from the educational point of view.

Classical rhetorical education knew four conventional forms of
spoken or written discourse: argumentation, exposition, description
and narration. These terms have been questioned on the basis that
neither a functional nor a formal linguistic definition could be found
for them in the context of written communication in modern society.
With the revival of interest in rhetorical education, new attempts were
made to classify discourse from a pragmatic point of view. Such
classifications were developed by Moffett (1968), Kinneavy (1971),
D'Angelo (1975), Britton, Burges, Martin, McLeod, & Rosen (1975),
and Applebee (1981), with the explicit aim of defining *educationally
relevant* writing situations (task situations) and discourse types. We
have, on the other hand, the terminology of linguistics, which
enables us to describe texts in terms of grammar, style, and more
recently, text grammar. This "in vitro" analysis, however, does not

help us in selecting prototypical texts on which the relationships between the aspects of the communicative situation and the linguistic features of the produced text can be studied. It seems there is a missing link between discourse classifications developed with the practical aims of rhetorical (writing) education, and the classifications used in descriptive linguistics. The former may be considered as theoretical summaries of practice in "language therapy," whereas the latter can be regarded something like "the anatomy of language." I propose that the missing link is provided in Werlich's (1976) book *A Text Grammar of English*, which is a "physiological" description of the independent written text. Werlich uses a text-internal point of view in his analysis and shows how text, as a functional unit of linguistic elements, is organized to fulfill various communicative purposes. His text typology is, therefore, uniquely suitable for the analysis of the curriculum from a formal educational point of view.

Werlich shows in many examples that, in the process of writing, the writer constructs text from a limited number of text constituents, and that these text constituents are responses to certain elements (parameters) of the writing situation, which competent readers and writers can recognize. From Werlich's analysis, which is detailed to the level of syntax and covers questions of content, text organization, and style, we shall recite here only his classification of texts by text type, text groups, and text forms, which seems most relevant from the point of view of curriculum planning. In an example, which roughly corresponds (in a somewhat idealized form) to the Hungarian curriculum, we will show how text forms fit into the communicative situations offered by the school in various subject matters on various grade levels.

Based on a model he calls "the cognitive matrix of the communicant's mind," Werlich distinguishes five *text types* as "idealized norms of text structuring . . . which serve as a matrix of rules and elements for the encoder when responding linguistically to specific aspects of his experience" (Werlich, 1976, p. 39). The five text types correspond to five aspects of experience. *Description* deals with factual phenomena in space. *Narration* deals with phenomena in time. *Exposition* is a text type that analyzes concepts or builds concepts by presenting the constituent elements in their logical relation to each other, and thus it deals with comprehension. *Argumentation* is a text type in which the writer "proposes relations between concepts of phenomena," and presents these in opposition to alternative propositions. *Instruction* is a text type in which the writer tells himself or others what to do in order to reach a certain goal.

Werlich further distinguishes two *text groups* on the basis of the relation of a text to its (cultural) context: fiction, which is largely independent of its cultural context; and nonfiction, which is interpreted in its cultural context.

Werlich proposes that text types and their variants appear in all languages in situation-specific *text forms*. He makes a basic distinction between situations in which the writer uses a personal point of view and those in which the writer takes an objective point of view.

On this basis he distinguishes the following major text forms:

(1) Descriptive text forms
    (1.1) impressionistic description (personal)
    (1.2) technical description (objective)
(2) Narrative text forms
    (2.1) the narrative (personal)
    (2.2) the report (objective)
    (2.3) the news story (objective but related to the writer's personal view)
(3) Expository text forms
    (3.1) the expository essay (personal)
    (3.2) the definition (objective)
    (3.3) the explication (objective)
    (3.4) the summary (objective)
    (3.5) summarizing minutes (objective)
    (3.6) the text interpretation
(4) Argumentative text forms
    (4.1) the comment (personal)
    (4.2) scientific argumentation
(5) Instructive text forms
    (5.1) instructions (with reference to personal authority)
    (5.2) directions, rules, regulations, statutes (with reference to impersonal authority).

On the basis of this classification we may ask ourselves: Which of these text groups, text types, and text forms may appear in the educational context of the school, and in what order? From the study of one standard (centralized national) curriculum, namely that of Hungary for general basic (grades 1-8) and academic secondary (grades 9-12) education, we can conclude that traditional school

TABLE 1.1

Text Forms Appearing in the Standard Textbooks of the
Compulsory General School and the Selective Academic
Secondary School in Hungary

| | Reading Mother Tongue: | | | Writing Mother Tongue: | |
	Language and Literature	History Social Studies	Sciences	Language and Literature	Other Subjects
			General		
Lower level grades 1-4	1.1 (fiction)	2.2	1.2	2.1	
	2.1 (fiction)	2.3	2.2	3.4	—
			School		
Upper level grades 5-8	1.1 (fiction)	2.2	1.2	1.1	1.2
	1.2	2.3	3.2	2.1	3.2
	2.1 (fiction)	3.2	3.3	3.4	
	2.2	3.4	3.4	3.6	
	3.2	4.1	4.2		
	3.3		5.1		
	3.4				
	3.6				
	5.2				
			Academic Section		
Grades 9-12	1.1 (fiction)	2.2	1.2	3.1	3.2
	2.1 (fiction)	2.3	3.2	3.6	3.3
	2.2	3.2	3.3	4.1	3.4
	3.1	3.3	3.4		
	3.2	3.4	4.2		
	3.3	4.1	5.1		
	3.4				
	3.6				
	4.1				

subjects offer a situational context to almost all text forms. (A
different question is, and it will not be discussed here, whether these
text forms appear in sufficient quality, with sufficient frequency, and
in sufficient variety, and whether they are made objects of intensive
study and are a starting point of adequate reading and writing
activities to ensure success of literacy education.) Table 1.1 indicates
which text forms are meant to appear at each of the three educational

levels (lower level of the general school: grades 1-4; upper level of the general school: grades 5-8; and the academic secondary school: grades 9-12).

The text forms dominating reading education on the lower or elementary level of basic education are narration and description. Tales and poems (2.1, 1.1), narrative passages on the episodes of national history, descriptive and narrative passages on the child's environment (2.2., 2.3, 1.2) constitute the longer texts to be read. (Instructive texts [5.1] in the form of task instructions are contained in almost all schoolbooks on this and all further levels and these are therefore shown only in the cells in which they have a further specific function. They could, however, be added in all cells of the "reading activity" column.) In composing, the writing of personal narrative (2.1) and summarizing of stories (3.4) starts with the help of the teacher usually from the third or fourth grade.

From Grade 5, when teaching by subject-matter specialist teachers begins, new text forms are gradually introduced. Besides stories and poems (2.1 and 1.1), interpretative passages on the works of literature (3.6), summaries giving complementary information to the excerpts of longer pieces of literature in the textbooks (3.4), and short biographies of writers (2.2), constitute the literature textbook. Grammar textbooks contain narrative and descriptive passages on "how language works" (1.2, 2.2), definitions (3.2), explications (3.3) of the basic grammatical notions, and summaries thereof (3.4). Rules (primarily spelling and usage rules) represent the instructive text form (5.2). In history classes, students are required to read narrative text forms: the report (2.2) and the news story (2.3). Comments (4.1) to interpret historical facts, definitions (3.2) of basic historical notions, and summaries (3.4) of chapters are also included in history books. In science textbooks the most common text forms are the technical description (1.2) (for example, in geography and biology), the definition (3.2), the explication (3.3), and the summary (3.4). The text form of scientific argumentation (4.2) and the instructive text form (5.1) appear in the context of mathematics and scientific experimentation. Text forms in which composition skills are practiced and developed are the impressionistic description (1.1) and the personal narrative (2.1). Besides these, summarizing (3.4) is frequently required and text interpretation (3.6) is occasionally required. In subjects other than mother tongue, technical description (1.2) and definition (3.2) are sometimes required writing tasks.

The text forms appearing in the academic secondary school are basically the same as those of the upper level of the general school, but the frequency of their occurrence is greater and they cover a larger area of (more abstract) topics. In addition to fiction, students also read passages which can be classified as essays (3.1), comments (4.1), and text interpretations (3.6) in literature classes. Definitions (3.2), explications (3.3) and summaries (3.4) can be found in the textbooks of almost all subjects related to their specific topics. In written composition, which is mainly taught and practiced in mother-tongue classes, the essay (3.1), text interpretation (3.6), and the comment (4.1) are the most frequently written text forms. In other subjects, the definition (3.2), the explication (3.3), and the summary (3.4) are tasks occurring with some likelihood.

This analysis suggests that nearly all text forms fit in the context of traditional subject matters.

Reading and Writing
Activities in the School

The availability of texts is only one condition of the acquisition of reading and writing literacy. Ultimately, the actual reading and writing activities related to texts and other learning experiences determine the success and level of literacy education. School activities, if well organized, are interrelated and multifunctional. Here, we shall point out three kinds of interrelationships.

Two types of reading and writing activities have to be distinguished. Those performed by the child with the direct aim of improving his reading and writing competence form part of reading and writing *instruction*. Those performed as means of subject-matter learning form part of literacy *education*. The former are organized by the mother-tongue teacher, the latter are a *shared responsibility of all teachers of a school*. Literacy instruction and literacy education are interrelated in the sense that the experiential basis needed for effective writing instruction has to be provided by the varied communication situations of subject-matter instruction and the elementary reading skills acquired in mother-tongue classes have to be developed into advanced reading competence in the instrumental use of reading in subject-matter learning.

Furthermore, reading and writing activities themselves are interrelated in the development of reading and writing competence.

Writing activities are often aimed at better understanding of texts (e.g., note making or summarizing for subject matter learning purposes), whereas reading or the study of text also serve the acquisition of modes of text organization that lead to different text forms.

Our third remark concerns the interrelationship of the acquisition of literacy values and literacy skills. Values are shared views of what are desirable goals in a community. In learning, values function as motives for setting learning goals. It follows from the above that only those literacy values that are shared by the adult community of the school (all teachers) are transmitted to students, and this common denominator of literacy values sets a limit to the students' motivation to acquire competence in written communication. Two examples may illustrate how the school's value system is indicated to the student.

Schools that take responsibility for developing language loyalty, usually have a unified language policy. This is realized, for example, in uniform requirements for spelling correctness: Not only the mother tongue teacher but all teachers correct the eventual spelling errors of the student, and correct spelling is a basic criterion of school success. Schools that adopt a community responsibility for developing writing competence usually have a policy for using essay tests in subject matter learning.

CONCLUDING REMARKS

Literacy education is a complicated and long process whereby one is taught to appreciate, comprehend, and use the language of literacy in a wide range of semipublic or public communication situations. It follows from the nature of the alphabetic writing system that oral skills and literacy interact, and both oral and written communication events affect the acquisition of the language of literacy. European languages and literatures, which have traditionally had strong interconnections, appear to have developed common rhetorical traditions. These can be detected in the similarity of the structures of school systems, school subjects, learning material, and traditional agreement over the criteria of erudition. Unity of cultural and communication values integrated multilingual Europe. This cultural integrity has been challenged only recently. This pluralism, suggested as an alternative view of educational and communication values, is threatening a communication chaos both within and outside the school; interestingly enough, at a time, when a new "lingua franca"—English—is linguistically integrating Europe in the spheres of science, business, and tourism, and in some areas, even politics.

Education for the literate use of language(s) is the shared responsibility of all teachers of the school. Teachers and students all use the language of literacy as the language of instruction. The norms and criteria of literate usage are acquired through analysis and comparison of communication situations in the school in which teachers and peers participate. Unity of cultural and communication values develops only in so far as agreement over these values can be negotiated among the teachers themselves, and between teachers and students. Provision of a representative sample of coherent texts—a text corpus representing the features of written communication to be acquired—is the shared responsibility of all school subjects. Since text types vary according to the segment of reality that forms the topic of communication, and text forms vary further according to the function of communication and the author's approach, school subjects and their contents are to be designed also with a view of full representation of important text forms. This is a requirement of formal literacy education.

Language and literature studies seem to have taken over the role of "the arts of the word": the trivium of the Middle Ages. Of all school subjects, mother tongue and foreign languages are those which can pay attention to explicit language *instruction*. With adequate cooperation, they should be able to develop in the students both loyalty toward the language of instruction and a sense of the multilingual character of our cultural traditions. This, I think, is vital for the survival of human culture in our complicated world.

REFERENCES

Applebee, A. N. (1981). *Writing in the secondary school. English and the content areas.* Urbana, IL: National Council of the Teachers of English.

Britton, J., Burgess, T., Martin, N., McLeod, A., & Rosen, H. (1975). *The development of writing abilities.* London: Macmillan.

D'Angelo, F. J. (1975). *A conceptual theory of rhetoric.* Cambridge, MA: Winthrop.

Gumperz, J. J. (1962). Types of linguistic communities. *Anthropological Linguistics* *4*, 28-40.

Kinneavy, J. L. (1971). *A theory of discourse*. Englewood Cliffs, NJ: Prentice-Hall.

Kiss, A. (1969). *Muveltseg es iskola*. (Culture and education). Budapest: Akademiai K.

Lambert, W. (1968, February 22-24). *Motivation and language learning: Psychological aspects*. Paper presented at the Southern Conference on Language Teaching, New Orleans, Louisiana

McKeon, R. P. (1964). The liberating arts and the humanizing arts in education. In A. A. Cohen (Ed.), *Humanistic education and western civilization* (pp. 159-181). New York: Holt, Rinehart and Winston.

Mead, M. (1978). *Culture and commitment. The new relationships between the generations in the 1970s*. New York: Columbia University Press.

Moffett, J. (1968). *Teaching the universe of discourse*. Boston: Houghton Mifflin.

Nystrand, M. (1982). Rhetoric's "audience" and linguistics' "speech community": Implications for understanding writing, reading, text. In M. Nystrand (Ed.), *What writers know* (pp. 3-28). New York: Academic Press.

Passow, A. H. (1974). Compensatory instructional intervention. In F. N. Kerlinger & J. B. Carroll (Eds.), *Review of research in education* (Vol. 2, pp. 145-175). Itasca, IL: Peacock.

Passow, A. H., Noah, H. J., Eckstein, M. A., & Mallea, J. R. (1976). *The national case study: An empirical comparative study of twenty-one educational systems. International Studies in Evaluation (Vol. VII)*. Stockholm: Almqvist & Wiksell.

Skutnabb-Kangas, T., & Toukomaa, P. (1976). *Teaching migrant children's mother tongue and learning the language of the host country in the context of the sociocultural situation of the migrant family*. Unpublished manuscript, The Finnish National Commission for Unesco, Helsinki.

Stenhouse, L. (1967). *Culture and education*. New York: Weybright and Talley.

Suhor, C. (1984). The role of print as a medium in our society. In Purves, A. & Niles, O. (Eds.), *Becoming readers in a complex society: Eighty-third yearbook of the National Society for the Study of Education, Part I* (1 pp. 16-46). Chicago: University of Chicago Press.

Takala, S. (1982). On the origin, communicative parameters and processes of writing. In Purves, A. C. & Takala, S. (Eds.). *An International perspective on the evaluation of written composition. Evaluation in Education: An International Review Series* (Vol. 5, pp. 207-230).

Thorndike, R. L. (1973). *Reading comprehension education in fifteen countries*. Stockholm: Almqvist & Wiksell.

Wann, L. (1939). *Century readings in the English essay*. (rev. ed.). New York: Appleton-Century-Crofts.

Weinreich, U. (1963). *Languages in contact. Findings and problems*. The Hague: Mouton.

Wells, G. (1985). *Language development in pre-school years*. Language at home and at school (Vol. 2.). Cambridge: Cambridge University Press.

Werlich, E. (1976). *A text grammar of English*. Heidelberg: Quelle & Meyer.

2

The Problem of Selection of Writing Tasks in Cross-Cultural Study

ANNELI VÄHÄPASSI

Since Kaplan (1966) developed the framework for contrastive rhetoric by emphasizing the close relationship between rhetoric and culture, it has been quite commonly realized that the society and culture to a high extent transcend and control the individuals. They can write meaningfully only by accepting and following the conventions of their own rhetorical culture. However, in most of the reported studies the relationship between culture, convention, and writing has been analyzed on the basis of compositions written in the nonnative language. One can argue, as does Hinds (1982), that the performance of a student may or may not reflect, for example, the organization of the composition in the native language. In consequence, in order to draw valid conclusions as to what extent writing is culturally and situationally influenced, compositions written in the native language and in national contexts, should be used.

One could also argue that there are some other sources of error in the studies of contrastive rhetoric. First, the conclusions have been based mainly on expository essays, which means that neither the audience nor the purpose of the writing have been specified explicitly enough. Second, the data bases used in the studies have been so limited that the researchers have not been able to investigate the problem of sub-cultures inside the same rhetorical culture. Therefore, many important questions have not been answered, for example, the following:

> To what extent are the different rhetorical patterns related to the gender of writers or the social background of writers, rather than to the certain culture?

To what extent are the conventions and rhetorical patterns influenced by the school systems and the development of literature in different cultures?

These questions cannot be investigated and answered without such a data base, which, on the one hand, allows the generalization to the whole population and, on the other hand, gives researchers opportunities to validate their results with regard to different subgroups in the population investigated.

At the present time there is such an opportunity available, namely on the basis of the data obtained in the IEA International Study of Achievement in Written Composition (the IEA Writing Study). The idea of investigating the nature, mastery, and instruction of writing skills in different school systems and cultures was born in the comparative mind of one researcher, namely the editor of this volume. In this study the data describing students' writing skills can be examined in relation to several factors. The IEA Writing Study has emphasized that student writing must be related to the development of literary culture in the participating countries and school systems as well as the functions of writing in each culture and school system. On the other hand, the study has paid special attention to cognitive processes developed by writing and to their stimuli (the writing assignments and situations in particular). The study also focuses on the importance of written expression as the means of education in different cultures.

The countries and school systems that have participated in the investigation of the writing outcomes of their school systems in the framework of a cross-cultural study are self-selected: the National Centers, which are the members of the IEA-organization (International Association for the Evaluation of Educational Achievement) were, in 1980, able to decide for themselves whether they were interested in the cross-cultural study of writing or, for example, in the international study focused on the achievements in science. According to their own decisions, the following National Centers were willing to participate in the IEA Writing Study: Chile, England and Wales, the Federal Republic of Germany, Finland, Hungary, Indonesia, Italy, the Netherlands, New Zealand, Nigeria, Sweden, Thailand, and the United States. Australia, Kenya, Israel, Ivory Coast, and Scotland were involved in the study during the stages described in this chapter, but could not collect and analyze data because of a lack of funding.

Populations investigated in the study are selected in such a way that the outcomes of school systems can be compared. The main population consists of students at the end of compulsory schooling. The other populations are students at the end of primary education and students at the end of preuniversity schooling. (For example and further information, see Takala and Vähäpassi, 1985, 1987).

SEARCHING THE COMMON FRAME OF REFERENCE FOR COMPARISON AND SELECTION OF WRITING TASKS

Once Alan C. Purves's proposal for an International Study of Achievement in Written Composition was accepted by the General Assembly of IEA, many problems with regard to comparability between school systems and cultures had to be discussed and solved. One could, for example, assume that different cultures would differ in terms of (a) What functions of writing are emphasized in school? (b) What are typical writing assignments? (c) What are appropriate topics to write about? (d) What is the appropriate form of task instruction (e.g., mere title versus detailed prompting)?

When discussing these questions one of the most difficult problems was to establish a common frame of reference and terminology. In this discussion the study's Steering Committee and International Study committee clearly faced the question of comparability of concepts and their meanings. The members of the committees began more and more to understand how different cultures verbalize different aspects of the same concepts. For example, in the vocabulary of some committee members, *to learn* meant "to repeat and demonstrate the acquisition of knowledge" whereas the others understood it as "the process of discovering new knowledge by writing" or "to acquire new concepts by expressive, exploratory writing." There were also different notions of concepts *expository, expressive, argumentative* or *pragmatic, functional* writing, which is quite understandable, because in many languages, for example, Finnish, such concepts have been adopted and translated from English. In such languages it is difficult to find the equivalent concept, because the whole phenomenon may be different than in the English speaking countries. Semantic fuzziness among representatives of different cultures became so evident, that one wondered whether cultural differences might be so great that valid comparisons between student writing are feasible. Very little was known of cultural patterns and preferences in this area.

Semantic fuzziness of concepts among representatives of the same culture, however, also became evident. One had to ask whether the selection of writing tasks in writing investigations is based on well-established theory or well-defined concepts in any single culture. Rationally thinking, it should be associated with the general approach of education in a particular school system, especially with the justification given for the teaching of writing at school. It should also be based on the overall orientation that has been adopted for writing as a construct. Unfortunately, it seems to be the normal situation that the tasks used to measure student writing are not given the kind of attention they deserve. Views on which aspects of the writing skill to measure and how to measure them tend to differ from one study to another (Baker, 1982; Purves, Söter, Takala, & Vähäpassi, 1984). Consequently, the results of different investigations are not easy to compare (see Wesdorp, 1982). The difficulty of task selection and the considerable variation in assignments from one writing study to another are probably owing to the fact that there is no general consistent theory of what constitutes language ability, including writing ability.

The question of selection and comparability of tasks, however, had to be solved before the IEA Writing Study could proceed to collect descriptive data and explore relationships between student performance in writing and various factors related to students' cultural backgrounds, home backgrounds, language contacts, teaching practices, and so on. It seemed reasonable to approach the issue from two different points of view (see Warwick & Osherson, 1973):

First: How congruent are the national concepts describing task types?

Second: How can the problem of linguistically equivalent task formulation be solved?

In the planning phase of the IEA Writing Study it soon became evident that in order to answer the two questions and establish a common framework, a conceptual analysis of the potential domain of school-based writing was necessary. A mere collection of tasks and topics from different school systems could not lead to an advance in our knowledge, nor to the formation of a theory (see Raivola, 1985).

It also soon became obvious that for the conceptual analysis, a feasible tool should be found, namely, a model of writing that could be applied to the specification of writing tasks or assignments. The model was needed also for the analysis of teaching. Work on such a model was undertaken, even though it was recognized that, like all models, it would no doubt be a simplification of reality. However, the merit of a model is that it helps to give due account of the central variables in school-based writing situations and of their relationships as they are realized in actual writing assignments.

A common framework for the selection of tasks was indispensable because the steering committee of the study did not accept any idea of being able to assess the writing competence of individual students and the productivity of school systems with a single writing task. The earlier work done by the committee members on national assessments has clearly revealed the importance of adequate content sampling. Thus, from the very beginning, it was decided that each student should write on several different tasks in order to cover the main goals of written communication, as well as the main cognitive tasks with respect to language and content generation.

THE GENERAL MODEL OF WRITING DOMAIN

An understanding of the psychological construct of writing and the educational value and uses of writing led to the development of a general model of the writing domain (Vähäpassi, 1982). Its development was guided by the view that several concepts and dimensions must be considered when selecting and sequencing writing tasks in teaching and/or investigating learning outcomes. My analysis of the concept of writing (1982) showed that the important contextual factors in a writing situation are (a) cognitive demands related to the topic and content, (b) social and intersubjective demands of writing concerning the purpose and audience of writing, and (c) linguistic and rhetorical demands of writing concerning the mode of discourse.

The domain of writing in this model is characterized by means of a two-dimensional typology using the first two factors as the main dimensions. The diffuse concepts and the different interpretations of the third dimension, the linguistic and rhetorical demands, make it inappropriate in a model for a cross-cultural study. However, these aspects of writing are reflected in the dimension called modes of discourse, in which documentative, reportorial, or exploratory discourse are realized in a variety of text types. Thus the model presents *dominant intention/purpose* as one main dimension, *cognitive processing/demands* as the other, with *modes of discourse* as a complementary dimension.

The purposes of writing (to learn, to convey feelings and emotions, to inform, to persuade, to entertain, delight, play with language, to keep in touch) were defined according to Roman Jakobson (1960), who distinguished six primary functions of written and oral discourse, as follows:

(1) metalingual function emphasizing the language code used to carry the message (in this classification, the function was considered to involve also the learning function in two meanings: to report and acquire knowledge)

(2) emotive function emphasizing the writer's thoughts and feelings, the internally experienced world of the writer

(3) referential function emphasizing the externally observable world outside writer and reader

(4) cognitive function emphasizing the reader's thoughts feelings and attitudes

(5) poetic function emphasizing the expression itself, for poetic purposes language use can also be multifunctional

(6) phatic function emphasizing the social contacts between writer and reader

Although the cognitive processes underlying writing and thinking are very complex, the following three stages in the cognitive processing/cognitive demands of writing tasks can identified: to *reproduce* internal or external reality, to *organize* or *reorganize* reality, to *invent* or *generate* a new possible world (see Bloom, 1956; Flower & Hayes, 1977; Rumelhart & Ortony, 1977; Bereiter, 1980).

In this context

—*reproduce* means receptive, recognizing and recalling modes of processing information, in which the writer copies, cites, takes notes etc.

—*reorganize* and *organize* means analyzing and structuring modes of processing information, in which the writer narrates, describes, explains, summarizes etc.

—*invent* and *generate* means evaluating and generating modes of information processing, in which the writer analyzes, expounds, argues, creates new possible world etc.

Primary content is related to the levels of cognitive processing and *primary audience* to the purpose of writing.

Taking into account the two main dimensions of the model and the connection between cognitive processing and mode of discourse, we obtained a typology that can be tested by trying to place different types of written products within its cells. Figure 2.1 illustrates such a trial classification, although it is by no means meant to be an exhaustive listing of the possible types of written discourse. Nor are the text types used to illustrate the system limited to the particular cells in which they are shown. For instance, a summary can be written for many purposes, such as to learn or to inform or to persuade. The same is true of many, perhaps most, text types.

The model is based on semiotic structure in that it considers the relationship between the writer, the reader, and the message. Recent models relevant to school writing, especially those by Moffett (1968), Kinneavy (1971, 1980), and Britton, Burgess, Martin, McLeod, and Rosen (1975), also reflect a similar understanding of the inter-relationships between writers, readers, and texts. In adopting this approach we avoid the basic weakness of many models of writing instruction, namely that the purpose and mode of writing have been considered largely synonymous. On the other hand, the semiotic models proposed by Moffett, Britton et al., and Kinneavy, when emphasizing the purpose of writing, tend to neglect the other important dimension, the cognitive processes. The close connection between thinking and writing is noted, but the relationship is not elaborated on in a manner that would be very useful for writing in an educational context.

I would also like to emphasize the difference between this model and the process model developed by Flower and Hayes (1981). The latter focuses on the actual writing activity on a given writing task and is therefore most useful in investigating and guiding the actual writing process. The present model focuses on the sequencing of writing tasks to be used in instruction and in the curriculum. This model is also a useful guide for investigating the coverage and the approach of the curriculum in different school systems.

Figure 2.1 General Model of Writing Discourse

Cognitive Processing → Dominant Intention/Purpose ↓	Primary Content / Primary Audience	I REPRODUCE Linguistically Precoded/Predetermined Information	II ORGANIZE/REORGANIZE Known Spatial/Temporal	Known Phenomena, Concepts or Mental States	III INVENT/GENERATE New or Alternative Spatial/Temporal, Phenomena, Concepts or Mental States	
1. To learn (meta-lingual)	Self	Copying Taking dictation			Comments on book margins	The traditio[nal]
2. To convey emotions, feelings (emotive)	Self / Others	Stream of Consciousness	Personal story	Portrayal Personal diary Personal letter	Reflective writing -- Personal essays Metaphors Analogies	literary genr[es] and modes
3. To inform (referential)	Others	Quote Fill in a form	Narrative report News Instruction Telegram Announcement Circular	Directions Description Technical description Biography Science report/experiment	Expository writing -- Definition -- Academic essay/article -- Book review -- Commentary	can be placed
4. To convince, persuade (conative)	Others	Citation from authority/expert	Letter of application	Advertisement Letter or advice Statement of personal views, opinions	Argumentative/ persuasive writing -- Editorial -- Critical essay/article	under one or more
5. To entertain, delight, please (poetic)	Others	Quotation of poetry and prose	Given an ending- create a story Create an ending Retell a story	Word portrait or sketch Causerie	Entertainment writing -- Parody -- Rhymes	of these four purposes.
6. To keep in touch (phatic)	Others	Postcards	Postcards, letters			
		DOCUMENTATIVE DISCOURSE	REPORTORIAL DISCOURSE		EXPLORATORY DISCOURSE	

The cognitive demands of writing tasks (that is, the horizontal axis of the model) can also be interpreted according to process characteristics. Tasks differ in the planning process required. Flower and Hayes (1981) distinguish processing in terms of (a) cognitive load of generating, (b) organizing of content, and (c) setting the purpose of communication (see de Glopper & Kádár-Fülop, 1986). On the horizontal axis of the model we notice that the first two demands increase as we move to the right. Students progress from the reproduction of ideas and language on the left, creating their own ideas with appropriate rhetorical and linguistic forms on the far right. This progression must be taken into account when selecting writing tasks and guiding the composing processes.

This model does not attempt to cover the whole complex domain of the activity of writing. However, the model seeks to illustrate this complexity and the multidimensional character of the domain of school writing. In consequence, the school has a demanding task in introducing children into the world of written communication. Clearly, the school is responsible for providing varied writing situations (varied writing purposes, cognitive demands, audiences). At the same time the model shows how many factors must be considered when we try to secure domain representativeness in tasks used in the evaluation of writing skills. Consequently, it can be used by different cultures and school systems for the analysis of the approach in teaching and evaluation in terms of selecting and sequencing writing tasks—but not in terms of guiding actual writing processes.

WRITING IN SCHOOL SYSTEMS

Written language has always played a dominant role in education. Typically, the acquisition of literacy is considered to be one of the most important tasks of the school. Literacy is not only one of the main goals of schooling, it is essential for the achievement of other goals as well.

While it is true that the four basic skills of general verbal ability, reading, writing, speaking, and listening are interrelated (Wells, 1981; Perera, 1984), writing is a much more school-based activity than are any of the other skills. Some children may know how to read when they start school, but relatively few know how to write. Reading is also quite a popular pastime outside the school, but few students write for pleasure. It has been maintained (e.g., Britton et al., 1975) that a school system has a decisive effect on the development of writing.

The writing instruction approach adopted in different cultures and school systems is related to the general goals of education, the conception of language functions, and the process of writing. Fundamentally, educational views, including the goals of education, are shaped by the nature of the society in which the school system is embedded, including the goals of writing instruction.

The goals of education as well as writing instruction can be examined on many levels (see Spencer, 1981; Applebee, 1981; Vähä-passi, 1982; Kádár-Fülop, Pezeskhpour, & Purves, 1982). According to a fairly concrete approach we can, with some simplification, distinguish three main groups of writing objectives. One set of objectives is associated with the documenting, acquisition, and recitation of knowledge, the second set is related to expanding reality and the developing of logical and divergent creative thinking, and the third set is related to activities in society, to the ability to communicate with people by writing. The purposes of writing to be practiced and cognitive processes to be developed are in the school systems selected according to these objectives.

These, in turn, influence the teaching approach, the sequence of writing tasks and criteria, individual writing tasks and their stimuli. The relationships between the different elements are outlined in Figure 2.2. On the basis of Figure 2.2 and the general model of writing, three main questions with regard to comparability and task selection will be discussed:

(1) Are the different school systems in different cultures, after all, somewhat alike? In other words, is the school a system, which functions in the same way in every culture, disregarding partic-ular/specific features of the culture in which the school is functioning?

(2) Or is the situation the opposite: Do different school systems and cultures emphasize different cells of the domain presented in Figure 2.1?

(3) How is the concrete selection and wording of writing stimuli decided in different school systems? Is it possible that the purpose and cognitive demand of one writing task might produce different phenotypes in different cultures?

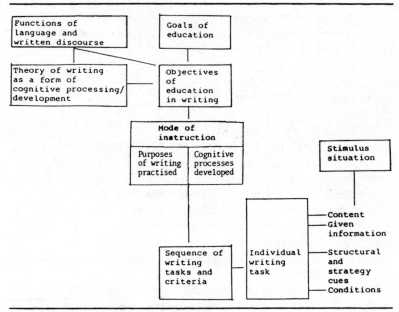

Figure 2.2   Determinants of School Writing Assignments

The data needed for answering these questions were collected from the National Centers involved in the IEA Writing Study in the first research stage when they were asked to send the topics used in school-leaving examinations during 1980-1983. In the second stage, both during and after the task selection, National Research Coordinators were asked to analyze the familiarity of the tasks selected from the point of view of their own school system, culture, and curriculum.

These data have been analyzed according to the general model of writing, and at this stage the conclusions are presented without statistical support. The reason for this is understandable: The tasks and topics used in different school systems are not comparable in such a way that one can force them into the same tables. The concepts presented in the domain of writing have been put into practice in different combinations in different school systems.

Later, as the data from the teaching practices become available, these questions will be reexamined. It is possible that when all the data have been analyzed, the conclusions drawn will change.

CONCLUSIONS BASED ON THE
FIRST STAGES OF RESEARCH

Relating School-Leaving Exams
to the Domain of Writing

Writing in order to learn in the meaning "to demonstrate one's knowledge" is emphasized in all the school systems that participated in the IEA Writing Study. Their school-leaving examinations, both in the language of instruction and in other school subjects, require the presentation and demonstration of knowledge using the conventional written code of the culture. In this case the cognitive demand of tasks is the ability to organize or reorganize the knowledge. It can be assumed that instruction differences do exist, however, whether the aim is to acquire concepts and new knowledge by writing, or only to repeat or to demonstrate knowledge.

The most emphasized purpose in school-leaving examinations of the language of instruction (mother tongue) was *writing in order to inform* in all investigated school systems. This applies especially to school-leaving examinations at the preuniversity level. At its best the tasks given to students demand reflective (or epistemic, in Bereiter's, 1980, sense of the term) writing in which the cognitive demand is *to invent and generate.* Students have an opportunity to consider the topic from their own point of view and to shed some new light on recognized problems. By means of this kind of writing, students may structure reality, create a mental representation of it, and expand their thinking. The topic is the focus of the tasks, however, referring to the writer's external reality, not to the emotions or attitudes of the writers themselves.

The tasks that presuppose writing for informative, referential purposes have also been presented in such a way that their cognitive demand is *to organize/reorganize.* This applies especially to the school-leaving examinations for the population of 16-year-old students (the Netherlands, Nigeria, and Sweden) or examinations for nonacademic tracks (the Netherlands), although preuniversity-level examinations in some school systems (Finland and Hungary) also contain tasks that are close to the writing tasks intended only to show the students' knowledge and learning. In Hungary these tasks require knowledge of language and literature, in Finland that of religion, historical or social issues, or science.

The frequent appearance of *writing in order to learn and to inform* in school-leaving examinations is supported by the results obtained by Britton et al. (1975) in British schools, and Spencer (1983) in Scottish schools. Referential (Britton uses the term *informative*) tasks constituted 62% of Britton's empirical data, and according to Spencer, 75% of all school writing in Scotland was informative. This applies to writing across the curriculum. Similarly, according to Applebee (1981a, 1981b), writing activities in American high schools were dominated by mechanical and informational uses of writing, whereas personal and creative uses of writing had little place in the high school curriculum.

The neglected tasks in school-leaving examinations, however, seem to be pragmatic, functional tasks, the purpose of which is to inform a given audience. This includes all school systems participating in the IEA Writing Study at the preuniversity level. However, the school-leaving examinations in the Netherlands and Nigeria contain some pragmatic tasks. In the Netherlands, the examinations also contain tasks that allow students to *write in order to convince or persuade* a given audience.

In general, the most neglected function in school writing appears to be the cognitive function, although in some school systems (e.g., Finland and the Netherlands) there is a growing emphasis on persuasive writing. In real life, as opposed to a school-like setting, however, persuasion and argumentation appear to pervade practically all discourse. the cognitive function may, in fact, be dominant in out-of-school situations.

Writing in order to convey emotions and feelings appears to be a very rarely used task in school-leaving examinations, let alone *writing in order to explore experience in literary forms, or entertain or delight by means of language.* On the other hand, there are some school systems that are exceptions of this general rule. In Australia and New Zealand and Wales students have more freedom to express their ideas and emotional needs in writing than in the other school systems. The cognitive demand of the tasks given to them is *to invent, generate.*

This analysis indicates that school writing in different school systems tends to restrict the use and practice of writing purposes when evaluated on the basis of school-leaving examinations. In this respect, school systems seem to be more alike than different.

Writing Stimulus Types
Used in School-Leaving Exams

When students are asked to search for meaning and seek a personal solution to large-scale problems, as happens in most school-leaving examinations at the preuniversity level, they are recalling what they know about their topic from their long-term memory, and are judging their experience with the topic and with the writing task in general (see Augustine, 1981). One has to assume that an important factor influencing the success of processing is the information given in the assignment. It is quite a different task to write on the basis of a short rubric like *High performance sports* than to write on the basis of several brief texts in which the viewpoints on the topic vary, as happens in the writing assignment presented in Appendix 2.A.

Cultural differences are not very great when evaluated in the light of school-leaving examinations. The approaches at the general task level do not seem to differ as much as one would expect. However, the stimuli used seem to vary considerably.

The most common type of stimulus appears to be some version of the following prototypes:

"People seldom stand up for what they truly believe; instead, they merely go along with the popular view."

Do you agree or disagree with this statement? Write an essay in which you support your opinion with specific examples from history, contemporary affairs, literature, or personal observation. (United States, 1982)

"Krakers" ignore verdicts pronounced by judges and they barricade the houses they have taken into use.

Demonstrators at nuclear plants don't carry police orders into effect: they maintain their blockades. Groups of political activists arrange places of abode for illegal immigrant workers.

Some people say: You have to acquiesce in decisions taken by an authority that was formed in a democratic way.

Other people put it this way: injustice supported by democratic decisions remains injustice all the same.

What is your opinion and how do you judge actions like the ones described above? (The Netherlands, 1981)

Comment on the following statement by Gandhi: "It is a deplorable habit, that of judging false other people's thoughts and then claiming ours to be true. It is equally deplorable to consider those who have opinions different from ours as our country's enemies." (Italy, 1980)

By contrast, quite seldom is the stimulus for writing given only as a mere title as seems to be the case in Finland, New Zealand, and Wales. For example:

The Spring Migration of Birds, the Festal Time of Northern Nature

Is the Law the same for Everyone?

Men's and women's jobs (Finland, 1980)

My first love

A day to forget

Parents are a nuisance (Wales, 1980, 1981, 1982)

WHY?

THE FUTURE (New Zealand, 1980)

The titles presented to the students in New Zealand, however, are often illustrated. For example, the picture reproduced in Appendix 2.B was included with the title, The Future. Using pictures together with titles is not the only difference between New Zealand and other school systems. In New Zealand there seems to be a trend toward a greater variety of school writing, particularly through increasing the variety of information given to students. There also seems to be a trend to increase the degree of freedom of students when selecting the mode of writing. In several tasks used in New Zealand, as well as in experimental tasks used in Australia, the student can choose the approach for writing on a topic. In contrast, titles or assignments given, for example in the Federal Republic of Germany, Finland, and Hungary, require a specific kind of writing and presuppose that students keep to the topic.

Thus we have seen that students in different countries are given varying amounts of information of information as stimuli for their writing in school-leaving examinations. The least amount of information is provided to Finnish, German, Hungarian, and Italian students. The richest information is provided in writing assignments used in Australia, the Netherlands, and New Zealand.

In those school systems in which the stimuli are many-sided the students also get an opportunity for personal, digressive, metaphorical, and multiple writing. In other school systems, again, the topics anticipate abstract, impersonal, and plain writing (compare Takala, Purves, & Buckmaster, 1982). One is tempted to ascribe this difference in the approach to writing and the support given to students to the whole verbal interaction in that particular culture and, therefore, it is also relevant in cross-cultural rhetorics.

CONCLUSIONS MADE FROM
THE SELECTION OF
ACTUAL WRITING TASKS

The tasks used in school-leaving examinations were analyzed by comparing them to the general model of written discourse. In this analysis two main dimensions of the model, namely the communicative purpose and cognitive demands of tasks, were evaluated and considered. The same dimensions were considered in the actual task selection.

The analysis of school-leaving examinations has led to the conclusion that the task used in the IEA Writing Study should give students an opportunity to show the ability *to organize and reorganize in order to inform, and to organize or reorganize in order to learn.* Tasks with an informative orientation were also designed to include socially needed pragmatic writing activities, although their emphasis varies considerably from one school system to another. These assignments were chosen to tap the so-called functional basic skills of writing. Although the cognitive function is not very dominant in school-leaving examinations it was decided to include in the study such tasks in which students have to demonstrate an ability *to invent/generate in order to convince/persuade,* because of the importance of this function in out-of-school situations.

The analysis of school-leaving examinations indicated that the opportunity to create and expand reality through writing played a part in several examinations. For this reason, it was decided to give students tasks that require them *to invent or generate in order to inform.*

The emotive function, that is, that which is involved in the tasks of *organizing/reorganizing, or inventing/generating in order to convey feelings and emotions,* was deemed so important for the evaluation of a school system it was decided that such a skill should be assessed. This decision was supported by the fact that some experts suggest that other forms of writing are based on it (see Britton et al., 1975; Kinneavy, 1980). By contrast, we did not include in the compulsory assignments any task that would require students to write *in order to entertain/delight* (poetic function) because it seemed to be only an occasional school task, although it is quite usual as an extra-curricular activity. On the other hand, we felt that the emotive and poetic functions of language are not very clearly distinguished in school-based writing. In practical situations these two functions often overlap. Therefore, it was decided to include one very open task among the international options, a task that would allow the opportunity of an artistic (poetic, literary) response as well as an opportunity *to entertain/delight.*

Such considerations led to a final number of 14 writing tasks (see Appendix 2.C). Using the model of the domain of writing as a theoretical background they can be classified as follows:

I. *Tasks in which students organize or reorganize in order to inform (seven in all).* These are *pragmatic* tasks (letters) addressed to a known audience. One of them also has a persuasive purpose. In these tasks there is systematic variation with regard to the topic and the social and psychological relationship of the reader and the writer. They emphasize the perspectives of both the topic and the reader.

II. *Tasks in which students organize or reorganize in order to learn (three in all).* These represent usual *learning* tasks such as summarizing, paraphrasing thoughts and events, transforming oral language into a narrative summary, describing phenomena and observations. All these skills are important in developing analytic perceptions of reality. Although learning skills and the perspective of the topic are the main focus of these tasks, the tasks also presuppose the writer's awareness of the reader.

III. *Tasks in which students organize/reorganize or invent/generate in order to convey feelings or emotions or to entertain (two in all).* These represent tasks in which students have to organize and generate their own view of externally observable and internally experienced reality.

Students have to write either *a personal story* or *narration* or they can choose the mode of writing. The tasks can be interpreted by them and by the scorers either as audience-oriented (entertaining) or addresser-oriented, which allow different solutions. Both tasks are addressed to an unknown readership.

IV. *Tasks in which students invent or generate in order to convince/persuade or to inform (two in all).* These represent writing tasks in which students have to generate and develop their own point of view of reality. One task (*reflective essay*) is topic-oriented with an attempt to balance varying views on the topic. The other task is primarily audience-oriented (*persuasive composition*), but students must choose the addressee themselves. Both tasks have been formulated so that student scripts can be analyzed to investigate young people's world-views and perceptions of reality.

The stimuli given in writing assignments were standardized in such a way that every assignment mentioned the purpose, audience, and text types presupposed in the assignment. The audience, however, was not mentioned if it was an unknown readership—representative of written culture. Furthermore, evaluation criteria and some structural cues were given in all the assignments. Three of the tasks included pictures.

The specification of task formulation gave students an opportunity to undertake task analysis. For example, when examining the summary task they must consider the following aspects:

Aspect	Question	Answer
text type	What form of text am I supposed to write?	a summary of a short given text
audience	To whom am I supposed to write?	an addressesee who has not read the text
purpose	Why should I write?	to aid learning

It was not considered possible to assess the writing competence of individual students and the productivity of the school system or the role of writing in different school systems with a single writing task. Thus, it was decided that each student should write on several

different tasks in order to cover the main goals of written communication as well as the main cognitive demands with respect to language
and content generation.

Since it was practically impossible for the students to respond to all
the tasks in the amount of class time available for testing, it was
decided to rotate the tasks so that each student wrote on three
assignments, each of which related to a different area of writing
ability. This design has the additional advantage of enabling us to
contribute to the research of writing ability as a construct. With data
based on different tasks written by the same student, we can
investigate to what extent writing is a general ability and to what
extent it is task specific.

CONCLUSIONS WITH REGARD
TO COMPARABILITY

The reader may wonder whether this task selection might favor
some school systems while being unfair to others. How valid is the
measurement if a given task is not used or is regarded as a secondary
activity in one or another school system? This question was carefully
discussed when the proposed selection of tasks was reconsidered by
the National Research Coordinators on the basis of the data described
earlier. Although we had this data available, we were fully aware of
the possibility that individual teaching practices may differ considerably from what the curriculum recommends, from what school-
leaving examinations demand, and from what the National Committees estimated to be prevailing practices (see Linnakylä, 1983).

Such considerations led to the following conclusion: Although
school systems did differ to some extent in the emphasis given to
different tasks, the National Research Coordinators and the National
Committees of such school systems were in favor of a many-sided set
of tasks. Their motivation was twofold: (1) the tasks illustrate to
teachers how varied the domain of writing actually is; and (2) the
tasks reveal what the actual results of teaching written composition
are, including the possibility of tasks that were *taught but not
learned,* or *not taught but learned.*

In other words, the National Committees of the school systems
participating in the IEA Writing Study were willing to interpret the

results of their school systems on the basis of the theoretical domain of writing. They realized how important the purposes of writing are in a particular community and wanted to investigate for which purposes the members of their community are able to write. They also wanted to see which level of cognitive processing is favored in their school system (compare Heath, 1983; Scribner & Cole, 1981).

All this conceptual reflection undoubtedly led to better (i.e., more controlled and theoretically based) writing tasks than the ad hoc procedures based on mere empirical consensus-seeking. One has to confess, however, that in terms of task instructions we faced problems in spite of a careful pilot studies. The concepts used or the situations described in them are not equally familiar in every culture. The problem was greatest when formulating the so-called pragmatic tasks. For example, in some cultures it is not usual that the child returns from school to an empty house, and therefore there is no need to leave a written message for a family, or it may be unusual that a student communicates with the principal or writes letters of application. There are circumstances in which direct personal argumentation about a delicate topic is not common. In selecting tasks and formulating their instructions we had to make compromises to make sure that we would not put some systems at a disadvantage in comparison with other systems.

The IEA Writing Study is the first attempt to assess writing skills across cultural contexts and across languages, and this is an audacious undertaking. We attempt to describe the outcomes of different school systems that have been measured by using a theoretically representative set of tasks and evaluated by means of a common scoring scheme and a commensurable scale.

It may be, however, that the most sensible way to compare the outcomes of different school systems is to ask groups of experts in each participating country to assess what portion and which groups of students have achieved the kind of writing skills that are needed in that particular country and culture. In countries like Finland or the United States, where telecommunication via computers will probably be an omnipresent activity the acquisition of writing is a condition of survival (Kádár-Fülop, in this volume). In other countries, such as Indonesia and Nigeria, the demands of literacy acquisition are different because of the addition of language problems. Therefore, we do not presume that the scores given in different countries can be directly compared with each other. Each country or school system must draw its own conclusions, comparing the scores given with the actual compositions (see Takala & Vähäpassi, 1987).

On the basis of the exceptional data collected, however, we have an opportunity to provide illuminating descriptions of possible differences in student writing. We can investigate questions that do not yet have satisfactory answers. The main questions to be set and answered in terms of contrastive rhetorics will be: To what extent are there actually distinct cultural patterns in writing, or to what extent is such a notion only a stereotype based on anecdotal evidence? To what extent is there general pattern or variation within each culture, and to what extent is their overlap between cultures? For example: Is the achievement profile of girls and boys similar in different cultures? Or, is the achievement profile of students from corresponding social groups similar in different countries?

The data collected in the IEA Writing Study provide numerous possibilities for future studies in contrastive rhetorics. Detailed text analyses within and across languages are possible, in order to find out how students at various grades and age levels cope with the cognitive, rhetorical, and linguistic demands set in the writing tasks (de Glopper & Kádár-Fülop, 1986). Several signs indicate that there is a growing interest in moving from the assessment stage to a stage in which we can take a closer look at the compositions themselves. A number of cognitive, linguistic, rhetorical, and cross-cultural studies have been tentatively sketched during recent meetings of the steering committee (Takala & Vähäpassi, 1987). On this data-base, research work can continue on one of the greatest challenges of the IEA Writing Study: to determine if and to what extent writing is culture bound.[1]

APPENDIX 2.A

Elaborate the assignment, given under A.

A. High performance sports

Following you'll find a number of quotes that talk about the advantage and disadvantages of high performance sports. Write an essay with the title "High performance sports," in which you consider some of the mentioned advantages and disadvantages and make clear what is your attitude concerning high performance sports.

(a) Some people condemn "in (high performance) sports the tough games and competition. Instead of offering compensation for these phenomena in society, sports rather emphasize them. Furthermore, ruthlessness with regards to opponents is thus increased. The person who practises high performance sports becomes less fit to function within a community." (W. van Zijll, "Sports and Society in the 20th Century," *Mirror of History,* November 9, 1974)

(b) Practising (high performance sports) demands great sacrifices that are accompanied by psychological and social stress. Solutions are demanded for, for example, loss of wages and pay, education and jobs, military service, career and also return to "normal" society after the conclusion of the activity in high performance sports. (In "High Performance Sports, Whose Responsibility? *Union of Dutch Municipalities,* Green Series nr. 10)

(c) "It is self-evident and justified that in sports young people want to achieve something. It is completely wrong to resent performance sports. In sports, too, people are allowed to search for the limits of their capacities. High performance sports and the achievements therein are very welcome to us if they function as an example for other sports practitioners and, for instance, to the large numbers of people who enjoy them passively." (Dr. B. J. Crum, "Criticism of High Performance Sports" AO-booklet, nr. 1465, May 25, 1973)

(d) Dr. Wildor Hollman, staff member of the sports college in Cologne: "With the training methods we are using now we have almost reached the limit. It has become almost impossible to prevent damage to the heart muscle under low oxygen conditions, in which high altitude training takes place. Serious injuries—many permanent—for sportsmen were every day occurrences in this year of preparations for the Munich Games. Broken tendons of Achilles, degenerated knee joints and heart attacks were the result of the pitiless overburdening of the body."

(e) Eef Kamerbeek (successful Dutch decathlon athlete in the fifties; fifth in the decathlon at the Olympic Games in Rome in 1960, a performance that hasn't been repeated by any other Dutchman): "Advantages? You learn some languages because of the many tournaments in which you compete. You are not so impressed any more by all kinds of officials and other people. You get somewhat better in dealing with people. Your name provides you with an easy introduction. And if you're faced with a tough situation, you can deal with it faster and more insistently than the average Dutchman. As a sportsman you have more endurance, you tend to be more optimistic and you have trained yourself in dealing with problems and resolving them. I think those would be the advantages.

"Sometimes they gave me some extra time off. But social support... no, of course they weren't able to give me that. Colleagues, with whom I was on a level in those days, have surpassed me in those years as a result of that. I could say, that because I occupied myself with sports, I got five years behind in my career" (In *What Are Sports?* Malmberg, 1972).

(f) Piet Keizer (played soccer for years for Ajax, where he started very young; played 34 times for the Dutch national team and won the European Cup with Ajax three times (1971, 1972, 1973), was often mentioned in the same breath with Johan Cruijff: "Holland has become a diploma country. If you get two diplomas they give you a third one for that accomplishment. But through playing soccer I learned and I saw a lot in a very practical way."

(g) Ada Kok (one of the world's best female swimmers from the 1960s; set European and world records on the 100 and 200 meters butterfly; a highlight in her career was the Olympic Games in Mexico 1968 where she won a gold medal in the 200 meters butterfly): "You are always surrounded by people, who associate with you only because you have a name. The moment you quit, people start withdrawing from you. And that is indeed felt as loneliness. That can sometimes hurt."

(h) Piet Kruiver (famous soccer player in the 1960s; played 22 times for the national team for which he scored 12 goals, but in 1968 he had to interrupt his career prematurely because of a serious injury of the groin: "I have two sons—But if they don't turn out to be real sportsmen I'd rather say: 'Son, why don't you go to school to learn a profession. Then you get something for life. Soccer is only a career for a very short time.'"

(i) Wim van Est was the first Dutch cyclist who wore the yellow sweater (indicating the leader) in the Tour de France (1952); one day later he fell in the precipice of the Col d'Aubisque but was only slightly hurt; in 1953 he won, together with other famous cyclists, like Wout Wagtmans, Gerrit Voorting, Daan Nolten, and Hein van Breenen, the competition for national teams in the Tour de France; he won the traditional race Bordeaux-Paris four times: "I have three grand-children and as far as I am concerned they can do it. I hope to live to see them getting on a bicycle."

(The quotations from Piet Keizer, Ada Kok, Piet Kruiver, and Wim van Est are taken from the radio program "Is there life after sports," April 27, 1977. The personal data, including the data concerning Eef Kamerbeek, have been provided by the sports editors of the ANP [Dutch Press Agency], The Netherlands, MAVO, 1978.)

APPENDIX 2.B
Illustration of a Writing Assignment in New Zealand

APPENDIX 2.C

The actual tasks used in the IEA Writing Study

Group I   *Pragmatic tasks* (7)

Task 1a: describe a desired bicycle to an uncle who wishes to buy one as a birthday present

Task 1b: describe oneself to a pen friend who the student is going to visit so as to make it possible for the pen friend to identify the student as he comes to meet the student

Task 1c: write a note to the principal/headmaster canceling a scheduled meeting

Task 1d: leave a message at home telling where the student has gone after school

Task 1e: write a letter applying for an advertised summer job

Task 4b: *describe a process doing something

Task 9:   write a letter to a younger student who is coming to study at the same school as the writer, telling the new student how he/she should write in the new school to get good grades

Group II   *Learning tasks* (3)

Task 2:   summarize a text*
Task 3:   retell a story (in a shorter way)*
Task 4a: describe a ritual mask*

Group III   *Personal/emotive tasks* (2)

Task 5:   write a personal story or narration (unknown readership)
Task 8:   write a "free" composition on an ambiguous and evocative pictorial stimulus (unknown readership)

Group IV   *Reflective, argumentative tasks* (2)

Task 7:   write a reflective essay (unknown readership)
Task 6:   try to persuade the reader to share the writer's strong view about something

*The instructions for these tasks specify that the reader is not familiar with the tests, the process, or the mask to be summarized or described.

NOTE

1. In order to preserve this exceptional data base, a representative sample of student scripts has been collected in an international text corpus. This corpus has been created with the financial support of Stichting voor Onderzoek van het Onderwijs (SVO), the Netherlands, and will be available at the end of 1987 to researchers from all over the world. Extensive notice of the availability of the corpus will be given in international research journals at the time of completion. Up to that time enquiries can be directed to Dr. de Glopper and Dr. Kádár-Fülop. Their addresses are given below.

Dr. J. Kádár-Fülop
National Institute for Education
Gorkij Fasor 17-21
Budapest 1071
Hungary

Dr. K. de Glopper
University of Amsterdam
Grote Bickersstraat
1013 KS Amsterdam
The Netherlands

REFERENCES

Applebee, A. N. (1981a). National study of secondary school writing. In A. Humes, B. Cronnell, F. Lawlor, & L. Gentry (Eds.), *Moving between practice and research in writing.* (Proceedings of the NIE-FIPSE Grantee Workshop; pp. 71-74). Los Alamitos: SWRL Education Research and Development.

Applebee, A. N. (1981b). *Writing in the secondary school: English and the content areas.* Urbana IL: National Council of Teachers of English.

Augustine, D. (1981). Geometrics and words: Linguistics and philosophy: A model of the composing process. *College English 43*(3).

Bain, A. (1890). *English composition and rhetoric.* New York: Appleton.

Baker, E. L. (1982). The specification of writing tasks. In A. C. Purves & S. Takala (Eds.), *An international perspective on the evaluation of written composition* (pp. 291-297). Oxford: Pergamon.

Bereiter, C. & Scardamalia, M. (1981). Schooling and the growth of international cognition: Helping children take charge of their own minds. In Z. Lamm (Ed.), *New trends in education* (pp. 1-45). Tel Aviv: Yachev United.

Bereiter, C. (1980). Development in writing. In L. W. Gregg & E. R. Steinberg (Eds.), *Cognitive perspectives of writing* (pp. 73-93). Hillsdale, NJ: Lawrence Erlbaum.

Bloom, B. S. (Ed.). (1956). *Taxonomy of educational objectives: The classification of educational goals. Handbook 1: Cognitive Domain.* New York: McKay.

Britton, J., Burges, N., Martin, A., McLeod, A., & Rosen, H. (1975). *The development of writing abilities.* London: Macmillan.

Carroll, J. B. (1960). Vectors of prose style. In T. A. Sebeok (Ed.), *Style in language* (pp. 283-292). Cambridge: MIT Press.

Carroll, J. B. (1975). Logic and conversation. In P. Cole & F. L. Morgan (Eds.), *Syntax and semantics: Vol. 3. Speech acts* (pp. 41-58). New York: Academic Press.

de Glopper, K., & Kádár-Fülop, J. (1986). *The IEA student composition corpus: Description and backgrounds.* (SCO Cahier 38). Amsterdam: Stichting Centrum voor Onderwigjsonderzoek van de Universiteit van Amsterdam.

Diederich, P. B. (1977). *Measuring growth in English.* Urbana, IL: National Council of Teachers of English.

Eckstein, M. (1983). The comparative mind. *Comparative Education Review, 27*(3), 311-322.

Flower, L. S., & Hayes, J. R. (1977). Problem solving strategies and the writing process. *College English, 39*(4), 449-461.

Flower, L. S., & Hayes, J. R. (1981). A cognitive process theory of writing. *College Composition and Communication, 32,* 365-387.

Gregg, L. W., & Steinberg, E. R. (1980). *Cognitive perspectives of writing.* Hillsdale, NJ: Lawrence Erlbaum.

Heath, S. B. (1983). *Ways with words.* New York: Cambridge University Press.

Hinds, J. (1982, May). *Contrastive rhetoric: Japanese and English.* Paper presented at the annual convention of Teachers of English to Speakers of Other Languages, Honolulu.

Jakobson, R. (1960). Linguistics and poetics. In T. A. Sebeok (Ed.), *Style in language* (pp. 350-376). New York: John Wiley.

Kadar-Fulop, J., Pezeskhpour, & Purves, A. C. (1982). Perspectives on the curriculum in written composition. In A. C. Purves & S. Takala (Eds.), *An international perspective on the evaluation of written composition* (pp. 247-264). Oxford: Pergamon.

Kaplan, R. B. (1966). Cultural thought patterns in intercultural educational. *Language Learning 16*(1-2), 1-20.

Kinneavy, J. L. (1971). *A Theory of discourse.* Englewood Cliffs, NJ: Prentice-Hall.

Kinneavy, J. L. (1980). A pluralistic synthesis of four contemporary models for teaching composition. In A. Freedman & I. Pringle (Eds.), *Reinventing the rhetorical tradition* (pp. 37-52). Fayetteville: L & S Books, University of Central Arkansas.

Leonard, S. (1914). As to the forms of discourse. *The English Journal, 3.*

Lewis, E. G., & Massad, C. E. (1975). *The teaching of English as a foreign language in ten countries.* Stockholm: Almqvist & Wiksell.

Linnakylä, P. (1983). *Kirjoittamisen opetuksen ja opiskelun strategiat peruskoulun keskiluokilla ja ylaasteella.* (Strategies of writing instruction and studying in the middle and upper grades of the comprehensive school). Doctoral dissertation (Turun yliopiston julkaisuja, Sarja—SER. C OSA—TOM. 39), Turku University, Finland.

Lucisano, P. (1987). Task analyses or writing tasks (Appendix B). In T. P. Gorman & A. C. Purves (Eds.), *The international writing tasks and scoring scales.* Oxford: Pergamon.

Moffett, J. (1968). *Teaching the universe of discourse.* Boston: Houghton Mifflin.

Perera, K. (1984). *Childrens' writing and reading: Analysing classroom language.* Oxford: Basil Blackwell.

Purves A. C., Söter, A., Takala, S., & Vähäpassi, A. (1984). Towards a domain-referenced system for classifying composition assignments. *Research in the Teaching of English, 18(4),* 385-416.

Purves, A. C. (1975). Culture and the deep structure of the literature curriculum. *Curriculum Theory Network 5(2).*

Purves, A. C., & Takala, S. (Eds.). (1982). *An International perspective on the evaluation of written composition.* Oxford: Pergamon.

Raivola, R. (1985). What is comparison? Methodological and philosophical considerations. *Comparative Education Review, 29(3),* 362-374.

Rumelhart, D., & Ortony, A. (1977). The representation of knowledge in memory. In R. C. Anderson, R. J. Spiro, & W. E. Montague (Eds.), *Schooling and the acquisition of knowledge* (pp. 99-136). Hillsdale, NJ: Lawrence Erlbaum.

Scribner, S., & Cole, M. (1981) *The psychology of literacy.* Cambridge, MA: Harvard University Press.

Spencer, E. (1981). *A categorisation of school writing.* Unpublished manuscript, Scottish Council for Educational Research, Edinburgh.

Spencer, E. (1983). *Writing matters across the curriculum* (SCRE Publication 79). Edinburgh: Hodder & Stoughton.

Takala, S. & Vahapassi, A. (1985) *International study of written composition.* Eric Documents 257 096.

Takala, S. & Vahapassi, A. (1987). Writing as an object of comparative research. *Comparative Education Review, 31(1),* 88-105.

Takala, S., Purves, A. C., & Buckmaster, A. (1982). On the interrelationships between language, perception, thought and culture and their relevance to the assessment of written composition. In A. C. Purves & S. Takala (Eds.), *International perspective on the evaluation of written composition* (pp. 317-342). Oxford: Pergamon.

Vahapassi, A. (1982). On the specification of the domain of school writing. In A. C. Purves & S. Takala (Eds.), *An international perspective on the evaluation of written composition* (pp. 265-289). Oxford: Pergamon.

Warwick, D., & Osherson, S. (1973). Comparative analysis in the social sciences. In D. Warwick & S. Osherson (Eds.), *Comparative research methods.* Englewood Cliffs, NJ: Prentice-Hall.

Wells, G. (1981). Language, literacy and education. In G. Wells (Ed.), *Learning through interaction: The study of language development* (pp. 240-276). Cambridge: Cambridge University Press.

Wesdorp, H. (1982). *De didactick van het stellen. Een overzicht van het onderzoek naar de effecten van diverse instructie—variabelen op de stelvaardigheid* (SCO Rapport). Amsterdam: SCO.

3

Developing a Rating Method for Stylistic Preference: A Cross-Cultural Pilot Study

R. ELAINE DEGENHART
SAULI TAKALA

Ever since Robert B. Kaplan published his seminal article on cross-cultural rhetoric (Kaplan, 1966), there has been a continuous flow of publications on matters related to communication across borders, cultures and languages. There are practical guides and courses that the foreign offices have prepared for diplomats and military personnel and similar materials that multinational companies are providing to their overseas employees. There are a variety of scholarly articles ranging from the macrolevel sociological studies by the Norwegian sociologist and peace researcher Johan Galtung (Galtung, 1979, 1983) to linguistic studies (e.g., Connor & Kaplan, 1987; Kaplan, 1983).

Stated very briefly, all of this activity and research stems from Kaplan's observation that students organize paragraphs in different ways in different cultures. It was felt intuitively that this variation in paragraph organization reflects cross-cultural differences in the structure of writing and divergent patterns of organization, not only of writing, but of thinking as well. Other research in the field has consisted primarily of attempts to test this basic hypothesis.

As the implications of such investigations have become more apparent, researchers from a variety of specialties have taken an

AUTHORS' NOTE: The authors wish to acknowledge the developmental work of Alan C. Purves, Avon Crismore, and Annette Buckmaster during the planning of the study and the invaluable contributions of Graeme Withers (Australia), Anneli Vähäpassi (Finland) and Hildo Wesdarp (the Netherlands), who collected the data and, in Finland and the Netherlands, spent many hours producing very careful translations.

interest. The more sophisticated methods being developed in text analysis have been incorporated into the continuing inquiry (Connor & McCagg, 1987). Enkvist's (1987) discussion of text linguistics, in which he points out the importance of the internal context and the information structure of a text to understanding, has clear implications for contrastive rhetoric. In recognition of the contribution of related fields to this study he has coined the cover term "discourse linguistics" to include discourse analysis, text linguistics, and conversational analysis. The 1982 volume of the *Annual Review of Applied Linguistics* was devoted to contrastive rhetorics and included studies in which comparisons were made between the written discourse of English and several other specific languages. These studies "call attention to particular tensions between the uses of written text (and all of the implications of the uses of written texts regarding information storage, information transfer, and information retrieval) and the older oral traditions in many cultures" (Kaplan, 1983). In addition to these studies which analyzed essays from a variety of cultures, Grabe (1987) has investigated different text types in expository prose. From his studies he has concluded that expository prose can be defined as a distinct major text genre containing a number of text-type distinctions, which may provide a real basis for rhetorical comparisons.

As interesting and informative as these linguistic studies are, however, Kaplan (1983) has stated that the real value of the contrastive approach is its concern with practical issues, in particular pedagogical problems. With this perspective of practical application, Söter (1985) has studied the writing of students enrolled in an educational system which uses a language other than their mother tongue. Such studies are seen as contributing valuable insights into the special needs of these students for curriculum planning, teacher training, and material development.

Although the newer methods of gathering and analyzing information have encouraged larger investigations in this important field, a major handicap to large-scale studies is still the costly necessity of working from direct samples of student scripts. An important area of inquiry is to explore the possibility of developing a new methodology, that would bypass the actual discourse linguistic analysis of scripts and still produce reliable data.

The present case study discusses some of the developmental work in this area done during the early stages of the large-scale IEA

International Study of Achievement in Written Composition begun in 1980 and involving 14 different countries and their school systems. As in all other comparative studies carried out by IEA, the writing study is assessing national school systems in terms of student achievement, and interpreting the results in the light of contextual factors such as school characteristics and teaching practices. This evaluative interest has been accompanied by a continuous curiosity concerning the exploration of possible cultural/national preferences in patterns of written communication.

One of the constant concerns of the IEA Written Composition Study has been that of describing certain nonlinguistic aspects of composition, which appear to form a focus of instruction, but which cannot be said to be internationally constant, because they are individual to countries or even to schools of thought within countries. One obvious example is the encouragement or discouragement given the student to inject his or her personality into the composition (see Takala, Purves, & Buckmaster, 1982).

The purpose of this chapter is to report some of the early work done in exploring the possibility of complementing the evaluation study with a more descriptive study of cross-cultural rhetorics. It is not intended to present a detailed report of the students' responses, since the number of students included in the trial of the instruments was much too small to allow any kind of generalizations. The evidence from these small trials, however, contributed to the development of the international writing study in the areas of task selection, test administration, scoring, and the analysis of student reponses.

The most difficult, time-consuming, and therefore expensive aspect of any study of student composition is the analysis and rating of direct samples of their writing. Although it is doubtful that this task can be eliminated entirely in a major study, the Steering Committee for the IEA Study of Written Composition hoped that some useful and reliable analyses could be done using direct questions and quantifiable rating scales. If such a system could be devised for the exploration and identification of national/cultural variations and preferences of, for example, paragraph aspects and organization, it could have an important impact on research directed toward instruction in multicultural educational systems.

With this goal in mind, the limited study reported here sought to determine (a) whether it is possible to assess students' writing style preferences directly using a rating scale procedure; and (b) whether students are able to recognize and report teacher preferences and patterns in school writing instruction.

DESCRIPTION OF THE PILOT STUDY

After examining earlier empirical investigations of writing style (e.g., Carroll, 1960; Diederich, 1977) and the traditions of literary theory and criticism, the following stylistic dimensions were considered relevant to the analysis of short student scripts:

multiple—single
abstract—concrete
linear—digressive
metaphorical—plain
personal—impersonal
humorous—serious

Using these dimensions as a basis, two kinds of scales were produced to study the feasibility of using rating scales to determine stylistic preferences. One was a unipolar scale using a set of 24 descriptive adjectives or short phrases. The other was a bipolar scale consisting of six pairs of short sentences representing the pairs of stylistic dimensions. A 5-point scale was used in both cases.

In addition, two outlines for compositions were written to illustrate the multiple-single dimension, that is, to illustrate the distinction between an approach which favors the discussion of several subtopics and an approach which chooses one or only a few subtopics to discuss. The other stylistic dimensions were illustrated by 10 short paragraphs, each written to stress a specific style aspect. (These instruments are reproduced in the appendices.)

The stimulus material for the study, then, consisted of two rating scales and a set of two composition outlines and 10 paragraphs illustrating the six pairs of stylistic dimensions. These instruments were tested using a small "convenience" sample of upper secondary school students in Australia (N = 60), Finland (N = 50), the Netherlands (N = 60) and the United States (N = 40).

RESULTS

As a preliminary step to addressing these problems, a number of graduate students from several countries were asked to rate a set of compositions as they would be rated in their home countries, and to write comments on the essays. From these ratings and comments a list of 26 criteria were identified and defined. The research coordinators in the participating countries, and their national committees, were then asked to indicate the appropriateness of each quality on this list for each of the three populations in the study.[1] The result was a revised list of 23 criteria.

With this revised list, an attempt was made to develop a score sheet that would indicate whether a composition was superior, adequate, or inadequate on each aspect. The quality judgements made on the basis of these rather specific criteria would show to what extent different countries give different weight to these aspects. This exercise was abandoned, however, when trials of this system proved it to be too cumbersome and time-consuming to be used on a large scale basis either as a scoring method or as an indirect method of identifying national/cultural preferences in writing.

A Unipolar Scale of Descriptive Adjectives

The identification and definition of a list of rating criteria was an important and useful product of this early experiment, however. With some further refinement, a five-point unipolar rating scale was constructed with 24 criteria. Students were then given a composition topic and a target audience, and were asked to indicate on the rating scale the degree to which they thought each quality or aspect would contribute to creating a good composition on that topic (Appendix 3A).

This student rating scale was pilot-tested in Finland and in the Netherlands. The hypothetical composition topic was to write to a person who represented a school or community group that was planning to make a change that the student opposed and to try to convince the person to leave things as they were. In addition to rating the qualities themselves, the Dutch students were also asked to indicate the degree of difficulty in making these judgements for each aspect. The terms on the list were not discussed with the students nor was there an attempt to test their knowledge or understanding of these terms.

The researchers in both countries first had to translate the list of descriptive terms from the original English. Throughout this study, the problem of translating very specific and somewhat technical terms into equivalent words that could be understood by students (i.e., avoiding technical English loanwords) proved to be an extremely difficult task.

In the Finnish trial of this stylistic preference measure (Table 3.1), the sample consisted of 51 students. For the hypothetical topic given, they showed a very strong preference for a logically connected composition (51 students), which is precise (48), concise and focused (45) and tightly organized (43). They also reported that in order to get a good mark, the composition should be exhaustive (47) and include everything on the subject (45), and they should use varied sentences (44). The only strong opinion concerning qualities that the composition should not have was "narrowed to one point" (43), which supports the preference for an exhaustive treatment of the subject.

This brief sample of the results of this trial demonstrates that students do have definite ideas of what is expected of them and are able to recognize and use generally accepted and understood terms in reporting their perceptions. The next important step in this exercise was to determine whether or not the students were sufficiently consistent in their responses to allow reliable generalizations from a larger sample of the population.

In order to determine the reliability (stability) of the students' judgments, the exercise was repeated with the same students after an interval of about four or five weeks. Although the second trial showed basically the same preferences, the responses were considerably weaker, and many students had changed their answer by at least one degree on the rating scale. In most cases the change was toward the center, indicating a less definite conviction.

A similar double testing was conducted in the Netherlands with equally unstable responses, with correlations primarily around .40 but ranging from .20 to .58. These results seem to indicate that it is highly unlikely that students could give reliably consistent judgments on writing style using this type of rating scale.

The Dutch questions concerning the relative difficulty in making

TABLE 3.1
Student Responses to Unipolar Stylistic Preference
Measure in Finland, N = 51
(first trial response/second trial response)

	Should be as close to this quality as possible				Should be the opposite of this quality
	1	2	3	4	5
Narrowed to one point	1 / 0	3 / 2	3 / 1	10 / 26	33 / 22
Humorous	3 / 3	2 / 10	26 / 26	18 / 11	2 / 1
Formal	24 / 15	17 / 24	7 / 10	3 / 2	0 / 0
Precise	34 / 25	14 / 20	3 / 5	0 / 0	0 / 1
Like a conversation	1 / 1	7 / 5	9 / 20	26 / 19	7 / 6
Varied sentences	26 / 18	18 / 25	6 / 5	0 / 1	1 / 2
Concise and focused	30 / 17	15 / 27	6 / 3	0 / 2	0 / 1
Serious	7 / 6	16 / 5	22 / 24	4 / 15	2 / 1
Personal	11 / 15	22 / 17	14 / 15	3 / 2	1 / 1
Detailed	10 / 9	18 / 25	19 / 14	4 / 2	0 / 1
Logically connected	46 / 35	4 / 11	0 / 3	0 / 1	0 / 0
In plain style	2 / 2	14 / 7	19 / 26	10 / 13	6 / 3
Including everything on the subject	29 / 23	16 / 20	3 / 4	3 / 4	0 / 0
Funny	0 / 0	2 / 6	14 / 21	19/ 20	16 / 4
Using my feelings	7 / 6	20 / 26	13 / 15	6 / 4	5 / 0
General	1 / 0	10 / 8	27 / 22	9 / 18	4 / 2
Tightly organized	26 / 18	17 / 24	6 / 8	2 / 1	0 / 0
Figurative	10 / 2	16 / 19	16 / 23	8 / 7	1 / 0
Exhaustive	30 / 19	17 / 24	3 / 6	1 / 1	0 / 1
Sober	9 / 5	16 / 10	19 / 24	6 / 11	1 / 1
Keeping a distance	2 / 0	2 / 1	11 / 10	22 / 25	14 / 14
Abstract	2 / 0	8 / 10	23 / 21	16 / 19	2 / 0
With digressions as needed	0 / 1	9 / 10	11 / 15	21 / 20	9 / 5
Using ordinary language	3 / 4	13 / 10	14 / 16	13 / 15	8 / 6

these judgments showed that of the 60 students in the sample, 21 found it difficult, 25 found it easy, and 14 found it neither too difficult nor too easy. The individual qualities that were reported to be the most difficult to judge were "figurative" (16 students) and "with digressions as needed" (11 students).

It was interesting to note, however, that there did not seem to be a relationship between the perceived ease or difficulty in judging a quality and the students' consistency in reporting whether or not that quality should be included in a specific writing task. For example, 30 students indicated that the quality "figurative" was very difficult to judge, yet the consistency of this judgment had a correlation value of .45 (p < .001). At the same time, the quality "serious," with a similar correlation value (.43), had been considered very easy to judge by 40 students. In this study, there seems to be no relationship between high correlations of stability and easiness, or between low correlations and difficulty of judging.

A Bipolar Scale of Stylistic Dimensions

Another attempt to study approaches to writing by using a rating scale was based on the six pairs of stylistic dimensions discussed earlier. For this purpose a bipolar five-point scale was constructed using six pairs of short sentences, each representing one of the stylistic dimensions (Appendix 3B). Again the students were given a hypothetical essay topic, "What should be done to improve my community?" (In the U.S., the students actually wrote the composition before completing the stylistic dimension scale). This scale was pilot-tested in upper secondary school mother-tongue classes in Australia (60 students, Finland (51 students), and the United States (19 students).

The students in all three countries agreed that a composition on this topic should be personal and should use a logical, that is linear, organization. The degree of conviction varied however. The United States (84%) and Finland (75%) indicated a stronger preference for a personal approach than Australia (60%). Australia (92%) and the United States (89%) showed a very strong preference for a linear structure, while Finland's structural preference was less definite (53%). The United States (100%) and Australia (76%) also agreed that this topic should deal with concrete things and specific instances. (Finland did not use this dimension.) Australia (93%) and Finland (72%) felt strongly that the composition should cover a number of different points about the topic while the American students were evenly divided on this dimension (multiple, 47%; single 47%). The Australian students (75%) felt that this topic should be treated in a serious manner. The Finnish students tended to prefer a serious approach as well (46%), but they also indicated an acceptance of humor (35%). (The U.S. scale did not include this dimension.) The clearest indication of a possible difference in national preference appeared to be linguistic. Both Australia (63%) and the United States (58%) preferred plain language with simple sentences. Finnish students, on the other hand, had an equally strong preference for metaphorical language (66%).

These results seem to suggest that a rating instrument of this kind might be useful in studying approaches to writing, especially in relation to the notion of possible nationally preferred patterns in writing and writing instruction. To test the stability of these ratings, the exercise was repeated in Finland after five weeks with the same sample of students. The results of this replication showed that, at best, only 33 of the 51 students responded with the same opinion (multiple/single), and intraindividual agreement was as low as 19 on the conversational/logical organization dimension. Even with a more lenient interpretation, in which a response was accepted as the same if it appeared on the same side of the scale, only 38 of the 51 students gave the same reponse the second time. Therefore, it was concluded that student responses are not consistent enough on this type of rating scale to give a reliable report of preferred styles of writing.

Preference Measure with
Concrete Writing Samples

In the above trials, the students were asked to respond to hypothetical tasks using abstract terms in isolation. A final attempt to construct an indirect measure of writing patterns presented the students with actual samples of writing designed to illustrate the dichotomous set of six dimensions of style. In this exercise, the students were given examples of each aspect in pairs and asked to indicate the preferred outline/paragraph of each pair. As variations of this first test, other versions asked the students, in addition to indicating preferences, first, to describe the characteristics of each pair in their own words and then to match each set with the appropriate style dimension. (The complete exercise is reproduced in Appendix 3.C.)

The purpose of this exercise was three-fold. First, the selection of one paragraph style over the other along the six dimensions was intended to reflect style preferences that might indicate national patterns, or at least instructional emphases. Second, by describing the paragraphs in their own words, it was expected that the students would demonstrate the extent to which they were able to recognize writing characteristics and to verbalize what they found without cues or prompts. The third part of this exercise was intended to determine whether or not the students were able to recognize style dimensions in writing samples if they were given cues and prompts as to what they should look for.

The basic questionnaire, which asked for only a preference between each pair of outlines or paragraphs, was given to 22 students in an American public high school. As is shown in Table 3.2, the students were most definite in their agreement that in order to get a good mark, an essay (on this topic) should be serious (20 students). They also indicated that the language should be plain (18) and the tone impersonal (16). The most difficult pair to judge was logical organization/digressions as needed, with five students unable to make a choice. This coincides with the earlier findings of the Dutch study in which the students indicated that the descriptive phrase "with digressions as needed" was difficult to judge. It is interesting to note, however, that there is no clear preference between the abstract/concrete paragraphs, even though the earlier sample of American students had indicated 100% preference for a concrete treatment of this topic on the bipolar scale of stylistic dimensions.

At the end of this part of the exercise the students were asked to select the one paragraph they thought their teacher would rate the best and the one closest to what they would write themselves (Table 3.2). The results seem to suggest that, even though the students indicate that the teacher would probably prefer paragraphs H, the impersonal composition (5 students), and F, the plain composition (4), they feel free to write in a different style (K, serious (6) and C, abstract (4)).

When this initial exercise was repeated a few weeks later to check the stability of the students' answers, only the paragraph pair E/F (figurative/plain) remained the same (20 students). The judgments for paragraph pairs C/D (abstract/concrete) and K/L (serious/humorous) were also fairly stable (18 students), but the reporting of all other dimensions proved to be very unreliable. It is especially interesting to note that only 6 of the 21 students selected the same paragraph a second time as their own personal choice.

The replication of this exercise included a new section which asked the students to label or describe the most characteristic feature of each

TABLE 3.2
American Students' Perceptions of Style Preferences
Using Actual Writing Samples (N = 22)

	MULT A	SING B	ABST C	CONC D	FIG E	PLN F	PERS G	IMPR H	LOG I	DIGR J	SER K	HUM L
Higher mark	13	6	10	12	4	18	3	16	14	3	20	2
no choice	3		—		—		3		5		—	
stability of rating (%)*	48		86		95		67		52		86	
Best paragraph												
teacher**	N/A		—	—	3	4	—	5	3	—	2	2
student	N/A		4	3	—	1	—	1	2	2	6	2

*Percentage of ratings that remained the same on a second trial; **Students' report of assumed teacher preference.

outline/paragraph (Appendix 3.C, Variation 1). A second class of students of the same age was added to this part of the study, raising to 42 the total number of students responding. Without any cues or prompts to suggest possible descriptive terms, the majority of the responses were surprisingly accurate, and in some cases used quite sophisticated language. The paragraph pair that seemed to be the easiest to describe was figurative/plain (E/F), with 35 responses relating to the actual dimensions. This pair also elicited the most rhetorical terms, such as "metaphoric"; "uses analogy"; "has imagery"; "realistic"; "straight-forward." It would seem from this decisive identification of a figurative writing style, although that specific term was not used, that students can easily recognize concrete examples of this style even though, as reported in the earlier Dutch study, they find it the most difficult concept in isolation.

The second dimension that the Dutch students had found to be difficult to judge, "digression as needed," continued to elude their American counterparts in these sample paragraphs, however. Seven students were unable to give any descriptive terms for this pair (I/J— logical/digressive), and of the 14 who did use accurate terms, it was the logically organized paragraph that was identified.

Of the remaining pairs, 29 students described the abstract/concrete pair (C/D) using such terms as "general"; "vague"; "analytical"; and "specific"; "descriptive"; "blunt." Twenty-eight students described the personal/impersonal pair (G/H) using variations of the exact terms, and 21 students noted the number of topics as the difference between the two outlines (A/B—multiple/single). Only 12 students considered the tone in the pair K/L (serious/humorous) to be the outstanding characteristic, while 19 suggested that the formal/familiar style of this pair was the distinguishing dimension.

When these same two classes were given the list of six pairs of stylistic dimensions, however, and instructed to match them to the outlines/paragraphs (Appendix 3.C, Variation 2), they were most successful in recognizing the serious/humorous (K/L) and multiple/single (A/B) dimensions (40 students out of 41). The logical/ digressive pair continued to be the most difficult to identify (29), followed closely by the abstract/concrete (C/D) paragraphs (30). The prompts made the personal/impersonal paragraphs more obvious to the students (38), while identification of the figurative/plain pair also increased slightly (37).

In general, this exercise would indicate that students are capable of recognizing different characteristics and stylistic dimensions of writing samples. However, their preferences as reported on the various types of easily scored rating scales used in this pilot test did not prove to be consistent enough to give a reliable picture of national or cultural styles of writing. Their ability to describe samples of writing fairly knowledgeably in their own words, on the other hand, encouraged the researchers to try again to use the students' own perceptions to describe writing instruction in schools.

For this exercise, the students were asked to write a letter to a younger student who would be attending the same school in two years. The letter was to include advice to the younger student on how to write a composition in order to get a good mark in the new school (Appendix 3.D). Although this task required assessment of direct samples of student writing, it proved to be successful when pilot tested on a large scale in all of the participating countries. (Since this task became a part of the main testing, it is discussed in Vähäpassi, this volume.)

DISCUSSION

The original purpose of the exercises described in this chapter was to try to develop an easily scored instrument, based on accepted rating criteria, which would reliably report national/cultural writing styles as reflected in student perceptions of instructional practices in school writing. The experience with both types of rating scales indicated that this indirect method of measurement was not sufficiently reliable for cross-cultural comparisons. When actual writing samples were used, the students demonstrated a fairly good knowledge of stylistic choices and an ability to express their perceptions of what they read. Even in this trial, however, the stability of responses proved to be too low to be reported with confidence.

A useful outcome of this study for researchers is the very fact that the pilot tests in general did not produce the hoped-for easily-scored rating instrument. It has been demonstrated that continued efforts in this area would not be a fruitful direction of inquiry. Each exercise has contributed in other ways to the development of various phases of the International Writing Study. For example, the identification of the specific rating criteria used in several countries led to a better understanding of the breadth of expectations in school writing. The reduction of these criteria to descriptive terms allowed the researchers to determine how much the students themselves were aware of the variety and appropriateness of these aspects of composition. Attempts to combine these criteria into related and meaningful categories led to the development of a "holistic/analytic scoring scale" for rating the compositions of the main study. This scale provides an overall impression score for each composition supplemented by scores for content, organization, and style and tone. (For a further discussion of the scoring system, see Takala & Vähäpassi, 1987; Wesdorp, Bauer, & Purves, 1982)

Perhaps the most importance outcome of these exercises, however, was the reinforcement of the idea that students can recognize and describe what is expected of them when they are asked to write a composition in school. Unfortunately the easily scored rating scales did not prove feasible, but the students were able to describe writing characteristics and the writing process. Rather than to continue the developmental work on rating scales to get an indirect measure of student writing, it was decided to assess both the quality and style of student writing directly from samples of their own compositions. The limited testing of the letter of advice to another student (Appendix 3.D) was extended to a full pilot testing of the revised instructions and became a major writing task of the final set of 14 tasks included in the main study. (For a further discussion of these tasks, see Vähäpassi in this volume.) Based on the resulting compositions and a thorough search of related literature, a comprehensive system for coding student responses was developed.

The main testing of the International Writing Study has now been completed and the student responses to this task are still being coded. It is expected that when the international data have been fully coded and analyzed, they will report student perceptions of instructional practices and rating criteria. It is hoped that they might also reveal whether or not there are in fact national/cultural differences in writing style preferences and instruction.

APPENDIX 3.A

STYLISTIC PREFERENCE MEASURE

People have different ideas as to what good writing is. We would like to know what you think is good composition. In order to make it easier for you to give your opinion, we would like you to consider that you have been asked to write a composition on some aspect of your school or community that you do not think should be changed. You are to write the composition for someone who has proposed making a change and you want to convince that person that things should stay as they are. You do not have to write the composition, but give your opinion of what a good composition on this topic would be like. Below is a list of words or phrases that people have used to describe what they think is a good composition. After each word or phrase is a scale on which you should indicate the extent to which you agree that the quality helps create a good composition. Please put an X in the space after *each* word or phrase to indicate your opinion.

	Should be as close to this quality as possible				Should be the opposite of this quality
Narrowed to one point	____	____	____	____	____
Humorous	____	____	____	____	____
Formal	____	____	____	____	____
Precise	____	____	____	____	____
Like a conversation	____	____	____	____	____
Varied sentences	____	____	____	____	____
Concise and focused	____	____	____	____	____
Serious	____	____	____	____	____
Personal	____	____	____	____	____
Detailed	____	____	____	____	____
Logically connected	____	____	____	____	____
In plain style	____	____	____	____	____
Including everything on the subject	____	____	____	____	____
Funny	____	____	____	____	____
Using my feelings	____	____	____	____	____
General	____	____	____	____	____
Tightly organized	____	____	____	____	____
Figurative	____	____	____	____	____
Exhaustive	____	____	____	____	____
Sober	____	____	____	____	____
Keeping a distance	____	____	____	____	____
Abstract	____	____	____	____	____
With digressions as needed	____	____	____	____	____
Using ordinary language	____	____	____	____	____

APPENDIX 3.B

STYLISTIC DIMENSIONS

What do you think a good composition on the topic "What should be done to improve my community?" would be like? What would your teacher want to see in it? Below are five scales. Place an X in the space that indicates what you think a good composition would be like.

	Definitely Like this	Probably Like this	Uncertain	Probably Like this	Definitely Like this	
It would cover a good number of different points about the topic.	—	—	—	—	—	It would deal with only *one* aspect of the topic and go into it thoroughly.
It would stick to points that any person might make.	—	—	—	—	—	It would show the writer's personal feelings.
It would use metaphors, images, and elaborate language with complex sentences.	—	—	—	—	—	It would use plain language with simple straightforward sentences.
It would be organized to follow the way people talk in conversation, or as if someone were telling a story.	—	—	—	—	—	It would have a clear logical organization using a technique like comparison, cause-effect, if-then, or logical definition.
It would deal with the topic in a serious way.	—	—	—	—	—	It would deal with the topic in a humorous way.

APPENDIX 3.C

On the pages following there are two outlines of compositions and ten paragraphs from compositions written on the topic: *What should be done to improve my community*. The outlines and paragraphs were written by people in different countries. Each example came from a composition that received a high grade from a teacher, but some of them are different from each other. We would like to find out which ones you think would receive a high grade if it were to be marked by a teacher in your school. There follow a pair of outlines and five pairs of paragraphs. After each pair is a question asking which you think would get the higher grade. Please answer each question.

APPENDIX 3.C *(continued)*

SET I

OUTLINE

A. Multiple*

    1. My community has a shortage of housing
        a. There are many families crowded in too small buildings
        b. The community should build more houses
    2. The streets and buildings are not repaired
        a. Every street has holes full of water
        b. The public buildings need paint
        c. The community should make repairs
    3. The schools are located away from where people live
        a. As the community has grown the schools have not moved with the new housing
        b. The schools should be moved or transportation should be improved
    4. There is little opportunity for young people
        a. There are few jobs outside of one factory and some shops and young people must move away
        b. The community should attract new businesses

OUTLINE

B. Single

    1. As my community has grown in size, it has not provided enough opportunity for work
        a. There is only one factory which has jobs and these jobs are dull
        b. Young people can only work for their families if they want to stay
        c. As a result, young people leave the community
    2. The community should provide more opportunities
        a. It could attract new factories and shops
        b. It could create an employment center
        c. It could provide training for young people to get ahead

Which outline would lead to a composition that would get a high mark?

A _____   B _____   No choice _____

*The stylistic descriptions are included here for the convenience of the reader and were not given on the original forms.

APPENDIX 3.C *(continued)*

SET II

C.   Abstract

The most serious problem my community faces is that people do not care for the appearance of the community. It seems that both the individual citizens and the local government consider other things more important than making the community an attractive place to live. Buildings that are older are allowed to deteriorate and when new buildings are erected the signs of construction may remain for long periods after the work is finished. This lack of care can be seen in the streets and the various public places around the community. The problem does not appear to be one of a lack of money but a lack of interest.

D.   Concrete

The most serious problem in my community is the ugliness and mess which makes the community an unattractive place to live. A person can walk down any street and see houses with broken windows or with junk piled around them. In the main part of town, the old public buildings are dirty and the paint is peeling from the walls. The new town garage was finished a year ago and it is being used, but the piles of lumber for construction are still sitting there and the dirt around the building is still piled in the mound the bulldozer made. There is not a street that does not need to have a hole filled, the benches in the town park are mostly broken, and the plumbing in the public lavatory has not worked for a year. The community seems rich enough; they buy new trucks. They just do not seem to care and so nobody else does.

Which paragraph would get a higher mark?

C_____   D_____   No choice _____

APPENDIX 3.C *(continued)*

E.   Figurative

The bluebird flits from one dry perch to another nervously. Butterflies search for budded sweet nectar blossoms while the young bear, thick-coated, paces his cage. North to south paces, over and over, watched intently by the old mother bear. Nearby the peacock, tail spread, beady-eyed. My best friend, Kara, wanting so much to flee. She darts from here to there to me—looking for escape, a reason to fly from this place. Who can blame her? Who cannot understand her need? Hope, growth, life is impossible. The poison in the air pervades all—places, people. She suffocates, she gasps for breath, she droops. And my community? I weep. Where are the sweet smelling blossoms and the clear tinkling bells from the high parts? The insistent drone of work whistles hypnotize, and the moan of the wheels blot the song. The press of gray brown despair tortures the souls of the bluebirds. Peacocks droop as the poison works, enveloping and endangering and ending. I must run to the blossoms and bells tinkling. The wheels crush the spirit, and helpless, tortured, cries drown the hope song. Spew out the poison, my community, and open the cage doors.

F.   Plain

My friend Misa feels as I do that our community offers no opportunity for us and our friends. We often talk to each other and discuss the arguments and reasons we will present to our families for leaving here. There are no jobs for us here. No future is possible here except to join the crowds of other people, young and old who are hungry and listless. The old factory whistle sounds at the same time every day, signaling old, tired, bored workers to produce the exported goods. The work days are long, the money is little but the boredom is great for those fortunate enough to have a job. The officials accept the situation here as inevitable and fixed. Life goes on as it always has with no changes except declines in the quality of life. Opportunities are lacking for young people in all areas, personal, social, economic and political. The youth are doomed here to a life worse than their mothers and fathers had. The community has no plans and goals for the future, no leaders to guide. The problems are great.

Which paragraph would get a higher mark?

E_____   F_____   No choice _____

APPENDIX 3.C *(continued)*

G. Personal

In order to describe the main problem in my community, I shall tell you about my family. I live at home with my mother and father and an older brother. I have two older sisters but they have left home and gone to the city, one to work as a secretary, the other to work in a bank. My older brother is about to leave also. You see, my father is foreman in the factory and my mother works at home taking care of the family and the small garden. The factory is the only place where there are jobs unless one wants to be a farmer or unless you happen to own one of the shops. My uncle owns a shop and his children work for him so that there are not jobs for others. The factory is not very big and the work is dull. If a person wants to improve, the way my sisters and brother do, a person has to leave. I really like this town, and I have many friends here, but I also want to do something different. I suppose I will move away when I finish school.

H. Impersonal

The major problem of the community is a lack of opportunity for young people. The community has three shops: a grocery, a small clothing shop, and a small hardware and tool shop, as well as a branch of the bank. There is also a small factory that employs about seventy-five people. Apart from that the only other work that people do in the community is farm work, and teaching in the school. There are more young people than there are jobs, and many of the jobs are boring, particularly if people want to get ahead in the world. Some of the young people are content to work in the factory or for their parents in a shop or on the farms. Only a few, however, want to teach in the school. As a result of this situation, about half of the young people who finish school leave the community.

Which paragraph would get a higher mark?

G _____   H _____   No choice _____

APPENDIX 3.C *(continued)*

I.   Logical

One of the first things the leaders in my community could do to make the community more attractive is to create a campaign to make the houses more attractive. If the leaders were to award prizes for the family that did the best job of fixing its house and cleaning the surrounding grounds, most families would accept the challenge. After first giving awards to families, the community could then expand the plan to public buildings and parks. Prizes and awards could go to groups of volunteers who would undertake the work of fixing these places and making them pretty. One might argue that these volunteers would not want to pay money for materials such as tools and paint. The cost to an individual or a group would, therefore, only be the cost of time. If everyone were to join, moreover, the amount of time would not be too great for any one person. By following a process of individual awards to group awards, the leaders could help make my community attractive.

J.   Digressive

The leaders of the community could make the place more attractive by helping people fix up and clean up their own houses and community buildings. I mean that people probably just need a start. Imagine what would happen if the leaders gave prizes to the people who help the most. One prize might go to the neatest garden area. Then another prize might go to the prettiest house. It would not be for the original design, but for the best cleaning, fixing, and painting. Then, other people could win an award for picking up the rubbish in the town square. It is usually filthy, with trash in the bushes. The town leaders could give out paint and tools to help, by the way. They could lend them to people to work on their own homes on days when the town workers do not need them. At the end, it would be nice to see banners and flags above the streets. The whole community would be bright and shiny. You would agree it would be a pleasant place to live, and the leaders and the people would have a common goal and a sense of pride.

Which paragraph would get a higher mark?

I _____   J_____   No choice _____

APPENDIX 3.C *(continued)*

K. Serious

There are a number of problems in my community but most of them would take a lot of time and money to solve. There is, however, one problem which is an acute one but which could be resolved without spending large sums of money. That is the problem of boredom. Nothing exciting ever seems to happen in the community. Yet, this need not have to be so. With some creative ideas and community spirit a lot could be done. The mayor could set up a committee consisting of both older and younger people to recommend new activities. These might include choirs for children and for adults and perhaps an amateur orchestra or band and an amateur theater group. There might be challenge matches or games between blocks or districts. People might revive old handicraft skills and show how different things were done in the past and what the things looked like. People might help to lay out jogging track in a park or in a forest. These are only a few examples of what might be done to resist the boredom of inactivity. Different kinds of solutions would have to be devised to suit local circumstances.

L. Humorous

Any problems in my community? Are you kidding? There are nothing but problems. We have so many problems that we could easily organize a sale and sell a lot at a bargain and still have more than enough for home consumption. The greatest problem is boredom. Griping about problems never did any good, however. What we need is a lot of action backed with a pinch of thinking. We have to be careful with thinking though. It might develop like a habit and nothing good ever came from too much thinking. Never fear. These are some ideas produced with very little thought. The mayor might set up a committee consisting of the greatest bores in town. They would never be able to finish their work and we would never hear from them again. That alone would go a long way to improve local conversation. Those with no near for music but with a great desire for performing in public might be asked to form a choir or a band to be led by a very exacting musician. They would spend all their time practicing and torturing each other but not the rest of us. Other bores might be encouraged to take up football or skiing. Soon most of them would be lying in hospital with a broken leg. Several weeks of relief! These are only a few examples of what might be done to combat boredom. Different kinds of solutions would have to be devised to cope with the local variety of bores.

Which paragraph would get a higher mark?

APPENDIX 3.C *(continued)*

Look back over the paragraphs and answer the following questions.

Which one paragraph do you think teachers would rate as the best? _____

Which one paragraph do you think is closest to one you would write?_____

VARIATION 1

1. Please indicate which outline would lead to a composition that would get a high mark.

   A _____   B _____   No choice _____

2. Which paragraph would get the higher mark?

   C _____   D _____   No choice _____

   E _____   F _____   No choice _____

   G _____   H _____   No choice _____

   I _____   J _____   No choice _____

   K _____   L _____   No choice _____

3. Which one paragraph do you think teachers would rate as the best? ___

4. Which one paragraph do you think is closest to one you would write?

   _____

5. The two outlines and the ten compositions all dealt with the topic of ways a community could be improved. When you read the paragraphs and rated them, you may have noticed that there were some differences between each pair and also between the pairs. What do you think distinguishes the two outlines and the ten compositions? Can you give a *label* to them or *describe what characterizes* them? Choose either the left-hand side or the right-hand side to write your answer, whichever you feel is the easiest for you. If you cannot think of anything, check the "Don't know" column in the middle. Do not spend more than one minute to suggest a label or to write a brief description.

APPENDIX 3.C *(continued)*

LABEL/ADJECTIVE (Don't use 'good' or 'bad')	DON'T KNOW	DESCRIPTION
A is _____ B is _____		The difference between A & B has to do with how _____
C is _____ D is _____		The difference between C & D has to do with how _____
E is _____ F is _____		The difference between E & F has to do with how _____
G is _____ H is _____		The difference between G & H has to do with how _____
I is _____ J is _____		The difference between I & J has to do with how _____
K is _____ L is _____		The difference between K & L has to do with how _____

Appendix 3.C *(Continued)*

VARIATION 2

The persons who wrote the two outlines and the ten compositions had in mind the following stylistic choices or dimensions:

1. Metaphorical (ornamental) — Plain (straightforward)
2. Logical — Digressive
3. Multiple (several subtopics) — Single (only a few suptopics)
4. Serious — Humorous
5. Personal — Impersonal
6. Abstract — Concrete

Now that you have read the outlines and paragraphs and thought about them, indicate how the one pair of outlines and the five pairs of paragraphs are related to the stylistic choices or dimensions shown in the above (match the two sets).

A/B_____   C/D_____   E/F_____

G/H_____   I/J _____   K/L _____

APPENDIX 3.D

Write a letter of advice to a student two years younger than you who is planning to come to your school and has asked you to tell how to write a composition on the topic *What should be done to improve my community* that will get a good grade in your school. In your letter first briefly indicate five hints as to what you think teachers in your school find important in judging compositions. *Illustrate them with a model composition on the topic *What should be done to improve my community.*

*Because the testing time was limited and the writing of a model composition did not seem to add anything of value to the analysis, the final instructions were modified to eliminate this part of the assignment.

NOTE

1. The populations sampled for this study included 12-year-olds, 16-year-olds, and preuniversity students. For a more detailed description of the population, see Takala & Vähäpassi, 1987.

REFERENCES

Carroll, J.B. (1960) Vectors of prose style. In T.A. Sebeok (Ed.), *Style in Language* (pp.283-292). Cambridge, MA: MIT Press.

Connor U. & McCagg, P. (1987). A contrastive study of English expository prose paraphrases. In U. Connor & R. B. Kaplan (Eds.). *Writing across languages: Analysis of L2 text* (pp. 73-86). Reading, MA: Addison-Wesley.

Connor, U. & Kaplan, R. B. (Eds.). (1987). *Writing across languages: Analysis of L2 text.* Reading, MA: Addison-Wesley.

Diederich, P. B. (1977). *Measuring growth in English.* Urbana, IL: National Council of Teachers of English.

Enkvist, N. E. (1987). Text linguistics for the applier: An orientation. In U. Connor & R. B. Kaplan (Eds.), *Writing across languages: Analysis of L2 text* (pp. 23-43). Reading, MA: Addison-Wesley.

Galtung, J. (1979). Deductive thinking and political practice: An essay on Teutonic intellectual style. In J. Galtung (Ed.), *Papers on methodology* (pp. 194-209). Copenhagen: Christian Eijlers.

Galtung, J. (1983). Struktur, Kultur und intellektueller Stil. *Leviathan 11(2),* 303-338.

Grabe, W. (1987). Contrastive rhetoric and text-type research. In U. Connor & R. B. Kaplan (Eds.), *Writing across languages: Analysis of L2 text* (pp. 115-138). Reading, MA: Addison-Wesley.

Kaplan, R. B. (1966). Cultural thought patterns in inter-cultural education. *Language Learning 16,* 1-20.

Kaplan, R.B. (Ed.). (1983). *Annual review of applied linguistics, 1982* (Vol. 3). Rowley, MA: Newbury House.

Purves, A.C., & Takala, S. (Eds.). (1982). *An international perspective on the evaluation of written composition* (Evaluation in Education: An International Review Series, Vol. 5, No. 3). Oxford: Pergamon.

Takala, S., & Vähäpassi, A. (1987). Written communication as an object of comparative research. *Comparative Education Review, 31,* 88-105.

Takala, S., Purves, A.C., & Buckmaster, A. (1982). On the interrelationship between language, perception, thought and culture and their relevance to the assessment of written composition. In A. C. Purves & S. Takala (Eds.), *An international perspective on the evaluation of written composition* (Evaluation in Education: An International Review Series, Vol. 5, No. 3; pp. 317-342)). Oxford: Pergamon.

Wesdorp, H., Bauer, B.A., & Purves, A.C. (1982). Toward a conceptualization of the scoring of written composition. *An international perspective on the evaluation of written composition* (Evaluation in Education: An International Review Series, Vol. 5, No. 3; pp. 299-315). Oxford: Pergamon.

PART II
National Differences in Writing Styles

4

Writers in Hindi and English

YAMUNA KACHRU

This study presents an analysis of selected pieces of written expository texts in Hindi to illustrate the differences between the conventions of writing in English and in Hindi. Hindi is an Indo-Aryan language used in South Asia in several varieties by approximately 300 million people. It is one of the four major world languages in terms of the number of speakers.[1]

This chapter is organized as follows: The first section identifies the theoretical approaches adopted in this chapter for the study of discourse in Hindi. The second section presents the traditional notions of expository writing in Hindi. Since a great deal of information is available on the tradition of writing and discourse features of English, the third section discusses these very briefly. The fourth section analyzes actual instances of Hindi texts and comments on their properties from a contrastive perspective. The final part of the chapter suggests further areas of research in order to confirm the conclusions drawn from these and similar previous analyses.

Since Hindi is typologically different from its distant cousin, English, and syntax and lexicon are an integral part of a text, a brief discussion of the major linguistic characteristics of the language is presented in Appendix 4.A.

AUTHOR'S NOTE: Part of the research reported herein was conducted during my sabbatical in the spring of 1986. I am grateful to the University of Illinois for granting me a sabbatical, to the American Institute of Indian Studies for awarding me a Senior Faculty Research Fellowship for field work in India, and to the Research Board of the University of Illinois for providing support for a research assistantship. I am grateful to the reviewers of this volume for their comments and suggestions on an earlier draft of this chapter.

THEORETICAL APPROACH

Recent publications in the field of discourse analysis suggest that two broad theoretical orientations have emerged in the study of discourse: the cognitive psychological approach and the sociocultural approach (Freedle, 1979). The first has been termed *schema-theoretic* (Adams & Collins, 1979) and assumes that a text in itself does not carry meaning. Rather, a text provides directions for hearers or readers only as to how they should retrieve or construct the intended meaning from their own previously acquired conceptual knowledge. The words of the text evoke in the reader associated concepts and their past and potential interrelationships. The structure of the text helps the reader in selecting among these conceptual complexes. The goal of the schema theory is to specify the interface between the reader and the text (Adams & Collins, 1979, p. 3). In contrast to schema theory, the sociocultural approach situates a text in a sociolinguistic context and focuses on how the interpretation of the text depends on factors such as participants, topic, setting, formal and functional aspects of language, and conventions of language use in the community. Notions such as "frame" (Minsky, 1975; used in Tannen, 1979, to discuss "structures of expectation") and "script" (Abelson, 1976) have been proposed to designate a culturally determined familiar activity within which texts are produced.

The two approaches are not mutually incompatible and, in fact, it can be argued that the sociocultural aspect provides a significant basis for the schema (e.g., as demonstrated in Heath, 1982; Scollon & Scollon, 1981; Scribner & Cole, 1981). In this study, insights gained from both the approaches are used. In particular, this study concentrates on selected discourse features of coherence and cohesion (Grimes, 1975; Halliday & Hasan, 1976). These are: culturally determined conventions of rhetorical structures such as "paragraph" and "episode" in expository prose (van Dijk, 1982), cohesive devices such as anaphora, lexical choice, and linkers (coordinating and subordinating conjunctions, participles, and so on), and stylistic choices that reflect "rhetorical stance" (Winterowd, 1975a, p. 136). Since all the three features, that is, culturally determined rhetorical structures, cohesive devices, and stylistic choices, are interlinked, they are discussed together. The discussions are necessarily brief in view of the limitation of space.

TRADITION OF WRITING IN HINDI

In the overall context of Indian literatures, even a cursory glance at the history of Hindi literature will make it clear that Hindi is not a name of a language, rather, it is used as an appellation for a group of related dialects and languages of the region known as "madhyadesha" (midland) in North India. The dialects and languages in which literature was created in this region since the tenth century AD were mainly Avadhi, Braj, Maithili, and Rajasthani, although some examples of compositions in KhaRi Boli (the dialect spoken around Delhi and Meerut, later standardized as Standard Hindi and Urdu), and a mixed language with elements of KhaRi Boli are also found.[2] The early literature predominantly consists of poetry, with genres such as bardic poetry, epics, devotional lyrics, and so on. There are a few works in prose, chiefly biographies of saints, that are more legendary than historical in nature. A few historical accounts also exist; their language, however, is not KhaRi Boli.

The major tradition that Hindi inherited was that of Sanskrit, and all the poetic conventions of Sanskrit are found in Hindi, too. Systematic development of prose in Hindi owes a great deal to the activities of the missionaries in the late eighteenth and early nineteenth centuries. All the genres in prose, whether in literary or journalistic register, developed in the nineteenth century, and the language was gradually standardized between 1850 and the early decades of this century.

There is no tradition of rhetoric in the sense of "conventions of writing effectively for various purposes" in Hindi or any other modern Indian language. Composition is taught in schools, and essay writing continues at the college level, but there are no textbooks exclusively devoted to rhetoric in the above sense. There are textbooks on grammar and composition, but these contain grammatical descriptions, instructions, and illustrations of parsing, a few remarks on organizing narrative, descriptive, argumentative, and personal essays, and a great many examples of "ideal" essays. Sometimes, a list of idioms and descriptions of prosody are included. Frequently, topics and outlines for writing essays are provided for teachers to use as homework assignments. The tradition of rhetoric in the sense of effective ways of conducting logical argumentation owes much to the tradition of the classical language, Sanskrit.

Existing accounts of Sanskrit tradition suggest that Indians

"think" in "a circle or a spiral of continuously developing poten-
tialities, and not on the straight line of progressive stages" as do the
westerners (Heimann, 1964). This nonlinear thought pattern of
Indians has been justified by pointing out the following facts: the
Indian concept of time is cyclic rather than linear; Indian logical
syllogisms have a nonsequential structure (Das Gupta, 1975, p. 117);
the melodic structure of classical Indian music is based on 10 scale
types, which can be diagrammed as a circle (Jairazbhoy, 1975, p. 225);
Indian art, especially the Buddhist frescoes of Ajanta are nonlineal
(Lannoy, 1971, p. 49), and so on.

The nonlinear structure of writing is widely attested in New Indo-
Aryan languages as well. For instance, my earlier work on writing in
Hindi, English, and Indian English (Kachru, 1983) shows that the
structure of expository prose in Hindi is spiral rather than linear, and
the same pattern is encountered in Indian English expository prose as
well. Similarly, Marathi is claimed to exhibit a circular rhetorical
structure in expository prose (Pandharipande, 1983). The interaction
of the oral and the literate traditions in India, extending over more
than 3,000 years, has been said to be responsible for the conventions of
writing still followed in Indic languages (see Kachru, 1987b, for a
discussion of this point).

Although the relationship of "thought patterns" to linguistic and
rhetorical structures is debatable, it is clear that different language
speaking communities have developed different "conventions" of
speaking, writing, and other types of societal behavior. There is no
doubt that the Indian conventions prefer nonlinearity, and looked at
from the Western perspective, may seem to be "circular" and hence,
"illogical."

TRADITION OF WRITING AND
DISCOURSE FEATURES IN ENGLISH

According to Kaplan (1966; 1980), the tradition of writing in
English is based upon Platonic-Aristotelian thought patterns, which
are linear. This is reflected in the paragraph structure in expository
writing (Kaplan, 1980, p. 402):

The thought patterns which speakers of English appear to expect as an integral part of their communication is a sequence that is dominantly linear in its development. An English expository paragraph usually begins with a topic statement, and then, by a series of subdivisions of that topic statement, each supported by examples and illustrations, proceeds to develop that central idea and relate that idea to all the other ideas in the whole essay, and then to employ that idea in its proper relationship with the other ideas, to prove something, or perhaps to argue something.

An example follows, then:

Contrarily, the English paragraph may use just the reverse procedure; that is, it may state a whole series of examples and then relate those examples into a single statement at the end of the paragraph. These two types of development represent the common inductive and deductive reasoning which the English reader expects to be an integral part of any formal communication.

Although concepts such as "topic statement/sentence" and "inductive" versus "deductive" versus "mixed" movement of paragraph have come under increasing attack (see Winterowd, 1975a, p. 250), most texts on rhetoric still refer to the TRIPSQA elements of expository paragraphs (Winterowd, 1975b, p. 43) and recommend editing paragraphs for "clarity" and "completeness," which in turn involve the concepts of topic sentence and linear development of the topic (Young, Becker, & Pike, 1970, pp. 321-326).

For the discussion that follows, I will take the "norm," or as D'Angelo (1975) calls it, the "idealization" (p. 26) of rhetorical structure reflected in Kaplan (1980) as representing the accepted norms of writing in American English, and contrast the discourse features of Hindi with them. The fact that the norm is not always, or even most frequently, adhered to is not particularly relevant here, since the idealized norm generally determines a community's evaluation of other communities or their conventions. One just has to read the several contrastive rhetorical studies published in the area of teaching composition to the learners of English from various non-English-speaking regions of the world to be convinced of this (e.g., see the controversy generated by attempts at questioning the claims in Kaplan, 1972, in the 1985-86 issues of *TESOL Quarterly*).

DISCOURSE FEATURES OF HINDI

The texts selected for discussion in this study belong to two distinct registers (Halliday & Hasan, 1976): literary criticism and scientific-technical, the latter meant for lay educated readers. The selection is not random. While there has been a long tradition of literary criticism in Indic languages, scientific-technical writing in new Indo-Aryan languages has developed under the impact of the educational system introduced by the British. Thus, there is a potential for marked differences between literary criticism on the one hand and scientific-technical writing on the other. The following remarks are based on an examination of a relatively large corpus of published material. Several books on literary criticism were examined (over 75,000 words) and a corpus of approximately 24,800 words was examined for the scientific-technical register (in the references to this chapter). Only a few sample texts extracted from the material studied are presented in the following discussion. All the fragments from the register of literary criticism presented here are either beginnings of a new chapter/section from a longer work or the opening paragraphs of shorter scholarly papers. In many cases, the chapter/section headings, or the titles of papers are presented as well to show the relationship of the selected paragraph(s) to the topics reflected by the headings/titles. The material from the scientific-technical register is of varied kinds: In 5, a complete short text is presented whereas in 8, the paragraph comes from the middle of a longer article.

Note the paragraphing and the transitions in the text below:[3]

1. The Influence of Persian on Dakkhini Literature

The period between 1600 to 1750 AD is the Middle period of Dakkhini literature. Dakkhini literature developed a great deal in this period. From the point of view of language, in the Early period, the influence of local languages on Dakkhini was not negligible, but in this period the standard form of Dakkhini emerged. The writers of this period contributed significantly to the standardization of Dakkhini. Dakkhini assimilated the influence of Persian both in language and in sensibilities. The tatsama and tadbhava vocabularies [i.e., the words borrowed from Sanskrit and the ones derived from the Old Indo-Aryan by regular sound change and other processes] of Dakkhini progressively diminished. It has been explained in the Preamble as to why India accepted Persian influences in this period. In this period in the cultural sphere Iran became the leader of all those countries where there were Muslim populations in large or small numbers. From the literary point of view Persian had become so rich that its influence on literatures in other languages was inevitable. The Qutbshahi dynasty of Golkunda considered Iran its ideal. Bijapur did not remain untouched by Persian influence either. In the Early period, Dakkhini literature was completely the literature of Hindi, but in this period it derived full benefit from Persian language and literature as well. Nusrati is a poet of this very period. He used the compounds of Persian in his language. From the point of view of poetics also, Nusrati's poetry is a debtor to the Persian tradition. Some people have considered Vali the Father of Urdu, in reality, this credit should go to Nusrati. All those features which later proved to be so helpful in the development of Urdu are present in Nusrati's language.

Many genres of literature flourished in this period. This period will be considered memorable from the point of view of lyrics (Ghazal), but the main tendency was toward narrative poems. The narrative poems of this period can be divided into three types: (1) historical narratives, (2) romantic narratives, and, (3) legendary narratives (Sharma, 1972, p. 196)

The background knowledge that is required to interpret the two paragraphs is as follows. The schema is that of the history of Dakkhini language and literature. The seat of the early development of Dakkhini was the Qutbshahi court of Golkunda in the Deccan. The language, Dakkhini, was based upon the North Indian dialect of KhaRi Boli. The rulers of Golkunda were Muslims, and the majority of writers of Dakkhini were Muslims, too. In the Early period, the writers used a form of chaste Dakkhini free from large scale borrowings from either Sanskrit or Perso-Arabic. The themes were also drawn from the "little" tradition of popular culture. Later, in the Middle period, as the literature assumed more features of a "great" tradition, the language and the literary conventions became more Persianized (Sharma, 1972).

As regards the structure of paragraphs, the following features are worth noting. The section heading identifies the topic to be "the influence of Persian on Dakkhini literature," whereas the actual topic is the result of Persianization, namely, the standardization of Dakkhini (sentence 3). The first line sets the temporal limits on the Middle period of the literature under focus, the second line asserts that the literature developed greatly in this period. Exactly what the processes of development were, however, is not stated explicitly until the first line of the following paragraph: That is where it is explained that many genres flourished in this period. The third line of the first paragraph asserts the development of the standard form of Dakkhini, the fourth states the authors' contribution in this process, the fifth asserts that Dakkhini assimilated Persian influences, the sixth states loss of certain vocabularies in Dakkhini. Six subsequent sentences elaborate on why and how Iran influenced India, especially Dakkhini. The last five sentences are about the poet Nusrati, who used Persianized vocabulary and thus led to the development of the variety known as Urdu, which was later institutionalized as a separate language.

The following conclusions about conventions of paragraphing in Hindi can be drawn from the above example. First, unity of a topic is not a requirement for a paragraph. Second, a Hindi paragraph tolerates a great deal of digression. Third, in a Hindi paragraph, there is no need for an explicit topic statement. The relationship of Persianization to the standardization of Dakkhini is left unstated. It is only the background knowledge of the reader about the relationship between Hindi-Dakkhini-Urdu that leads to the intended inference. Fourth, a claim and its justification may be presented in separate paragraphs while material related to the background may be presented in the same paragraph as the claim.

There are at least four distinct "episodes" in the paragraph under focus: the development of various genres in the Middle period of Dakkhini literature, the factors responsible for Persian influence on Dakkhini, standardization of Dakkhini as a result of Persianization, and the role of the poet Nusrati as the Father of Urdu. All four are related in that the Middle period of Dakkhini coincides with the increasing Persian influence all over West and South Asia, increasing Persianization results in standardization of Dakkhini as well as the development of new genres in its literature, and Nusrati plays a significant role in the whole process. The relationship of these four to the second paragraph can be shown diagrammatically in the following:[4]

2. *Persian Influence on Dakhini Literature*

Paragraph 1

S 1   Period identification

S 2   Development of literature   Background

S 3   (clause 1)   Influence of local languages

S 3   (clause 2)   Emergence of a standard form ⎫
S 4   Writers'contribution in the process   ⎬ Sub-topic 1

[S 3 (clause 1)]   ⎫

S 5   Influence of Persian   ⎪
S 6   Supporting evidence   ⎬ Sub-topic 2
S 7 - 12   Reasons   ⎭

[S 3 (clause 2)]

S 13   Poet Nusrati   ⎫
S 14 - 15   His use of Persian elements   ⎪
S 16   Father of Urdu   ⎬ Sub-topic 4
S 17   Supporting evidence   ⎭

Paragraph 2

[S 1 and S 2 of Paragraph 1]   ⎫
S 18   Development of many genres   ⎬ Sub-topic 3
S 19 - 20   Enumeration of genres   ⎭

Topic that emerges from analysis: Standardization of the Dakhini language as a consequence of Persianization.

Subtopics: (1) Standardization as a consequence of Persianization (S 3 and S 5); (2) Factors responsible for Persian influence (S 7-S 12); (3) Development of genres in the Middle period (S 1, S 2, S 18-S 20); and (4) Role of Poet Nusrati in the development of Standard Urdu. Note that subtopic 4 is related to the others very indirectly. Dakhini and Urdu share the same source—KhaRi Boli—and developmental history—contact with Arabic and Persian. In contemporary times, Dakhini is considered a regional variety of Standard Hindi and/or Urdu.

The second paragraph in itself has a straight linear structure with an initial statement and its subsequent elaboration.

One other instance of the same genre is essential to illustrate a few other characteristics. Consider the excerpt in 3 below:

3. Contemporary Hindi Literature: Criticism

The main problem that any independent nation faces is that of new construction. The domain of this construction is not limited to economic, political and social reconstruction, it extends to literature, culture, etc., as well. Literature is an integral part of culture and cultural progress of a country depends mainly on literature. There are two aspects of literature—creative and critical. Creative literature is a measure of a country's sensibility, critical literature that of its intellect. A nation will be considered as intellectually enlightened as its criticism is deep and wide.

Four more paragraphs follow, then:

Although in the past one and a half decades a large number of books have been published under the name of criticism which can not be placed under criticism by any stretch of imagination, even so all in all Hindi criticism has widened its path, has realized its heritage, has discovered something new. (Singh, 1967, pp. 297-298)

The next paragraph states what the essay is about, and is followed by several paragraphs detailing the historical facts about the major critics and criticism in Hindi.

Notice that the main topic of the essay, the state-of-the-art of contemporary criticism, does not appear until the sixth paragraph. Writing such elaborate "global" introductions is acceptable in Hindi essays on literary as well as social, economic, political, educational, and other topics. In addition, it is not inappropriate to express affective involvement of the writer with the topic as is clear from the following excerpt:

4. smriti kii rekhaaē (Lines of Memory)

Mahadeviji's personal reminiscences are collected in *smriti kii rekhaaē*. Her first book, *atiit ke calcitra* was a collection of similar reminiscences. These days, the type of reminiscences that is most prevalent in our literature is the so-called "literary reminiscences!" One author writes a memoir of another, more famous, author known to him and thus spreads his own and his deity's fame far and wide. It is allright to write literary memoirs, but the aim of such writers should not be to wave the flag of one's own or one's mentor's fame. He should attempt to draw the character in such a way that the human aspects of the subject is revealed fully. But a majority of present memoir writers pay no attention to this requirement.

The reminiscences collected in *smriti kii rekhaaẽ* are quite different. (Rai, 1977, p. 108)

After the first two sentences, the author introduces a digression— the prevalent kind of reminiscences, and his own judgments about them. Sentences 5 and 6 contain an explicit prescription for the writing of memoirs, sentence 7 laments the fact that writers of memoirs do not follow the suggested rules. Such "prescriptivism" may be objectionable in a review in American English (note the text cited as the first example of Expository Essay in Winterowd (1975a), in which "the writer . . . has disappeared behind his subject matter and style," p. 140).

In addition to the paragraph structure, the cohesive ties (Halliday & Hasan, 1976) deserve special mention, too. Note the repetition of "this period" in the text in 1. The period between 1600-1750 AD is under focus throughout. It is more natural in English to contrast "the Early period" with "the Middle period" between lines 5 and 7 of the text. In Hindi, the repetition of "the Middle period" would hurt cohesion: once "the Middle period" is established as the topic in line 2, subsequent reference by the full noun phrase would break the coherence of the text. The demonstrative form with the head noun is used as a pronominal only because sentence topics shift frequently.

Note also the emphatic "this very period" in line 28 of the text. In English, it does not make much sense to have the emphatic phrase. In Hindi, the emphatic draws attention to the facts mentioned in preceding sentences—the period when Persian influence is on ascendancy, hence the use of Persian compounds by Nusrati.

Note the correlative "even so" in line 4 of the second paragraph in the text in 2. Again, the correlative performs no function in English, the conjunction "although" by itself signals the concessive meaning. In Hindi, the correlative is essential in the concessive construction.

It is interesting to compare a text from the scientific-technical register to the above to determine if there is a difference between the two registers in rhetorical structure and cohesion. Consider the following:

5. H.L.A.: The New Identity Card of Man

How biotechnology is becoming a boon to the mankind is known by the discovery and use of H.L.A. H.L.A. is the name of human leukocyte antigen. On the basis of types of H.L.A., diseases can be identified at birth. H.L.A. technology is the most appropriate and safe support during blood transfusion or selection of right organs for organ transplant.

In the nucleus of human cells there are 23 pairs of chromosomes. The sixth chromosome among these is responsible for the capacity to fight diseases. The steadily progressing developments in biotechnology have revealed that there are five special parts in the genes of the sixth chromosome. In order to identify them, scientists have called them A,B,C,D, and D-related or D-type. On the surface of the white blood cells of humans, there is provision for identifying unfamiliar or harmful material. The antigen present on the surface of the cell does this job. The presence, quantity and type of this antigen may differ because of even tissue, individual traits, race, and tribe. The responsibility of manufacturing these antigens rests with the D or D-like part. By now one hundred different antigens of this type have been identified in man. There is one definite hereditary theory about them that in any one man, there can only be two types of the said antigen. One comes from the mother, the other from the father.

Before the development of the human leukocyte antigen technology, man could also be identified on the basis of blood-group. If two people have the same blood group, then one's blood can be used for the other in transfusion, or one's organs may be transplanted into the other's body. Similarly, at the scene of crime, blood stains are lifted and their blood group identified so that it could be determined if the blood is of the person involved in the crime or of someone else. Similarly, many times, controversy arises as to the parentage of a child and it becomes difficult to determine the child's parents on the basis of blood group alone. Now all these problems have been solved by the development of the H.L.A. technology. The rate of success by this method is 93 to 98 percent.

As important as matching of H.L.A. is in medicine, it is equally important in criminology. At this point, there are facilities for H.L.A. matching in India in the All India Institute of Medical Sciences in Delhi and the Criminological laboratory located in Madras in Tamilnadu. (Singh, 1986, p. 40)

The organization of this piece does not seem to be very different from the texts belonging to the literary genre. The title promises the piece to be about the use of H.L.A. technology in identifying humans. The opening paragraph, however, starts with a general statement about the usefulness of the technology and expands the abbreviation of H.L.A. in the title. The second paragraph enumerates the benefits of the technology to elaborate on the statement in the first sentence of the first paragraph. The third paragraph introduces H.L.A. and has all the relevant information that explains how the H.L.A. could function as an identity card for humans. The fourth paragraph compares identification on the basis of blood group with that based on the H.L.A. antigen group. It also asserts the superiority of the latter type of identification technique. The last paragraph sums up the usefulness of the technology in two different areas of application and provides information about where it is available in India.

From the point of view of American English norms of paragraph development in academic writing, only the third paragraph of the piece, relatively speaking, is well organized. It is coherent, and gives all the required information without digressing into details not immediately relevant to the description of the H.L.A. antigen. One improvement that might be suggested is that the order of the seventh and the eighth sentences be changed to make the proper connections between sentences 6 and 8, and 7 and 9.

The structure of the essay in 5 is as follows:

6. *H.L.A.: The New Identity Card of Man*

Paragraph 1	
S 1 Gene technology and its usefulness for man, e.g., H.L.A.	Background
S 2 Expansion of the abbreviation H.L.A.	
Paragraph 2	
S 3 Use of H.L.A. in early diagnosis of diseases	
S 4 Reliability of H.L.A. in blood transfusion/ organ transplant	Sub-topic 3 (a)
Paragraph 3	
S 5 - S 15 Relevant biological information	Sub-topic 2
Paragraph 4	
S 16 Blood types and human identity	Sub-topic 4
S 17 - S 19 Applications of blood typing	Sub-topics 4
S 20 - S 21 Superiority of H.L.A. technology	and 3 (b,c,d)
Paragraph 5	
S 22 H.L.A. in medicine and criminology	Conclusion
S 23 Location of facilities	

(continued)

Topic that emerges from analysis: H.L.A.: Description and application
of typing in medicine and criminology.
Subtopics: (1) What is H.L.A.? (2) Relevant biological information (3)
Applications of typing in (a) early diagnosis of diseases, (b) identification of criminals or their victims, (c) decisions regarding parent-
hood, (d) blood transfusion and organ transplant; (4) Comparison with
blood typing, superiority of H.L.A. technology; (5) Conclusion:
Availability of technology and location of facilities.

Note also the use of tenses in the third paragraph. The transition
from past (sentence 1) to present (sentence 2) is sudden—it seems odd
in English. Since in Hindi, unlike in English, the point of speech and
the reference point (Reichenbach, 1966) coincide, this is perfectly
natural. The transition between sentences 3 and 4 is also strange from
the point of view of English. Sentences 2 and 3 describe normal
applications of the technology, sentence 4 suddenly brings up
"controversy" and sentence 5 implies there are problems with blood
transfusion and identification in criminal cases, too. Such leaps of
"inferences," required to make sense of texts, seem to be quite
common in Hindi.

The discussion so far may give the impression that there is no
paragraph structure comparable to the American norm in Hindi
writing. This, of course, is not true. Both in the literary and the
scientific-technical genres, there exist paragraphs with the property
of straight linear progression of thought. Two examples, one each
from the literary and scientific-technical writing, may illustrate this.
Consider the pieces in 7 and 8:

7. *Contemporary Hindi Literature: Novel*

Similar to life and the world, novel also has become progressively
manysided and complex. The novelist of today can not function by
simply showing the conflict between human circumstances and
propensities. He must also portray the transformation that takes place
in this conflict as a result of the experiences obtained from the ever-

changing inner and outer environment. The novel today has become
an expression of the relationship between man and his circumstances,
the progressive development of his viewpoint with regard to his
ecology. Hindi novel is not an exception to this process. (Rangra, 1967,
p. 145)

The structure of this paragraph is perfectly straightforward in that
it starts with a set of general observations and concludes with the
statement that these apply to the novel in Hindi, too. The paragraphs
following this one develop the theme of the novel in Hindi
portraying the relationship of man and the conflict between his inner
and outer environments further.

The following is an example of a paragraph in scientific-technical
register:

8. Care of Teeth

There is a special need to be particularly careful about the teeth for
this reason, too, because diseases of the teeth can lead to other diseases.
Diseased teeth do not function properly and impede the digestion of
and nutrition from food, and this affects one's entire health. Sometimes
pus or other contaminants from the teeth get into the blood stream and
spread all over the body, which causes diseases of the digestive system
such as gastric ulcer, coli cystitis, diseases of the joints and bone, heart
diseases, and diseases of the throat and lungs. Therefore, it is necessary
to take special care of one's teeth.(Saritaa, 1982, p. 146)

The above is a well-structured paragraph in that the orthographic
and the discourse paragraph coincide perfectly. The schema is that of
care of teeth; it concerns the neglect of teeth and how neglect can lead
to various diseases. The paragraph begins with the sentence that care
of teeth is necessary because neglect results in diseased teeth, and
diseases of the teeth in turn may lead to other diseases. Subsequent
sentences enumerate various unpleasant consequences of diseased
teeth, and the paragraph ends with the concluding sentence that it is
necessary to care well for one's teeth.

CONCLUSION

I have presented evidence to show that the conventions of writing
in Hindi seem to differ from those of American English in the two

registers I have quoted from in this study. The difference is not categorical in that the structure of a paragraph in Hindi is not always "circular" or "spiral" (Kachru, 1983). There are paragraphs that exhibit the straight linear structure said to be the "preferred" structure for expository writing in English (Kaplan, 1966), and there are paragraphs that exemplify the spiral/circular structure. Both seem to be fairly common. What is needed now is to determine if there are more than these two types of paragraphing in Hindi, and also what the distribution of these is in various registers and genres, as is being done for English (Grabe, 1987). A detailed analysis of a large corpus from Hindi, consisting of samples from several registers and genres as well as student writing, is in progress now. Once this current project (Kachru, n.d.) is completed, more definite information will be available on the relative distribution of various types of paragraphs and other structural features in Hindi. On the basis of the data analyzed so far, chiefly from the published sources, the frequency of the two types of paragraphs seems to be about equal in both the registers (e.g., 38% of the opening paragraphs in the scientific register and 40% of the opening paragraphs in the genre of literary criticism are nonlinear in structure).

In addition, claims about the "circular" or "spiral" thinking patterns of Indians and the reflection of these in Indian philosophy, art, music, literature, and so on (Lannoy, 1971), also need to be examined seriously. Appropriate methodology for this kind of research still awaits development.

APPENDIX 4.A
HINDI GRAMMAR AND LEXICON

Hindi is a verb-final language (i.e., it has the word order subject-object-verb). It has postpositions, the auxiliaries follow the main verb, and the modifiers—both adjectives and participials—precede the head noun. Nevertheless, it has, unlike Japanese, mixed characteristics of verb medial (subject-verb-object) and verb final languages. For instance, the relative clauses are of the correlative type, but do not always precede the head noun: In case the head noun is in a nonsubject function or is indefinite, the relative clause follows the entire main clause. Complement clauses also normally follow a lexical head noun. Standard Hindi, which is largely based upon the Western variety, has a split ergative syntax (see Kachru, 1980 for a description of the major syntactic characteristics of Hindi). In the verbal system, Hindi makes clear distinctions among three aspects, three tenses, and six moods, which cross-classify each other. The aspects are imperfect, progressive, and perfect; the tenses are present, past, and future; and the moods are indicative, interrogative, imperative, optative, contingent, and presumptive. The distinctions are made either by changing the form of the verb or with the help of the auxiliaries, except for the interrogative, which requires either a question particle or a distinct intonation. The verb phrase usually shows agreement with some noun in person, number, and gender in the sentence. Consequently, the paradigm of forms looks formidable to an English speaker. The forms, however, are regular; irregular verbs can be counted on the fingers of one hand. One consequence of the systematic difference in terms of moods is that Hindi expresses a clear distinction between actual versus potential, which is formally obscure in English. Also, Hindi makes clear distinctions among timeless general statements and general state of affairs in the present (present imperfect form), general state of affairs in the past (past imperfect form), and particular, completed events in the past (the perfect form, comparable to English simple past). In English the latter two are not distinguished consistently: The simple past in English is ambiguous between a general state of affairs in the past or a particular, completed event in the past.

In semantic terms, Hindi makes a distinction between volitional and nonvolitional acts, which interacts with the dynamic-stative and transitive-intransitive systems in complex ways. Thus, the distinctions that are expressed in English either lexically, or by adverbs, or by the passive (especially the get-passive) are expressed by verb-governed sentence constructions in Hindi (see Kachru, 1980, for a detailed description of Hindi verbs).

Hindi has a range of participial constructions that obviate the need for using full clauses with finite verbs. This leads to the perception that Hindi has a more nominal style as compared to English. In addition to full pronouns, Hindi makes extensive use of zero pronouns for anaphoric reference, which may lead to a perception of lack of coherence in Hindi texts on the part of an English-speaking reader. These have been discussed and illustrated in Kachru (1983).

In some sense, unlike an average educated English-speaker, an average educated Hindi-speaker uses a verbal repertoire with a unique set of features. Standard Hindi has at least three distinct varieties with phonological, lexical, and syntactic characteristics of their own: eastern, western, and southern. The western variety is the one used in education, literature, and media. The specialized lexicon (i.e., terms for literary criticism, law, science, and technology, and other disciplinary areas) is drawn from three sources:

Sanskrit, Perso-Arabic, and English. There is a great deal of code-mixing (B. Kachru, 1979) and code-switching (Gumperz, 1982) that involves linguistic elements from Sanskrit, Perso-Arabic, and English in Hindi texts, whether spoken or written. All the above features can be identified in the texts discussed in this study (see Appendix 4.B for the Hindi texts in transliteration).

APPENDIX 4.B

The numbers preceding the excerpts correspond to the numbers of the translations cited in the text; the diagrams are not repeated here.

1. <u>dakkhinii</u> <u>saahitya</u> <u>par</u> <u>faarsii</u> <u>kaa</u>   <u>prabhaav</u>:   1600
    Dakkhini literature on Persian of influence

   se 1750 ii. tak kaa samay   dakkhinii saahitya kaa
   from   AD till of time   Dakkhini   literature of

   madhyayug hai.   is yug mẽ dakkhinii saahitya kaa bahut
   middle period is this period in Dakkhini lit. of   much

   vikaas huaa.   bhaaSaa kii drSTi se aarambhik yug
   development happened language of view from early   period

   kii dakkhinii par kSetriiy bhaaSaaõ kaa kam prabhaav
   of   Dakkhini   on   regional languages of less influence

   nahĩĩ thaa, kintu is yug mẽ dakkhinii kaa pariniSThit
   not   was but this period in Dakkhini of   standard

   ruup prakaT huaa. is yug ke lekhakõ ne dakkhinii ke
   form emerged   this period of writers erg. Dakkhini of

   pariniSThiikaraN mẽ bahut yog diyaa. dakkhinii ne
   standardization in much cooperation gave Dakkhini erg.

   bhaaSaa tathaa bhaav donõ   driSTiyõ se faarsii kaa
   language and sensibility both   views   from Persian of

   prabhaav grahaN kiyaa. hindii ke tatsam tathaa tadbhav
   influence   acquired   Hindi of 'tatsama' and 'tadbhava'

   shabd kam hote gae. piiThikaa mẽ bataayaa gayaa hai
   words less become went preamble   in stated   been has

   ki is kaal mẽ bhaarat ne iiraanii prabhaavõ ko kyõ
   that this period in India erg. Persian influences DO why

   sviikaar kiyaa. is kaal mẽ iiraan saanskritik kSetra
   acceptance did   this period in Iran   cultural   field

   mẽ un sabhii deshõ kaa aguaa banaa, jahãã musalmaan kam
   in those all nations of leader became where Muslims less

   yaa adhik sankhyaa mẽ baste the. saahityik driSTi se
   or more numbers in lived   literary   view from

   faarsii itnii samriddha ban cukii thii, ki anya bhaaSaaõ
   Persian so prosperous become had   that other languages

   ke ssahitya par uskaa prabhaav paRnaa anivaary thaa.
   of literature on its influence fall   unavoidable was

golkunDaa kaa Qutbshaahii vansh iiraan ko aadarsh maantaa
Golkunda of Qutbshahi dynasty Iran DO ideal considered

thaa.   biijaapur bhii iiraanii prabhaavõ se achuutaa
was   Bijapur   also Persian influence from untouched

nahĩĩ rahaa. aarambhik yug mẽ dakkhinii kaa saahitya
not remained beginning period in Dakkhini of literature

puurNtayaa hindii kaa saahitya thaa, kintu is yug mẽ
completely Hindi of literature was but this period in

usne   faarsii bhaaSaa tathaa saahitya se bhii puuraa-
it erg. persian language and literature from too   full

puuraa laabh uThaayaa. nusratii isii yug kaa kavi hai.
full advantage derived Nusrati this period of poet is

isne faarsii ke samaasit padõ kaa prayog apnii bhaaSaa mẽ
he erg. Persian of compound phrases of use his language in

kiyaa. saahitya shaastra kii driSTi se bhii nusratii kii
did   poetics   of view from too Nusrati of

kavitaa faarsii paramparaa kii riNii hai. kuch logõ ne
poetry Persian tradition of debtor is some people erg.

valii ko urduu kaa janmdaataa maanaa hai, vastutah yah
Vali   DO Urdu of father   consider in reality this

shreya nusratii ko milnaa caahiye. nusratii kii bhaaSaa
credit Nusrati IO accrue should   Nusrati of language

mẽ ve sabhii tatva vidyamaan hãĩ, jo aage cal kar urduu
in those all elements present are which later   Urdu

ke vikaas   mẽ sahaayak hue.
of development in helpful became

     is yug mẽ saahitya kii anek vidhaaẽ samriddha
     this period in literature of many genres prosperous

huĩĩ. bhaavgiit (Ghazal) kii driSTi se yah yug
became lyrics   Ghazal   of view from this period

smarNiiya maanaa jaaegaa, kintu mukhya pravritti
memorable considered will be but   main   tendency

kathaatmak kaavyõ kii or thii. is yug ke kathaatmak
narrative poems toward was this period of narrative

kaavyõ ko tiin shreNiyõ mẽ bããTaa jaa saktaa hai --
poetry DO three classes in divided   can   be

1. aitihaasik kathaatmak kaavya, 2. premaakhyaanak
     historical narrative poems   romantic narrative

kaavya, 3. pauraaNik aakhyaanak kaavya.
poems   legendary narrative poems

3. aalocnaa (Criticism)

kisii bhii svatantra raaSTra ke saamne sabse
any   at all independent nation   of front all from

pramukh samasyaa navnirmaaN   kii hotii hai. is
main   problem new construction of happens   this

nirmaaN   kaa kSetra aarthik, raajniitik tathaa saamaajik
construction of area   economic political and   social

punarnirmaaN   tak hii siimit na ho kar saahitya-
reconstruction to only limited not being literature

sankriti aadi tak phailaa hotaa hai. saahitya sanskriti
culture etc. to spread   is   literature culture

kaa anivaarya anga hai aur kisii desh kaa saanskritik
of essential part is and any country of cultural

unnayan   mukhyatah saahitya par nirbhar kartaa hai.
awakening primarily literature on depend does

saahitya   ke do pakSa hote ha͂ĩ -- racnaatmak aur
literature of two aspects are   creative   and

aalocnaatmak.   racnaatmak saahitya   desh   kii
critical   creative   literature country of

samvedanshiiltaa kaa maapak hai to aalocnaatmak
sensitiveness   of measure is then critical

saahitya   uskii bauddhiktaa kaa. jis   raaSTra kii
literature its   intellect   of   which nations of

'aalocnaa' jitnii gahrii aur vyaapak   hogii
criticism as   deep   and extensive be will

bauddhik driSTi se vah utnaa hii prbuddha maanaa
intellectual view from it as emph. awake   consider

jaaegaa.
be will

4. smriti kii rekhaae̊ (Lines of Memory)

'smriti kii rekhaae̊' me̊ mahaadeviijii ke nijii
memory of lines   in Mahadeviji   of own

sansmaraN   sangrihiit ha̋ĩ. aise hii sansmaraNo̊
reminiscences collected are such emph. reminiscences

kii unkii pahlii pustak 'atiit ke calcitra' thii.
of her   first bokk   past of mobile pictures was

aajkal   visheS ruup se jis   sansmaraN   kaa pracalan
now a days especially   which reminiscences of prevalence

hamaare saahitya mẽ hai,   vah   hai   svanaamdhanya
our   literature in is   that   is   so-called

'saahityik sansmaraN'! ek saahityik apne paricit kisii
literary reminiscences one literatur self's known some

duusre adhik labdha-pratiSTha saahityik kaa sansmaraN
other more well-known   literatur of reminiscences

likhtaa hai aur is prakaar apnii aur apne aaraadhyadev
writes   and thus   own   and self's deity

donõ kii kiirti ko digdigant   mẽ prasaarit kartaa hai.
both of fame   DO all directions in broadcast does

saahityik sansmaraN likhnaa Thiik hai,   lekin   aise
literary   reminiscences write proper is   but   such

sansmaraNõ   mẽ lekhak kaa uddeshya keval apnii aur apne
reminiscences in writer of aim   only own and self's

vandya saahityik bandhu kii kiirtidhvajaa phahraanaa hii
respected literary friend of flag of fame unfurling only

nahĩĩ honaa caahiye. use   is prakaar   caritraankan
not   be   should him to this way   charcter drawing

karne kaa prayatn karnaa caahiye ki ankit caritra   kaa
do   of effort do   should that drawn character of

maanviiy pakSa puurii tarah ubhar kar saamne   aa jaae.
human   aspect fully   rising   front   come go

par aajkal   adhikaansh sansmaraN-lekhakõ kaa dhyaan
but now a days majority   memoir   writers of attention

is   baat   kii or kadaacit nahĩĩ jaataa.
this matter toward perhaps   not   go

5. ec. el. e.: maanav kaa nayaa pahcaan-patra (H.L.A.: The
    new identity card of man)

    jiin takniikii maanav ke liye ek vardaan kaise bantii jaa
    gene technology man   for   a blessing how become go

    rahii hai, yah pataa lagtaa hai   ec. el. e. kii   khoj
    -ing is this known   is   H L A of discovery

    aur upyogitaa se.   ec. el. e. hyuuman lyukosaaiT eNTijen
    and usefulness from H   L A human   leucocyte antigen

    ko kahte hai.
    DO call

        ec. el. e. kii qismõ ke aadhaar par biimaariyõ kii
        H   L   A of types of basis   on diseases   of

janm   hote   hii   pahcaan   ho   saktii   hai.
birth happen as soon as   diagnosis happen   can

raktaadhaan   ke vaqt sahii rakt ke cunnav   athvaa
blood transfusion of time right blood of selection or

ang-pratyaaropaN ke   vaqt sahii ang   ke   cunaav mẽ
organ transplant of   time right organ of selection in

ec. el. e. takniikii hii sarvaadhik upyukt   aur surakSit
H   L   A technology only most   appropriate and   safe

sahaaraa hai.
support is

     maanav koshikaaõ ke naabhik mẽ guNsuutra ke   23
     human   cells   of nucleus in chromosomes of 23

joRe   hote hãí. inmẽ   se   chaThaa guNsuutra maanav
pairs   are   these in from sixth   chromosome humans

mẽ rogpratirodhii   kSamtaa ke liye uttardaayii hai.
in disease resistance capcity for   responsible is

jiin takniikiyõ ke kramashah vikaas   se   yah   pataa
gene technologies of gradual development from this known

lagaa   ki chaThvẽ guNsuutra kii jiin mẽ pãac xaas
became that sixth chromosome of gene in five special

hisse hote hãí. pahcaan   ke taur par vaigyaanikõ ne
parts   are   identification for   scientists erg.

inhe 'e', 'bii', 'sii', 'Dii' aur 'Dii-rileTiD' athvaa
these a   b   c   d   and d - related   or

'Dii'-qism jaisaa kahaa hai.   maanav kii shvet rakt-
d- type   like called have humans of   white blood

koshikaaõ kii satah par anjaan yaa nuksaandeh padaarth
cells   of surface on unfamiliar or harmful   substance

kii   pahcaan   kii vyavasthaa hotii hai. koshikaa-
of identification of arrangement is   cell

satah par vidyamaan enTiijen ye kaam karte hãí. is
surface on present   antigen these jobs do   this

enTiijen kii upasthiti, maatraa aur qism maanav uutak,
antigen of presence   quantity and type human tissue

vyaktitva, jaati,   aur kabiile tak ke aadhaar par
personality species and .tribe even of basis   on

alag - alag ho saktii hai. in enTiijanõ ke   nirmaaN
distinct   be can   these antigens of production

kii zimmedaarii 'Dii' aur 'Dii'-samaan hisse kii hai.
of responsibility d   and d - like   part of is

ab tak maanav mẽ aise 100 vibhinna qism ke eNTiijanõ
now till humans in such 100 different types of antigens

kii pahcaan   ho cukii hai. inkaa ek   nishcit
of identification been has   these of a   definite

aanuvanshikii siddhant yah hai ki kisii ek   vyakti
geneological theory   this is that any one individual

mẽ keval do qism ke kathit   eNTiijan hii hote hãĩ. ek
in only two types of so-called antigen only are   one

maataa tathaa duusraa pitaa kii or se aataa hai.
mother and   other   father from comes

      hyuuman   lyuukosaaiT enTijan   takniikii   ke
      human   leucocyte   antigen   technology   of

vikaas   se pahle 'blaD-grup' (rakt-varg) ke hisaab se
development before blood group blood group according to

bhii vyakti   kii pahcaan   hotii thii. agar do
also individual of identification happened   if two

vyaktiyõ kaa blaD-grup samaan hai to   ek kaa rakt
individuals of blood group identical is then one of blood

duusre ko caRh saktaa hai, yaa ek kaa ang duusre ko
other   to climb can   or one of organ other to

pratyaaropit ho saktaa hai. isii tarah apraadh-sthal par
transplanted be can   this way   crime   place on

rakt-dhabbõ ko uThaa kar unke   blaD-grup   kaa
blood spots DO lifting   their blood group of

pataa lagaayaa jaataa hai taaki yah   pataa   lag jaae
knowledge found   is so that this knowledge found be

ki apraadh mẽ sanlipt vyakti   kaa hii yah rakt hai
that crime in involved individual of emph. this blood is

yaa kisii duusre kaa. isii tarah kaii baar   aulaad
or some   other of this just like many times progeny

ke masle bhii khaRe ho jaate hãĩ aur blaD-grup kii madad
of matters also rise be go   and blood group of help

se santaan ke maataa-pitaa kaa nishcay karnaa   kaThin
with progeny of mother father of decision do   difficult

ho jaataa hai. ab ye saarii samasyaaẽ ec. el. e. milaa
becomes   now these all problems H L   A   match

kar dekhne kii takniikii se   duur ho gaii hãĩ.   is
-ing see   of technology with remote became have   this

vidhi se saphaltaa ke aasaar   93 se 99 pratishat hãĩ.
method with success of possibility 93 to 99 percent are

      ec. el. e. milaan kaa jitnaa mahatva aayurvigyaan
       H   L   A matching of as much importance medicine

mẽ hai, utnaa hii apraadh vigyaan mẽ bhii hai. bhaarat
in is that much emph. criminology in also is   India

mẽ is samay dillii mẽ akhil bhaartiiya   aayurvigyaan
in this time Delhi in All   India   Medical Sciences

sansthaan aur tamilnaaDu mẽ madraas mẽ apraadh vigyaan
Institute and Tamilnadu in Madras in Criminology

prayogshaalaa mẽ ec. el. e. milaan kii suvidhaa hai.
Laboratory   in H   L A matching of facility is

7. <u>upanyaas</u> (Novel)

jiivan aur jagat ke samaan upanyaas bhii uttarottar
life   and world similar to novel   too progressively

bahumukhii   evam jaTil   hotaa gayaa hai. maanav kii
manyfaceted and complicated becoming been has man   of

paristhitityõ ke saath uskii manovrittiyõ kaa sangharS
circumstances with his   tendencies of conflict

dikhaa dene se hii   aaj ke upanyaaskaar kaa kaam
show   give with emph. today of novelist   of job

nahĩĩ caltaa. nirantar   badalte hue baahrii aur
not   moves continuously changing   outer and

bhjiitrii parivesh   mẽ praapt   anubhavõ   ke
inner   environment in obtained experiences of

phalsvaruup is sangharS mẽ jo   ruupaantar
result   as this conflict in which transformation

ghaTit hotaa hai, upanyaaskaar ko use bhii citrit
takes place   novelist dat. that too portray

karnaa hotaa hai. upanyaas aaj   maanav kii apnii
do   has to   novel   today man   of self's

paristhitiyõ ke saath uske sambandh   kii, apne
circumstances with his   relationship of   self's

paripaarshva ke prati uske driSTikoN ke uttarottar
environment   toward his   viewpoint of progressive

vikaas   kii, abhivyakti ban gayaa hai. hindii
development of   expression become has   Hindi

upanyaas is prakriyaa kaa apvaad nahĩĩ.
novel   this process   of exception not

8. dããtõ ke baare mẽ visheS saavdhaanii kii zaruurat
    teeth about   special care   of necessity

    isliye   bhii hai kyõki dããtõ kii biimaarii se
    this reason too is because teeth of disease   from

    anya rog   bhii ho sakte hãí. vikkaryukt dããt
    other diseases too happen can   diseased teeth

    Thiik prakaar kaary   na kar paane ke kaaraN bhojan
    properly   function not do manage of reason meal

    ke paacan   evam poSaN   mẽ baadhak   hote hãí. iskaa
    of digestion and nutrition in impediment are   this of

    prabhaav puure svaasthy par paRtaa hai. kabhii kabhii
    effect   entire health on falls   sometimes

    inse   niklaa mavaad yaa sankramaNyukt padaarth
    these from emerged pus or contaminated material

    khuun mẽ milkar saare shariir mẽ phail jaataa hai, jiske
    blood in mixing whole body in spread goes   which of

    phalsvaruup paacan sansthaan ke vikaar   jaise gaisTrik
    result as   digestive system of diseases like gastric

    alsar (amaashay kaa vraN), kolii sisTaaiTis (pittaashay
    ulcer stomach   of ulcer coli cystitis   gall bladder

    pradaah),   joRõ evam haDDiyõ ke vibhinn rog,   dil
    inflammation joints and bones of various diseases heart

    kii kuch biimaariyããa, gale evam phephRe ke phoRe ityaadi
    of some diseases   throat and lungs of blisters etc.

    utpann ho jaate hãí. atah   dããtõ kii surakSaa   kaa
    arise become   therefore teeth of protection of

    visheS dhyaan   rakhnaa aavashyak hai.
    special attention keep   necessary is

NOTES

1. For an introduction to the salient features of the language, see Kachru (1987a). For a history of the language and literature, see Handa (1978).

2. The R in KhaRi Boli represents a retroflex flap. The following convention of transliteration of Hindi has been used in this chapter: length of vowels and consonants is indicated by doubling, that is, ii represents a long tense high front unrounded vowel. The capital letters, for example, T and D, represent the retroflex consonants. The symbol above the vowels signals nasalization. The following abbreviations have been used in the glosses.in Appendix 4.B: erg. = ergative marker, dat. = dative subject marker, DO = direct object marker, and IO = indirect object marker.

3. The Hindi texts are quoted in translation for the convenience of the readers. All the translations are by the author of this chapter. The original texts are given in transliteration in Appendix 4.B.

4. The diagram (Persian influences on Dakhini literature) represents the relationships exhibited by the Hindi paragraphs; the relationships are not always reflected exactly in the same way in the English translation as the linguistic conventions of the two languages are so different. An examination of the texts cited in Appendix 4.B would help in confirming the analysis represented by the diagram.

REFERENCES

Abelson, R. P. (1976). Script processing in attitude formation and decision-making. In J. S. Carroll & J. W. Payne (Eds.), *Cognition and social behavior* (pp. 33-45). Hillsdale, NJ: Lawrence Erlbaum.

Adams, M. J. , & Collins, A. (1979). A schema-theoretical view of reading. In R. O. Freedle (Ed.), *New directions in discourse processing* (pp. 1-22). Norwood, NJ: Ablex.

Basham, A. L. (Ed.). (1975). *A cultural history of India*. Oxford: Clarendon.

D'Angelo, F. J. (1975). *A conceptual theory of rhetoric*. Cambridge, MA: Winthrop.

Das Gupta, S. N. (1975). Philosophy. In A. L. Basham (Ed.), *A cultural history of India* (pp. 111-123). Oxford: Clarendon.

Freedle, R. O. (Ed.). (1979). *New directions in discourse processing*. Norwood, NJ: Ablex.

Grabe, W. (1987). Contrastive rhetoric and text-type research. In U. Connor & R. B. Kaplan (Eds.), *Writing across languages: Analysis of L2 text* (pp. 115-138). Reading, MA: Addison-Wesley.

Grimes, J. E. (1975). *The thread of discourse*. The Hague: Mouton.

Gumperz, J. J. (1982). Conversational code-switching. In J. J. Gumperz (Ed.), *Discourse strategies* (pp. 59-99). Cambridge: Cambridge University Press.

Halliday, M.A.K., & Hasan, R. (1976). *Cohesion in English*. London: Longman.

Handa, R. L. (1978). *A history of Hindi language and literature*. Bombay: Bharatiya idya Bhavan.

Heath, S. B. (1982). *Ways with words*. New York: Cambridge University Press.

Heimann, B. (1964). *Facets of Indian thought*. London: Allen & Unwin.

Jairazbhoy, N. (1975). Music. In A. L. Basham (Ed.), *A cultural history of India* (pp. 212-242). Oxford: Clarendon.

Kachru, B. B. (1979). Code-mixing as a verbal strategy in India. In J. E. Alatis (Ed.), *International dimensions of bilingual education* (pp. 107-124). Washington, DC: Georgetown University Press.

Kachru, Y. (1980). *Aspects of Hindi grammar*. New Delhi: Manohar.

Kachru, Y. (1983). Linguistics and written discourse in particular languages: Contrastive studies: English and Hindi. *ARAL 3*, 50-77.

Kachru, Y. (1987a). Hindi-Urdu. In B. Comrie (Ed.), *The world's major languages* (pp. 470-489). London: Croom Helm.

Kachru, Y. (1987b). Cross-cultural texts, discourse strategies and discourse interpretation. In L. Smith (Ed.), *Discourse across cultures: Strategies in world Englishes* (pp. 87-100). Englewood Cliffs, NJ: Prentice-Hall.

Kachru, Y. (n.d.) *Discourse patterns and interpretation: A cross-cultural perspective*. Unpublished manuscript.

Kaplan, R. B. (1966). *Cultural thought patterns in inter-cultural education. Language Learning, 16*, 1-20. Also in K. Croft (Ed.), 1980. *Readings on English as a Second Language for teachers and teacher trainees* (pp. 399-418). Cambridge, MA: Winthrop.

Kaplan, R. B. (1972). The anatomy of rhetoric. Prolegomena to a functional theory of rhetoric. Philadelphia: Center for Curriculum Development (Concord, MA: Heinle and Heinle).

Lannoy, R. (1971). *The Speaking Tree: A study of Indian culture and society.* New York: Oxford University Press.

Minsky, M. (1975). A framework for representing knowledge. In P. H. Winston (Ed.), *The psychology of computer vision* (pp. 211-277). New York: McGraw-Hill.

Pandharipande, R. (1983). Linguistics and written discourse in particular languages: Contrastive studies: English and Marathi. *ARAL 3*, 118-136.

Rai, A. (1977). *naii samiikSaa* (New Criticism). Allahabad, UP, India: Hans Prakshan.

Rangra, R. (1967). *upanyaas* (Novel). In H. Bacchan, H. Nagendra and B. Agarwal (Eds.), *Samsaamyik hindii saahitya* (Contemporary Hindi Literature) (pp. 143-224). New Delhi: Sahitya Akademi.

Reichenbach, H. (1966). *Elements of symbolic logic.* New York: Free Press.

Scollon, R., & Scollon, S. (1981). *Narrative, literacy and face in interethnic communication.* Norwood, NJ: Ablex.

Scribner, S., & Cole, S. (1981). *The psychology of literacy.* Cambridge, MA: Harvard University Press.

Sharma, S. (1972). *Dakkhinii Hindii kaa Saahitya* (The literature of Dakkhini Hindi). Hyderabad, UP, India: Dakshin Prakshan.

Singh, B. (1967). *aalocanaa.* In H. Bacchan, H. Nagendra and B. Agarwal (Eds.), *Samsaamyik hindii saahitya* (Contemporary Hindi Literature) (pp. 295-346). New Delhi: Sahitya Akademi.

Singh, R. (1986. February 2). *aadmii kaa nayaa pahcaan-patra* (H.L.A.: The new identity card of man). *saaptaahik hindustan* (Weekly Hindustan) (p. 40).

Tannen, D. (1979). What's in a frame? Surface evidence for underlying expectations. In R. O. Freedle (Ed.), *New directions in discourse processing* (pp. 137-181). Norwood, NJ: Ablex.

van Dijk, T. (1982). Episodes as units of discourse analysis. In D. Tannen (Ed.), *Analyzing discourse: Text and talk* (pp. 177-195). Washington, DC: Georgetown University Press.

Winterowd, W. R. (1975a). *Contemporary rhetoric: A conceptual background with readings.* New York: Harcourt Brace Jovanovich.

Winterowd, W. R. (1975b). *The contemporary writer: A practical rhetoric.* New York: Harcourt Brace Jovanovich.

Young, A. E., Becker, A. L., & Pike, K. L. (1970). *Rhetoric: Discovery and change.* New York: Harcourt Brace Jovanovich.

5

Cross-Cultural Variation in Persuasive Student Writing

ULLA CONNOR
JANICE LAUER

Contrastive rhetoric, the comparison of the writing of students and accomplished writers from different linguistic and cultural backgrounds, has focused on expository writing. Numerous books and articles have dealt with contrasting patterns of expository prose between English and a variety of languages (Chinese, Japanese, Korean, Thai, Spanish, and French), for example, Kaplan (1966; 1972), Ostler (1987), Hinds (1980; 1983; 1987), Carrell (1984a; 1984b), Connor (1984), Connor and McCagg (1983), Eggington (1987), Grabe (1987), and Scarcella (1984). Much of the activity is reviewed in considerable depth in Kaplan (1987).

Despite this wealth of research on cross-cultural differences in expository writing, few researchers have examined other genres with the exception of the following research: Söter's (1985) study of the narrative writing of students of English as a second language in Australia; Tannen's (1980) research on oral narrative retellings by Greek and American adults; Connor's (1987) study of argumentative patterns in persuasive writing of English, German, Finnish, and U.S. high school students; Connor and Takala's (1984; 1986) research on argumentation; and Tirkkonen-Condit's (1986) research on Finnish and English editorial writing.

AUTHORS' NOTE: Research for this chapter was funded by a grant from the Exxon Education Foundation. Ulla Connor had the primary responsibility for the design of the study, analyses of superstructure and Toulmin's informal reasoning levels, as well as the statistical analyses. She was assisted in these analyses by the following research assistants: Mary Farmer, Vicki Byard, and Michael Patashnik. Janice Lauer was responsible for the analysis of the persuasive appeals, with the help of Barbara Glenn and Mark Simpson, graduate research assistants.

One reason for the lack of cross-cultural research into persuasive texts has been the confusion about the nature of the genre. From Greek times through the Renaissance, the education of a communicator was synonymous with instruction in persuasion. Rhetoric, the pinnacle of Greek education, focused on the development of three kinds of persuasive skill—political in the forum, legal in the court, and ceremonial at state occasions. Today, however, instruction in persuasive discourse occupies a tenuous and ambiguous position in the writing curriculum of many countries. In the nineteenth century, England, the United States, and New Zealand came under the sway of a different classification of discourse—description, narration, argumentation, and exposition. The story of the rise and domination of this quartet has been chronicled by many, including Connors (1981), Lunsford (1982), Britton et al. (1975), and Kinneavy (1971). One result of this situation was that argumentation replaced persuasion in the writing curriculum. Campbell (1776) and later Bain (1866) in an initial formulation of these classifications had distinguished argumentation from persuasion by means of faculty psychology, that is, argumentation appealed to the mind and persuasion to the will. When persuasion was dropped from the classification system, the teaching of argumentation focused almost exclusively on logic, particularly instruction in deductive and inductive reasoning. Lost was a concern for the two other appeals that had characterized effective persuasion—ethos and pathos, the credibility and affective appeals.

In the sixties, Moffett's (1968) reclassification of discourse into drama, narrative, exposition, and logical argumentation continued this neglect of persuasion. Britton et al. (1975), however, in their model of discourse, included the persuasive under the transactional function along with the informative. They defined the persuasive function as that in which "action, behavior, attitude and belief are influenced by reason, argument, and strategy; potential resistance is acknowledged, and an attempt is made to overcome it" (p. 146). Notice that this definition was devoted largely to the rational appeal. In their survey of student writing in England, they found that only 1.6% could be allocated to persuasion, noting that such writing was often close to informative because of the ambiguity of what constituted an argument.

In Kinneavy's (1971) classification, persuasion was distinguished from exposition as one of the four major aims. The basis for this distinction was the feature of the communication triangle that was being emphasized—the audience. Kinneavy spoke of the neglect by English departments of the teaching of the credibility and affective appeals. In his attempt to define persuasion, distinguishing it from his other aims of discourse, he cited the problem: "Despite the fact that there is little scientific empirical evidence on the nature of persuasion [Hovland et al., 1953], common sense and a long tradition have settled on some convincing attributes of such discourse" (p. 219). The major features he identified included: focus on the decoder, lower level of probability than in science or exploration, and the use of the enthymeme, example, images of the writer, and emotions, instead of formal deduction and induction.

More recently, there has been a growing interest in the analysis of argumentative/persuasive discourse. Linguists have studied structures both at the syntactic and discourse levels, and speech-act sequences in persuasion (Aston, 1977; Kummer, 1972; Tirkkonen-Condit, 1983; 1984). Rhetoricians have studied the prevalence of different appeals—logos, pathos, ethos (Berlin & Inkster, 1980; Connors, 1981; Kinneavy, 1971), while communication theorists and philosophers have been interested in issues such as the role of informal reasoning in argumentation (Reinard, 1984; Toulmin, 1958) and social-cognitive abilities in persuasion (Delia, Kline, & Burleson, 1979).

Even though a great deal of theoretical work exists in the above areas, very few applications have entered into the understanding, description, and evaluation of student essays, with the exception of some recent discussions and disagreements about the role of social-cognitive skills in different kinds of writing—narrative and persuasive (Burleson & Rowan, 1985; Connor & Lauer, 1985).

A third reason for the lack of analytic, theory-driven research on persuasive student writing is the inherent difficulty of operational-izing and quantifying new theoretical concepts. The development and application of any analytical method is further complicated because student essays do not fit neatly into patterns suggested by text models based on accomplished texts.

During the past couple of years, we have studied patterns in persuasive student writing using compositions from the set of the International Association for Evaluation of Educational Achievement (IEA) (Purves & Takala, 1982). The goal of our research has been to identify reliable and valid indicators of writing quality in persuasive

    There are several things people can like or dislike in their
life or the world around them. They might have noticed that
young people find work or that people smoke in public places, or
have noticed problems in their community that certain places are
unsafe, that certain opportunities are missing, or that
particular groups should get to understand each other better.

    In this writing task, you have to explain what you think is
an important problem in your community or in the life of the
people your age. You can use one of the examples described above
or choose a problem of your own.

    You have to imagine that you have to write to people who can
solve this problem but are not familiar with it.

    Therefore, you should explain the problem clearly in order
to convince your audience that the problem is an important one.
After that, describe your plan for improving the situation in
sufficient detail that they know what you want done. Be sure to
give enough details, facts, and examples to support your
description and suggestion.

    Your composition should be 2 or 3 pages long. Before you
give your composition in, reread it in order to see:

    1.   How clearly you have described the problem and your
         solution.
    2.   How convincing you have been in presenting your arguments.

    Your composition will be graded according to the above
criteria.

    If you want to change or correct something you may do it on
your original, you do not have to recopy the whole composition.

Figure 5.1 Assignment

compositions. Even though our complete analytic system to describe
and evaluate these compositions includes measures of syntax and
coherence, for the purpose of comparing persuasive patterns cross-
culturally, this chapter will focus on three analyses specifically
related to persuasion from linguistic, rhetorical, and communication
perspectives:

    (1) the superstructure of argument
    (2) a Toulmin analysis of informal reasoning
    (3) the persuasive appeals

Each of these components has a solid theoretical basis, related to
the nature of argumentation (superstructure, Toulmin analysis, and

part of the persuasive appeals). Our previous research shows empirical evidence that each of these components has an independent, additive effect on persuasive writing quality (Connor & Takala, 1986).

We will first describe three different theories, the accompanying text analyses, and the scoring procedures. The major part of the chapter, however, discusses the use of this system to detect cross-cultural differences found in student essays.

The data set in our study is unique; the compositions were randomly selected from among the IEA compositions. A total of 50 compositions were chosen randomly out of thousands of compositions written by U.S. high school students 16 years of age. Also randomly chosen were 50 compositions from among essays written by high school students of the same age in England and New Zealand, respectively. The composition task itself was a typical persuasive essay topic used in schools requiring students to describe a problem and offer solutions to it (see Figure 5.1).

All the subjects in our sample wrote their compositions in English, their first language. This enabled us to examine cross-cultural variation without the interference of differing languages. Much of previous contrastive rhetoric research has examined potential transfer of first language writing patterns when students write in their second language. Our data set is unique in that our subjects speak and write the same language—English—but live in different cultures.

TEXT ANALYSES

Problem-Solution Superstructure of Argumentative Text

Superstructure is the organizational plan of any text and refers to the linear progression of the text. Superstructures of narrative texts have been studied extensively by linguists and psycholinguists (Gulich & Quasthoff, 1985; Labov & Waletsky, 1967; Mandler & Johnson, 1977). Superstructures of expository prose have also received much attention (Grimes, 1975; Kintsch, 1974; Meyer, 1985). No such comprehensive analyses exist for examining superstructures of argumentation with the exception of the research conducted by Kummer

(1972) and, more recently, by Tirkkonen-Condit (1985). Kummer suggests that an argumentative text can be described as a sequence in which the structural units of situation, problem, solution, and evaluation can be identified. This kind of argument superstructure is based on the theory that the reader approaches argumentative texts as a cognitive process of problem solving. The goal of the writer is to change an audience's initial opposing position to the final position of the writer. Kummer shows that there are specific "slots" in the text for the initial, undesirable state: the problem, and for the desirable state: the solution. The evaluation slot is reserved for the evaluation of the outcome of the suggested solution. The situation slot is reserved for background material, that is, facts and views intended for the orientation of the reader to the problem area.

Tirkkonen-Condit has shown empirically that problem-solution structure exists in argumentative texts. She points out that even though some researchers, Hutchins (1977) and Hoey (1979), have applied the problem-solution structure to narrative and expository texts rather successfully, the particular type of problem-solution pattern, with situation and evaluation, is typical of argumentation and not of exposition or narration.

Since there is a wealth of evidence showing the important role superstructures play in the recall and comprehension of stories (Carrell, 1984b; Rumelhart, 1977) and expository prose passages (Carrell, 1984a; Connor, 1984; Connor & McCagg, 1987; Meyer, 1985), in addition to the emerging theories of argumentative superstructure, we included the problem-solution superstructure of argumentative text as one of the three independent variables in our model. In the present study, then, the situation-problem-solution-evaluation structure of the essays was identified. We hypothesized that, analogous to good accomplished persuasive writing, student essays given high scores by raters would include all four parts of an argument superstructure. Two independent raters achieved a 100% agreement in identifying the occurrence of the superstructure components in the sample essays.

Toulmin Analysis of
Informal Reasoning

The Toulmin (1958) model of informal logic has been found successful in the teaching of argumentative/persuasive writing

(Kneupper, 1978; Stygall, 1986; Toulmin, Rieke, & Janik, 1979). It is a three-part model, consisting of claim, data, and warrant.

A *claim* is an assertion, a thesis statement. Toulmin (1958) calls it "conclusions whose merits we are seeking to establish" (p. 97). Toulmin et al. (p. 29) define claims as "assertions put forward publicly for general acceptance." To score the strength of the claims in the essays, we considered whether the claim was relevant to the task, suggested a specific and clear problem, and presented a consistent point of view. We also identified subclaims, if any, and considered how well developed they were.

Data is support for the claim in the form of experience, facts, statistics, or occurrences. Data in the English classroom means "details" and "development." In evaluating the data used in the sample essays, we considered quantity as well as quality in the pieces of data. Good data needed to be specific; it was based on specific facts, not just on the writer's own experience. And data needed to be related to the claim for persuasive results.

Warrants are described by Toulmin as

> Rules, principles, inference-licenses or what you will instead of additional items of information. Our task is no longer to strengthen the ground on which our argument is constituted, but is rather to show that, taking these data as a starting point, the step to the original claim or conclusion is an appropriate and legitimate one. At this point, therefore, what are needed are general, hypothetical statements which can act as bridges; and authorize the sort of step to which our particular argument commits us. (p. 98)

In the sample essays, we rated warrants as to their explicitness, soundness (reliability and trustworthiness), and relevance to the case.

The rating of the compositions using the Toulmin model was done by one rater after the establishment of reliability with another rater. Prior to the rating, at three separate training sessions, criteria for scoring were determined using several IEA essays not in the present sample. The final scale, given in Figure 5.2, shows that claim, data, and warrant each received 0-3 points. The raters were instructed (1) to write down claim, data, and warrant and (2) to give a score for each component following the criteria. The reliability among the two raters on a subsample of 30 compositions was quite high, considering that ours is the first effort to quantify and build up reliability for the

Claim

1   No specific problem stated and/or no consistent point of view.
    May have one subclaim. No solution offered, or if offered
    nonfeasible, unoriginal, and inconsistent with claim.

2   Specific, explicitly stated problem. Somewhat consistent
    point of view. Relevant to the task. Has two or more
    subclaims that have been developed. Solution offered with
    some feasibility with major claim.

3   Specific, explicitly stated problem with consistent point
    of view. Several well-developed subclaims, explicitly tied
    to the major claim. Highly relevant to the task. Solution
    offered that is feasible, original, and consistent with
    major claim.

Data

1   Minimal use of data. Data of the "everyone knows" type,
    with little reliance on personal experience or authority.
    Not directly related to major claim.

2   Some use of data with reliance on personal experience or
    authority. Some variety in use of data. Data generally
    related to major claim.

3   Extensive use of specific, well-developed data of a variety
    of types. Data explicitly connected to major claim.

Warrant

1   Minimal use of warrants. Warrants only minimally reliable
    and relevant to the case. Warrants may include logical
    fallacies.

2   Some use of warrants. Though warrants allow the writer to
    make the bridge between data and claim, some distortion and
    informal fallacies are evident.

3   Extensive use of warrants. Reliable and trustworthy allowing
    rater to accept to bridge from data to claim. Slightly relevant.
    Evidence of some backing.

Figure 5.2 Criteria for Judging the Quality of Claim, Data, and Warrant

analysis. Interrater reliability using Cronbach's alpha for claim was 0.77, 0.56 for data, and 0.66 for warrant.

Persuasive Appeals Analysis

The Persuasive Appeals Analysis evaluates the use of three appeals—rational, credibility, and affective. The rational appeals are informal lines of reasoning categorized under Perelman's (1982) headings of quasi-logical arguments; arguments based on the structure of reality; argumentation by example, illustration, and model; and analogy and metaphor. The credibility appeals include the writer's personal experience, knowledge of the subject, and awareness of the audience's values. The affective appeals include the use of concrete and charged language, of vivid pictures, and of metaphors to evoke emotion in the audience. A discussion of these three appeals can be found in Lauer, Montague, Lunsford, and Emig (1985). Figure 5.3 shows the scale for the appeals analysis.

A more detailed version of this analysis was used in our previous study (Connor & Lauer, 1985), in which we found a significant (.001) relationship between ineffective use of the rational and credibility appeals and low holistic ratings on the essays. We also found that four specific appeals (of the 23 studied) also correlated significantly with highly rated essays.

In the present study, the compositions from each of the three countries were rated for the effectiveness of their appeals on a scale of 0-3 (see Figure 5.3) by two trained raters achieving interrater reliabilities of .90 on the rational appeals, .73 on the credibility appeals, and .72 on the affective appeals.

Holistic Ratings

The compositions were rated for overall impression by three independent raters, who were not connected with the IEA study. The scale was 1-5, 1 being the lowest and 5 the highest. The raters were third-year Ph.D. students in Purdue University's Rhetoric and Composition Program who had had several years' experience in teaching and evaluating writing. The raters were told to base their general impression markings on how well the composition fulfilled

Rational

0   No use of the rational appeal*

1   Use of some rational appeals*, minimally developed or use of
     some inappropriate (in terms of major point) rational
     appeals

2   Use of a single rational appeal* or a series of rational
     appeals* with at least two points of development

3   Exceptionally well developed and appropriate single extended
     rational appeal* or a coherent set of rational appeals*

*Rational appeals were categoried as (quasi-logical, realistic
structure, example, analogy).

Credibility

0   No use of credibility appeals

1   No writer credibility but some awareness of audience's values
                        or
     Some writer credibility (other than general knowledge) but
     no awareness of audience's values

2   Some writer credibility (other than general knowledge) and
     some awareness of audience's values

3   Strong writer credibility (personal experience) and
     sensitivity to audience's values (specific audience for the
     solution)

Affective

0   No use of the affective appeal

1   Minimal use of concreteness or charged language

2   Adequate use of either picture, charged language, or
     metaphor to evoke emotion

3   Strong use of either vivid picture, charged language, or
     metaphor to evoke emotion

Figure 5.3 Persuasive Appeals Scale

the task and topic requirements: in other words, how clearly the writer described the problem and solution, and how convincing the writer was in presenting his or her arguments. The raters were asked to work quickly at a single session supervised by the researcher. The agreement among the raters was high; the Cronbach's alpha coefficient was .83.

PROCEDURES

Scoring and Sample Essays

For the data analysis, the three independent variables were: (1) superstructure of argument, (2) informal reasoning, and (3) persuasive appeals. The dependent variable was the holistic score. The independent variables were measures by three analytic instruments. In the Superstructure Analysis, the essays received one point for each of the components: situation or introduction of problem, problem development, solutions, and evaluation of solution. For informal reasoning using the Toulmin Analysis, essays received a separate score (0-3) for claim, data, warrant following the criteria given in Figure 5.2. For the Persuasive Appeals Analysis, the essays were rated on a scale of 0-3 for each of the three appeals: rational, credibility, and affective.

To illustrate further the text analyses and scoring, we include here sample analyses of two compositions, Essay 1, a low essay with a holistic score of 1.7 and Essay 2, a high essay with a score of 5 (all three raters gave it a score of 5). Copies of the compositions are shown in Appendix 5.A.

The student in Essay 1 writes about abortion being wrong (introduction of problem in sentence 1) and develops his thesis by defending this point of view in the rest of the sentences (sentences 2-12). Neither solution nor evaluation is given, resulting in an incomplete argument superstructure with a score of 2. The Toulmin Analysis of the essay is given in Figure 5.4. The claim is consistent and clear, but because no solution is offered, the claim receives a score of 2. Although there are five pieces of data they are neither specific, well-developed, nor highly relevant, and thus merit a score of 2.

Claim	(score = 2)	:	Abortion is wrong.
Data	(score = 2)	:	Right after conception constitutes life. Abortion affects a whole community. Those who argue that they have a right to their own bodies should realize God gave them those bodies. Fetus' rights are ignored. Fetus can't talk, carry protest signs, or defend himself.
Warrants	(score = 1)	:	Abortion is a very serious issue. Abortion is a crime. To abort a child is to kill part of God and part of the mother. Fetus is innocent victim of modern cruelty.

Figure 5.4   Toulmin Analysis of Essay 1 (holistic score — 1.7)

Although the warrants are mostly explicit, they are neither reliable nor trustworthy even though they are related to the claim and data. In other words, there is no evidence of backing, resulting in a low score of 1.

On the Persuasive Appeals Analysis, Essay 1 received a score of 1 for rational appeals because it used the arguments of effect, definition, cause, and analogy, but with the exception of the second to last sentence, each appeal is only mentioned, never developed. For the credibility appeal, the essay received a score of 0, because the writer established no credibility. On the affective appeals, the essay was rated a score of 1 because the writer used a few charged terms such as "murderers," "cruel," and "innocent victim," but did not sustain such language throughout.

The problem discussed in Essay 2 is underage drinking in the student's community. All the parts of the superstructure are evident—situation or introduction of the problem (sentence 1), problem development (sentences 2-20), and solution and its evaluation (sentences 21-29). The Toulmin analysis in Figure 5.5 indicates a well-developed claim, data, and warrants.

For the Appeals Analysis, Essay 2 received a score of 3 for rational appeals because of the exceptionally well developed personal example and for the use of effect. The Essay received a score of 3 for the credibility appeal because of the use of personal experience and the demonstration of sensitivity to the audience's concern for their

Claim	(score = 3)	:	Underage drinking is a problem in our community. (Solutions: Parents should tell kids about alcohol. Schools should distribute information on alcoholism. Community needs AA group for teens.
Data	(score = 3)	:	I hear kids boasting about drinking on weekends. Kids think parents are stupid for not noticing. I'm teenage alcholic. I drank through junior high and high school. As freshman in high school, I need whiskey to get out of bed. I drank at school during lunch. I had to drink to feel normal. My grades and athletic performance lowered. My PE teacher sent me to a counselor. Counselor diagnosed me as alcoholic and put me on treatment plan. After year of struggling, I'm myself.
Warrants	(score = 3)	:	If only other teens knew the struggles of alcholism, they wouldn't boast about their drinking. Worth efforts to help one person. No good to cut alcohol off at source, because kids will get it from somewhere. Need to take action promptly in ways kids can understand.

Figure 5.5   Toulmin Analysis of Essay 2 (holistic score — 5)

children. For the affective appeal, the writer received a score of 2, based on an adequate presentation of a concrete picture.

RESULTS

Of overall interest is the type of topics the students in the sample selected. Table 5.1 shows that students wrote on 14 different topics. The most popular topics were "nuclear arms" (22 students), "animal cruelty" (14 students), and "racism" (9 students). It is interesting to note that there was no topic on which students from only one country

TABLE 5.1
Frequencies of Topics Written by Country

Topic	England	America	New Zealand	Total
Nuclear arms	11	7	4	22
Animal cruelty	13	0	1	14
Racism	1	3	5	9
Uniforms	3	0	3	6
Alcohol use	2	4	0	6
Parental control	0	3	3	6
Unemployment	1	1	3	5
Smoking	3	1	1	5
Abortion	0	4	1	5
School exams	3	0	1	4
School hours	0	2	1	3
School attendance	0	1	2	3
Motorcycles	1	0	1	2
Women	1	0	1	2

TABLE 5.2
Means and Standard Deviations for Holistic Scores
by Country

	X	s.d.
England	2.293	0.809
U.S.A.	1.747	0.685
New Zealand	2.484	0.817
	2.175	.770

wrote. Rather the topics were shared by students either from all three countries or from two countries.

Table 5.2 shows the means and standard deviations for the holistic scores for the compositions by students from the three different countries. The average mean score among all subjects was 2.18 with the standard deviation of .77. In each country, essay scores ranged from 1 to 5.

There was a significant difference in the holistic ratings among students from the three countries ($F = 12.31$, $p < .01$). The Scheffé post hoc test showed that U.S. students were significantly lower than the other two groups combined, while there was no significant difference between the English and New Zealand students.

No significant differences were found between the three countries in the use of argument superstructure. Table 5.3 shows low average scores on superstructure for each country suggesting that "eval-

TABLE 5.3
Means and Standard Deviations for Superstructure
by Country

	X	s.d.
England	2.78	.82
U.S.A.	2.54	.76
New Zealand	2.69	.91

TABLE 5.4
Means and Standard Deviations for the
Toulmin Categories by Country

	X	s.d.
Claim		
England	1.898	0.685
U.S.A.	1.600	0.728
New Zealand	1.784	0.702
Warrant		
England	1.286	0.817
U.S.A.	0.640	0.693
New Zealand	1.157	0.946
Data		
England	2.000	0.677
U.S.A.	1.260	0.653
New Zealand	1.765	0.764
Added (claim, data, warrant)		
England	1.728	0.480
U.S.A.	1.167	0.523
New Zealand	1.569	0.616

uation," which raises a composition to score 4, was not evident in the average performance of any of the groups.

In the Toulmin Analysis of informal reasoning using the average of claim, data, and warrant combined, there was a significant difference among the three groups ($F = 14.09$, $p < .01$). The Scheffé test showed that the U.S. compositions as one group were significantly lower than the English and New Zealand compositions as a group (see Table 5.4). The statistical analyses of the specific categories—claim, data, and warrant—revealed, as Table 5.4 indicates, that no significant differences existed between the three countries in the claim category, but that the U.S. compositions were significantly lower ($p < .01$) for both the data and warrant categories than the

TABLE 5.5
Means and Standard Deviations
for the Persuasive Appeals

	X	s.d.
Rational		
England	1.440	0.541
U.S.A.	1.100	0.544
New Zealand	1.804	0.693
Credibility		
England	1.020	0.714
U.S.A.	0.840	0.714
New Zealand	1.196	0.448
Affective		
England	1.000	0.833
U.S.A.	0.460	0.676
New Zealand	1.137	0.600

compositions written by the students from England and New Zealand.

On the Persuasive Appeals Analysis, Table 5.5 shows that there was a significant difference among the three groups of compositions on the rational appeals ($p < .01$), the credibility appeals ($p < .05$), and the affective appeals ($p < .01$). The Scheffé test reveals that on the rational appeals, the U.S. compositions were significantly lower ($p < .01$) than the New Zealand compositions.

On the credibility appeals, the U.S. compositions were significantly lower ($p < .05$) than both the English and New Zealand compositions. On the affective appeals, the U.S. compositions were again significantly lower ($p < .01$) than the English and New Zealand compositions.

DISCUSSION OF RESULTS

The results of our study show that an argumentative persuasive writing task is difficult for students from all three countries. The range of the average holistic scores was 1.75-2.49. Keeping in mind that the rating scale was 1-5, one can conclude that persuasive writing is indeed a demanding genre and not well developed among students of that age.

These results are not surprising in light of the fact that persuasive writing, as we discussed above, especially the use of credibility and affective appeals, has received scant attention in the curriculum of all three countries. Instead they have emphasized argumentation, privileging rational appeals, and devaluing appeals to values. Writing persuasive discourse that integrates these appeals requires training and practice. Even though some discourses for some audiences place emphasis on one or another appeal, the absence of any appeal, or its inept use, can destroy a text's persuasiveness. Students have not been placed in educational environments in which they can learn to make appropriate choices for specific rhetorical situations, nor have they been taught the rhetorical resources for achieving powerful persuasive texts. The results of the Persuasive Appeals Analysis support these observations. In each country, the highest mean scores were for use of the rational appeals, with the mean use of credibility and affective appeals much lower.

Two of the analyses—Superstructure and Informal Reasoning—also showed that some aspects of persuasive writing might have been more challenging for these 16-year-old students. For example, average scores on the Superstructure Analysis showed that students were not using the evaluation component—the highest level. Also, for the Toulmin Analysis, warrants were rated lower among the students from each country than were claims and data. Because warrants are more sophisticated elements of argument they either require higher levels or are learned later in development.

As to cross-cultural differences in persuasive writing skills, the U.S. students did more poorly along all the measures than the students from the two other countries. This finding of poorly developed persuasive writing skills is consonant with a report from the National Assessment of Educational Progress, which stated that "in 1984, 80 percent of in-school 17-year-olds could not write an adequate persuasive letter."

Future research needs to determine the reasons for the cross-cultural differences we found in student writing. We expect that studies examining school writing curricula in the three countries will reveal varying emphases on persuasive writing, which could explain some of the results.

In addition to revealing cross-cultural differences in writing, our research also contributes to the general knowledge on contrastive rhetoric. Instead of studying expository writing—the primary area of contrastive rhetoricians—we extended our analyses to persuasive writing—a genre not previously studied by contrastive rhetoricians.

It is also noteworthy that we focused on rhetorical features of texts rather than purely linguistic features typically studied in previous contrastive rhetoric research.

For the theory of writing evaluation, we have developed a system that evaluates components of persuasive essays rather than general features of text that constitute most other analytic scoring. This system allows us to examine the core components of what makes text persuasive. In comparison to "primary trait scoring" (Odell, 1977), we have advanced the theory of text analysis in that our components have been developed into analytic scales. These scales—Superstructure, Toulmin's Informal Reasoning, and Persuasive Appeals— are theory-based, objective, and quantifiable. Even though our project includes other components, such as analyses of coherence and syntax (Connor & Lauer, 1985), we feel that the components explained in the present research are the most pertinent to the content of persuasion. Further, even though we feel that the components we chose are valid and reliable measure of the persuasive task in the present study, we are fully aware that other persuasive tasks might necessitate slight adjustments in our text analysis system.

APPENDIX 5.A

Composition 1
(holistic score = 1.7)

The right to abortion is a very serious issue in these times affecting the decisions of teenage pregnancies resulting in many unwanted infants. However, first we must differentiate between living and non-living before accusing the abortion technique as murderous or cruel. There are many views, but I believe that right after contraception constitutes as a living mass of matter, no matter how small or undeveloped it is. It will eventually become a human being. Abortion is wrong and teenagers should realize that it is a crime that not only affects the person choosing to have an abortion, but affects a whole community. Many people against pro-life argue that they have a right to their own bodies and could do what they please in any matter. Well, who gave those people the right to live themselves in the first place? God made the human being from a reflection of himself to live and govern the material world he made in 7 days. To abort a child is like killing a part of God as well as a part of the mother. Everyone talks about their rights, but what about the fetus' rights. He can't talk, he can't carry protest signs, and he can't defend himself. Thus, he is an innocent victim of modern cruelty.

Composition 2
(holistic score = 5)

Underage drinking is becoming a problem in our community. Every Monday and Tuesday I hear kids telling each other about last weekend and how they went out and got "plastered" or "wasted," and how stupid their parents are for not noticing. For the rest of the week they go around planning what they are going to do next weekend. When I hear them talking I just think to myself, "If they only knew." I know.

I am a teenage alcoholic. All through my junior high and high school years I thought I was cool because I drank. Little did I know that the situation was getting out of hand. By the time I was a freshman in high school it was getting so I needed a shot of whiskey just to get me out of bed. It got worse. Next I started taking drinks to school and drinking them at lunch. I had to have a drink just to "normal." My grades went down and my athletic ability, which had always been excellent also went down.

Finally, at the end of my sophomore year in high school, someone noticed. He was my PE teacher. He asked if I had a drinking problem and I shot an innocent look at him and said, "Who, me?" He referred me to a counselor and I, after a heated inner struggle, went just to see what it was like. My counselor diagnosed me right away as an alcoholic and put me on a treatment plan. Today I feel, after a year of struggling with my disease that I am once again myself. When I hear my friends talking about their weekends I say to myself, "If they only knew."

I feel that parents should be open with their children and tell them the facts about alcohol. The schools should distribute pamphlets to students on alcohol and alcoholism. I know, most of them would just throw them away, but if just one person was saved by the effort wouldn't it be worth it? What if it were your child? I also feel that we as a community need an Alcoholics Anonymous group for teenagers like myself. Then maybe younger alcoholics wouldn't be too afraid to go to their meetings. Cutting the alcohol off at its source won't do any good. The kids will get it from somewhere else. We have to take action against this problem now, and in ways that the children can understand.

REFERENCES

Aston, G. (1977). Comprehending value: Aspects of the structure of argumentative discourse. *Studii italinai di linguistica teorica ed applicata, 6,* 465-509.

Bain, A. (1866). *English composition and rhetoric.* New York: D. Appleton.

Berlin, J. A., & Inkster, R. P. (1980). Current-traditional rhetoric: Paradigm and practice. *Freshman English News, 8,* 1-14.

Britton, J. et al. (1975). *The development of writing abilities (11-18).* London: Macmillan Education.

Burleson, B. R., & Rowan, K. E. (1985). Are social-cognitive ability and narrative writing skill related? *Written Communication, 2,*(1), 25-43.

Campbell, G. (1776). The philosophy of rhetoric. (New edition reprinted in facsimile, L. Bitzer, Ed.). Carbondale: Southern Illinois University Press.

Carrell, P. L. (1984a). The effects of rhetorical organization on ESL readers. *TESOL Quarterly, 18,* 441-469.

Carrell, P. L. (1984b). Evidence of a formal schema in second language comprehension. *Language Learning, 34,* 87-112.

Connor, U. (1984). Recall of text: Differences between first and second language readers. *TESOL Quarterly, 18.*

Connor, U. (1987). Argumentative patterns in student essays: Cross-cultural differences. In U. Connor & R. B. Kaplan (Eds.), *Writing across languages: Analysis of L2 text* (pp. 57-72). Reading, MA: Addison-Wesley.

Connor, U., & Kaplan, R. B. (1987) (Eds.). *Writing across languages: Analysis of L2 text.* Reading, MA: Addison-Wesley.

Connor, U., & Lauer, J. (1985). Understanding persuasive essay writing: linguistic/rhetorical approach. *Text, 5,* 309-326.

Connor, U., & McCagg, P. (1983). Cross-cultural differences and perceived quality in written paraphrases of English expository prose. *Applied Linguistics, 4,* 259-268.

Connor, U., & Takala, S. (1984). *Argumentative patterns in student compositions: An exploratory study.* Paper presented at the TESOL Conference, Houston.

Connor, U., & Takala, S. (1986). *Predictors of persuasive essay quality.* Unpublished manuscript. University of Indiana, Indianapolis.

Connors, R. J. (1981). The rise and fall of the modes of discourse. *College Composition and Communication, 20,* 297-304.

Delia, J. G., Kline, S. L., & Burleson, B. R. (1979). The development of persuasive communication strategies in kindergarteners through twelfth-graders. *Communication Monographs, 46,* 241-256.

Eggington, W. (1987). Written academic discourse in Korean: Implications for effective communication. In U. Connor & R. B. Kaplan (Eds.), *Writing across languages: Analysis of L2 text* (pp. 153-168). Reading, MA: Addison-Wesley.

Grabe, W. (1987). Contrastive rhetoric and text-type research. In U. Connor & R. B. Kaplan (Eds.), *Writing across languages: Analysis of L2 text* (pp. 115-138). Reading, MA: Addison-Wesley.

Grimes, J. (1975). *The thread of discourse.* The Hague: Mouton.

Gulich, E., & Quasthoff, U. M. (1985). Narrative and analysis. In T. A. van Dijk (Ed.), *Handbook of discourse analysis* (Vol. 2) (pp. 169-197). London: Academic Press.

Hinds, J. (1980). Japanese expository prose. *Papers in Linguistics, 13,* 117-158.

Hinds, J. (1983). Contrastive rhetoric: Japanese and English. *Text, 3,* 183-195.

Hinds, J. (1987). Reader vs. writer responsibility: A new typology. In U. Connor & R. B. Kaplan (Eds.), *Writing across languages: Analysis of L2 text* (pp. 141-152). Reading, MA: Addison-Wesley.

Hoey, M. (1979). *On the surface of discourse.* London: Allen and Unwin.

Hovland, C. et al. (1953). *Communication and persuasion.* New Haven: Yale University Press.

Hutchins, J. (1977). On the structure of scientific texts. *UEA Papers in Linguistics, 5,* 18-39.

Kaplan, R. B. (1966). Cultural thought patterns in intercultural education. *Language Learning, 16,* 1-20.

Kaplan, R. B. (1972). *The anatomy of rhetoric: Prolegomena to a functional theory of rhetoric.* Philadelphia: Center for Curriculum Development. (Distributed by Fleinle & Fleinle.)

Kaplan, R. B. (1987). Cultural thought patterns revisited. In U. Connor & R. B. Kaplan (Eds.), *Writing across languages: Analysis of L2 text* (pp. 9-23). Reading, MA: Addison-Wesley.

Kinneavy, J. (1971). *A theory of discourse.* Englewood Cliffs, NJ: Prentice Hall.

Kintsch, W. (1974). *The representation of meaning in memory.* Hillsdale, NJ: Lawrence Erlbaum..

Kneupper, C. W. (1978). Teaching argument: An introduction to the Toulmin Model. *College Composition and Communication, 29,* 237- 241.

Kummer, J. L. (1972). Aspects of a theory of argumentation. In E. Gulich & W. Raible (Eds.), *Textsorten* (pp. 25-49). Frankfurt am Main: Athaneum.

Labov, W., & Waletsky, J. (1967). Narrative analysis: Oral versions of personal experience. In J. Helm (Ed.), *Essays on the verbal and visual arts* (pp. 12-44). Seattle: University of Washington Press.

Lauer, J. M., Montague, G., Lunsford, A., & Emig, J. (1985). *Four worlds of writing* (2nd ed.) New York: Harper & Row.

Lunsford A. (1982). Alexander Bain's contributions to discourse theory. *College English, 44,* 290-300.

Mandler, J. M., & Johnson, N. S. (1977). Remembrance of things parsed: A story structure and recall. *Cognitive Psychology, 9,* 11-151.

Meyer, B. F. (1985). Prose analysis: Purposes, procedures and problems. In B. K. Britton & J. B. Black (Eds.), *Understanding expository text* (pp. 11-64). Hillsdale, NJ: Lawrence Erlbaum.

Moffet, J. (1968). *Teaching the universe of discourse.* New York: Houghton Mifflin.

Odell, L. (1977). Measuring changes in intellectual processes as one dimension of growth in writing. In C. R. Cooper & L. Odell (Eds.), *Evaluating writing.* Urbana, IL: NCTE.

Ostler, S. E. (1987). English in parallels: A comparison of English and Arabic prose. In U. Connor & R. B. Kaplan (Eds.), *Writing across languages: Analysis of L2 text* (pp. 169-185). Reading, MA: Addison-Wesley.

Perelman, C. (1982). *The realm of rhetoric.* (William Kluback, Trans.). Notre Dame: University of Notre Dame Press.

Purves, A. C., & Takals, S. (Eds.). (1982) *An international perspective on the evaluation of written composition.* London: Pergamon.

Reinard, J. C. (1984). Development in persuasive communication: Two experimental studies on attitude change. *Journal of the American Forensic Association, 20.*

Rumelhart, D. E. (1977). Understanding and summarizing brief stories. In D. LaBerge & J. Samuels (Eds.), *Basic processes in reading.* Hillsdale, NJ: Lawrence Erlbaum.

Scarcella, R. (1984). How writers orient their readers in expository essays: A comparative study of native and non-native English writers. *TESOL Quarterly, 18,* 671-688.

Söter, A. (1985). *Writing: A third language for second language writers.* Unpublished doctoral dissertation. University of Illinois, Urbana.

Stygall, G. (1986). *Rating writing with Toulmin*. Unpublished manuscript. Indiana University, Indianapolis, Department of English.

Tannen, D. (1980). A comparative analysis of oral narrative strategies: Athenian Greek and American English. In W. L. Chafe (Ed.), *The Pear stories: Cognitive, cultural, linguistic aspects of narrative production* (pp. 51-88). Norwood, NJ: Ablex.

Tirkkonen-Condit, S. (1983). Argumentoivan tekstin rakenteesta. In P. Roinila, R. Orfanus, & S. Tirkkonen-Condit (Eds.), *Nakokulmia kaantamisen tutkimuksesta*. Finland: University of Joensuu, Department of Languages.

Tirkkonen-Condit, S. (1984, September 10-11). *Towards a description of argumentative text structure*. Paper presented at the Second Nordic Conference on English Studies in Turku, Finland.

Tirkkonen-Condit, S. (1985). Argumentative text structure and translation. *Studia Philologica Jyväskylaensia, 18*. Jyväskyla, Finland: University of Jyväskyla.

Tirkkonen-Condit, S. (1986, June 5-10). *Persuasive editorial writing in Finnish and English*. Paper presented at the First International Conference on Argumentation. Amsterdam, Netherlands.

Toulmin, S., Rieke, R., & Janik, A. (1979). *An introduction to reasoning*. New York: Macmillan.

Toulmin, S. E. (1958). *The uses of argument*. Cambridge: Cambridge University Press.

van Dijk, T. A. (1973). Grammaires textuelles et structures narratives. In C. Chabrol (Ed.), *Semiotique narrative et textuelle* (pp. 177-207). Paris: Larousse.

Writing trends across the decade, 1974-84 (1986). Princeton, NJ: NAEP.

6

Cultural Variation in Reflective Writing

ROBERT BICKNER
PATCHARIN PEYASANTIWONG

The data provided for this descriptive study of reflective writing in English and Thai are essays chosen at random from among those written by high school students as part of the International Study of Achievement in Written Composition, conducted by the International Association for the Evaluation of Educational Achievement. A total of 90 essays were provided for the study, 40 from the United States written in English and 50 from Thailand written in what is known as Central Thai, the official language of the country and the required medium of instruction in the public schools. The essays were written by high school students and all deal with the same topic, selected by the student participants from among seven provided for them. The English language version of the task description is given below.

TASK 7

Below are a number of observations and questions. *Select one (1) and write an essay in which you reflect on what is said and state your own viewpoint.* However, in writing your essay you might also take account of different points of view. In your essay you may refer to personal observation, to books that you have read, to films, plays or whatever will contribute to what you want to say.

Your essay will be judged on what you have to say, how clearly you present and illustrate your thoughts and how effectively you express them.

Give your essay a title or use the title given. If you want to correct or change something, you may do it on your original; you do not have to recopy the whole essay.

(1) Does watching television make it more difficult to think indepen-
    dently?
(2) Many young people today find it difficult to talk to and understand
    middle-aged people.
(3) What might happen if students were to be given more control over
    what they study and how they study?
(4) What might the world be like if the role of women in society really
    changed?
(5) It is preoccupation with possessions, more than anything else, that
    prevents men from living freely and nobly.
(6) Doesn't the heart in the middle of crowds feel frightfully alone?

Note: When you have finished writing, answer the questions on page 6. You have one class period to complete the writing. SPACE FOR PLANNING (Notes, outline, draft).

There follows a blank page intended for preparatory work, then several blank pages, the first of which is labeled "START YOUR WRITING HERE." At the end of the booklet are five multiple choice questions and one essay question asking the participants to evaluate their preparation for and skill at completing the assigned task.

Although the description makes no connection between the essay and any regular classroom work, the setting and the presentation of the task must have encouraged the students to view their work as they would a school assignment or examination, and this must be considered in evaluating the writing. The essays were written in the classroom, with regular classroom instructors acting as monitors. The 8½" × 11" task booklet is similar to an examination booklet, and each student was asked to write his or her assigned identification number on the booklet. Space was provided for outlines and drafts, and the students were told that the essays would be evaluated and by what criteria those evaluations would be made. Finally, they were asked to evaluate their own work.

The Thai language version of the task description is even more like an examination than is the English version. The participants are several times addressed as *nákrian* (student), as in "The student should write an essay . . ." The term is commonly used by school teachers in addressing their classes, and would not normally be used as a noun of address outside of the classroom setting. While the English language description uses the term *judge* to refer to the evaluation of the essays, the Thai description uses Kaanhâykháneɛn (grading). The Thai version also asks for suggestions on how student writing, in general, might be improved, and closes the booklets with the statement "We are Thai. We must work together to improve the Thai language." Thus the Thai presentation of the task strongly suggests that the participants view their work as they would an examination or assignment, and in so doing calls for all the formality and attention to propriety that normally characterize relationships between teachers and their pupils in Thai schools. There is strong societal pressure for Thai students to be formal and polite in all dealings with their teachers, and the task description adds to this normal degree of formality a call to be attentive to a national priority—the use of the official language.

Even granted these differences between the English and Thai versions, however, it seems appropriate to assume that the students in both groups felt at least an implicit message that they were to interpret the task as they interpret normal class assignments. The presentation of the task and the setting in which it was to be carried out no doubt suggested to the students that they ought to produce an essay that their teachers would see as good examples of the form as it had been taught in the class.

The Essays in General

Both the English and Thai essays vary widely in length and in the depth with which they treat the topic. There is also wide variation in the degree of skill that the student writers display in their work. No background information on the individual participants was made available for this study, but in both sets some essays use nonstandard words and spellings.

The authors of the present study read and evaluated the IEA essays separately, and then again jointly, according to five factors discussed in Takala (1982). That work discusses the results of a 1980 study of compositions done in schools in 12 countries, Thailand and the United States among them, on the topic "My Native Town." That study compared five aspects of the texts, rating each according to the degree to which the writer revealed personal thoughts and feelings

("personal"), the presence or absence of figurative language ("ornamental"), the amount of specific information included in the text
("abstract"), the presence or absence of a single focus of interest
("single"), and the type of coherence devices used ("logical").

The most striking difference between the evaluations discussed in
the Takala study and the IEA essays was in the personal versus
impersonal dimension. In the earlier study the Thai compositions
were rated highly personal, whereas the IEA essays appeared to the
authors of the present study to be highly impersonal. This, and other
factors of interest that were noted during the evalution, are discussed
in this chapter. Some of the observations are stated in percentages.
These numbers are given only as indicators of general trends;
working with a small sample does not allow for more formal
statistical analysis.

Themes

All the essays address the issue raised in the task description,
although with varying emphasis. A number of essays in each set are
entitled "The Generation Gap," suggesting a neutral position, but
others indicate the starting point from which the writer works. Some
of the English language essays carry titles such as, "Talking to
Middle Aged People," "Understanding Adults," and "Talking to
Middle Agers." Many of the Thai essays, on the other hand, carry
titles such as, "The Feelings of Teenagers," "The Problems of
Teenagers," or simply "Teenage."

The difference in perspective indicated in the titles is generally
reflected in the essays. The English speaking writers tend to concentrate on adult behavior patterns and other influences outside of
themselves. Typical comments are that times and customs have
changed, that older people have had different experiences and faced
different problems in growing up, that older people are too talkative,
that older people are more knowledgeable about life but insensitive in
the manner in which they give advice or correction, and that older
people take teenagers' feelings for granted. Several writers point out
that teenagers are in a period of change and growth and that this leads
to erratic and sometimes troublesome behavior. The problem is
nearly always discussed in terms of the changes that adults need to
make in order to accommodate the needs of the teenagers. A few of the

writers say that adults have good intentions, but others state that adults are simply jealous of modern youth or are interested in demonstrating their dominance.

The Thai perspective is quite different in that nearly all the writers begin their essays by focusing on the characteristics of teenagers, a point that tends to receive, at best, only slight attention in the English essays. Typical statements are that teenagers are in a period of transition between childhood and adulthood and as a result are impulsive, impatient, emotional, curious, fashion-conscious, and so on. More than half of the writers balance their critique of the problem by including a treatment of the adolescent perspective and also one of the adult perspective, as they see it. Complaints commonly found in these sections are that adults are too strict, or are old-fashioned, or do not invest enough time in talking to their children. These complaints, however, are always softened by statements ascribing desire to see the children grow in proper directions or the pressures of supporting a family in a changing economy. Many of the writers call for a spirit of accommodation in which both adults and teenagers can strive for mutual understanding in order to assure the best possible guidance for the youth of the country.

Many essays in each set address the problem of language use. Some writers in each set mention a fear of seeming foolish or inarticulate that makes teenagers reluctant to talk to adults. But in other ways the perspective is very different. A common attitude in the English essays is that teenagers live in a dynamic linguistic environment that is beyond adults. A typical statement of the point is given below.

> The way we talk today, the grown-ups can hardly understand us. We add different words to the vocabulary just about every week. The grown-ups can't keep up with all those words that we keep saying and so they just tell us to stop saying them. I don't understand why they just couldn't learn to live with it.

The writers working in Thai acknowledge the rapid pace of change in the language of teenagers, but see it as a problem for the teenagers rather than for the adults, as is illustrated below.

> It can be seen that the difficulty and awkwardness that the majority of today's teenagers are likely to feel in conversing with the under-standing adults stems from [the fact that] the language that most teenagers use is unsuitable and inappropriate for use with adults.

Proper use of spoken Thai requires that the speaker be sensitive to the status relationship he or she shares with the addressee. The writers of these essays feel constrained in the use of slang not because their elders might not understand it, but because it is not sufficiently deferential for use with one's superiors.

The themes in both sets of essays tend to be treated in general and abstract terms. Many writers complain about parental rules for example, but with very few exceptions they do not cite specific examples. Several of the English essays complain of curfew restrictions, but only two specify what those restrictions are. The threat posed by drugs in society is mentioned in about one third of the English essays, but only one student gives specific details, saying that a brother has been arrested for drug-related misconduct. The Thai essays are even more abstract, and do not include anecdotal material or specific details of the points raised. Drugs are cited frequently, for example, but the deleterious effects of drug use are left unstated.

Attitudes Toward the Text

The student writers treat the text and the act of creating the text in different ways. Within each set of essays there is variation, but the English language compositions tend to be more personal than their Thai counterparts. The students working in English make greater use of personal pronouns and use more informal vocabulary and slang than do those working in Thai.

In the English language set, some of the essays are written as completely impersonal statements dealing with issues in a seemingly dispassionate manner. The writer avoids identification with either group, and so creates a text from which he or she is personally removed. The paragraph below is from one such essay.

Many young people today find it difficult to talk and understand middle-aged people. Those in their middle-ages are going through difficult times. Many come to a crisis over the lives they have made for themselves. Middle-aged persons are faced with responsibilities of money, shelter, and often family. The teenager also goes through difficult and stormy times. At this stage of life, young people are searching to find their identity and are beginning to have to accept responsibility. Furthermore, teenagers are going through hormonal changes.

Some of the English essays are very personal statements in which the writers deal directly with their own lives and make it clear that they are discussing the problem from their own perspective. An example paragraph is given below.

> I find it hard to talk to middle-aged people because they do not really understand the way youths act. I know they were young once too, but things are different now. We talk different and act different than they ever did.

Some of the English language essays use the expressions "young people" and "middle-aged people" from the task description. Others discuss "adults" and "teenagers" as impersonal groups, and some use generic forms such as "the adult" and "the teenager." A few of the writers who begin this way sustain this level of usage. Most of the essays that begin with impersonal terms, however, soon shift to more personal ones, or alternate between personal and impersonal terms. In one essay, for example, the writer begins with "young people" and "middle-aged people" but then says that "older people" can't understand "our" problems. The writer then uses "teenagers" and "parents," followed by a statement that "we" don't understand why "they" refuse "us." One is left with the impression that these writers appreciate the distinction between impersonal and personal writing, but are not yet in complete command of that distinction.

Some of the English essays make no use of the impersonal terms found in the task description and instead use personal pronouns throughout the text. These essays are usually very conversational in tone and the writers often refer to themselves as "kids" and "we kids" and to their parents as "my parents" or "mom and dad." In a few of the essays such terms are placed in quotes, suggesting that the writers feel that the terms are not completely suitable for the task at hand, but still are not ready to abandon their use. One writer asks rhetorically "Yet, what kind of a responsible adult cannot make important decisions and need their 'mommy' to tell them what to do next." Clearly this writer feels that the word "mommy" would not normally be considered proper in this essay, but sees that it can be used for effect if it is marked properly.

Other expressions more commonly associated with informal speech than with writing appear in these compositions as well, but they are not marked in the texts with quotes. Examples are "dumb," "ditching school," "weird," "so bizarre its pitiful," "just yell at the kid" and so on. Other vocabulary choices in the essays in which these expressions appear are not slang or colloquial and are more common to writing. The presence of these expressions suggests that the writers are not able to create a text of uniform formality, and inadvertently mix spoken forms with the written forms that they study in the classroom.

Two essays contrast with the others and indicate the variation in the degree of constraint that the English speaking writers feel in performing the task as it has been assigned. In one of these essays the writer devotes only three short sentences to the chosen topic and then, clearly not happy with the choices given in the directions and perhaps not happy to be participating at all, concludes with, "I think the topics you picked were very uninteresting. How can you make an evaluation on writing where the effort wasn't even there." Thus the student follows the task directions in expressing a personal viewpoint, but it is about the quality of the assignment instead of the topic assigned. None of those writing in Thai make any such negative comments.

In the second of these essays the writer does address the topic directly and at some length, but the approach taken is very different from that taken by others. The essay is entitled "Pure Gruesomeness Dudes, Severe," and the first sentence reads "Middle aged people can be like such geeks!" In commenting on adult behavior the writer says, "They can be sooo [sic] weird!" The rest of the essay is similar. The themes touched on here are also found in the more conventional essays: different life styles, different tastes in music and speech, and teenagers' embarrassment at talking with adults. The text is what the task directions have requested, and it is a good example of the essay form. It follows the accepted English pattern of introduction, body and conclusion, and there is a uniformity of tone throughout. Also, the writer does include his or her own opinion of the situation. The obvious command of the expected form, and the almost complete reliance on slang terms not normally considered suitable for written class work, makes for a striking essay. By following the conventional format in such an unconventional way the writer creates a text that both follows and plays with the directions. None of those writing in Thai took such liberties.

The Thai essays are, in general, far less personal than are their English counterparts, which is the opposite of the evaluation of the Thai essays quoted in Takala (1982). Also, the Thai essays done for the IEA study are far more formal than are those done in the United

States. Personal pronouns are used extensively in spoken Thai to establish and express status relationships between speakers. Of the many pronouns available, however, only a few appear in the essays, and those in very limited ways, and the sentence particles, which are characteristic of all speech and are used to indicate degrees of intimacy and formality, do not appear in the essays at all.

In most of the essays the writers maintain a neutral stance and make no use of either first or second person pronouns. Reference to the groups of people under discussion is usually made with impersonal forms, primarily the nouns *wayrûn* (teenagers) and *phulûyày* (adults). When the writers feel called upon to express a complaint about adult behavior they often introduce the complaint with the equivalent of "Teenagers might feel that . . ." This phrasing allows the writer to state the negative opinion without being overtly associated with the group said to hold the opinion.

When text constraints do call for pronominal reference, third person pronouns are the ones most often used. The pronoun most commonly used to refer to teenagers is *khǎw* (they), which is neutral or mildly deferential. Some writers use the same word to refer to adults, but others choose *thân* (they) which is more strongly deferential, and also nonintimate. Use of these forms suggests that the writers are avoiding involving themselves in any sort of relationship either with the teenagers or adults that they are discussing.

A few writers do include themselves in the group they are discussing by using the word *raw* (we), and the texts they create are somewhat more personal than the other Thai texts, but do not approach the personal nature of the English essays. Interestingly, it is in these essays that one sees a lack of command of the essay form. Like their English speaking counterparts, these writers tend to begin their essays using the most abstract terms, then shift into the use of the pronouns, causing an unevenness in the tone of their writing.

The other first person pronoun commonly used in the essays is *Khâaphácâw* (I), which is strongly marked for formality and nonintimacy. The pronoun is normally used only in printed documents, such as application forms, and in making certain public statements or declarations. Several of the essays use the term primarily when the author wishes to identify his or her opinions, for example, to separate them from generally held opinions. Use of the term suggests that the writer is imagining an abstract audience, one with which he or she has only the most distant of relationships.

By far the most common strategy is to use no pronoun forms at all. Thai makes extensive use of noun phrase deletion, especially in subject position, so that long stretches of text can be attributed to a group, teenagers for example, by mentioning that group once at the start of a paragraph and continuing without any further mention of a subject. This leaves the writer free to express his or her opinions without an overt commitment to membership in that group. English patterns, which demand a subject for each sentence and include a constraint against redundancy, create a much different situation. Students writing in English who begin with a nonspecific form like "teenagers" soon must find other suitable nouns to use, or face a choice between the pronouns "we" or "they" if they wished to continue the discussion. The Thai writers are not similarly bound, and can create texts without having to decide whether or not to include themselves in the group under discussion.

There are no terms found in the Thai compositions that are comparable to the terms *mom, dad, kids, weird* or *ditchin' school,* and so on, that are found in the English essays. References to parents are nearly always done in generic form, and the more intimate forms equating to the English *mom* and *dad,* for example, do not appear in the essays. One or two of the Thai compositions make very limited use of slang terms, but other than that they are far more formal than are the English essays, and are more uniform in tone.

Structure of the Essay

The vast majority of the English essays begin with a topic sentence and follow that sentence with others that give examples illustrating the point. Most of this material explains the activities or attitudes of the parties discussed. One exception to this pattern begins with a brief anecdote from the writer's personal experience that illustrates the problem of mistrust between teenagers and adults. The rest of that essay is like the others.

The essays generally continue into a second paragraph with additional examples or support for the original topic sentence. In some cases this additional material is in contrast to the first paragraph, focusing on adults instead of teenagers, for example, but in most the distinction between paragraphs is not clearly drawn. The concluding material is generally set off in a separate paragraph. Most of the essays are three to four paragraphs in length.

The Thai essays are similar in some respects. They commonly begin with a topic sentence followed by supporting material. Subsequent paragraphs provide elaboration or a different perspective. One major difference between the English and Thai compositions, though, is the nature of the material given in support of the topic sentence. The English writers all accept the terms used in the task description as given information, not needing elaboration or clarification. Nearly all the Thai writers, however, devote significant space to defining terms. These definitions are generally presented as lists of characteristics, and special attention is usually given to those characteristics of teenagers that contribute to the difficulties of communication between the generations. These lists are composed of parallel structures, as illustrated below.

One frequently used technique lists characteristics of teenagers in several sentences that begin with the term *wayrûn* (teenagers). One of the essays, for example, states that the teen years are those from 12 to 19, and that people in this time turn in on themselves and disregard others. Following next is the list of characteristics of teenagers, which in translation reads, "Teenagers want freedom, and do not want help in what they do. Teenagers want privacy, and those around them should respect their rights in this matter. Teenagers are often confused, and so adults are unhappy with what they do. Teenagers are in a period of difficult adjustment, [and] are in a period of important transition." Each of the four statements begins with the noun *wayrûn* followed by a verb construction, and the last sentence is a smaller version of the larger structure in that two verbal constructions refer to the subject of the sentence. The rest of the essay focuses on the implications of these points for teenagers and for those around them.

Some of the lists are quite simple and straightforward. In the following example the list items are nouns: "Fashion and speech styles are points of group recognition for teenagers, and so they do not like to talk in front of adults, elders, teachers and older relatives."

Some of the lists are made up of complex structures that in English translation do not appear parallel. One example is also built on the noun *wayrûn*, which translates both of the English terms *teenage* and *teenagers*. Unlike the previous example the word is not repeated here. It begins the sentence and serves as the referent for the following six clauses, each of which begins with a verbal element. The link between each clause and the noun is established by zero anaphora, an important coherence device in Thai, and one of sufficient scope to link syntactic units that differ considerably in length and complexity. The different clauses have been numbered in the translation below to show the point at which each one begins. The example reads, "Teenage (1) is a time of transition in the passage from childhood to adulthood. (2) [It is] likely to have strong emotions (3) [and] stubbornness. (4) [It] dislikes the direction and control of others. (5) [It] acts [from] self-will [and] (6) likes to experiment with different fashions." English structures do not tolerate this sort of linking, and so the translation has been broken into several sentences, but the original Thai wording is a single sentence.

The presence of these lists in so many of the Thai essays suggests that part of the role of the essay in Thai is to specify precisely the various aspects of the problem under discussion by gathering together all of the relevant details. One also gets the strong impression that, at least to these writers, the presence of such lists makes their prose forceful and elegant. Recent study has suggested that the creation of lists in the form of catalogs is a major coherence device in Thai poetry dating back as far as the fifteenth century (Bickner, 1986). The presence of the lists in these student essays suggests that the phenomenon is worthy of study in the present day as well.

There are significant differences between the two groups of essays in the way in which the composition is brought to a close. All but one of the English essays end with a clearly identifiable concluding section. In 10% of the essays this concluding section is simply a restatement of the problem as originally presented in the title or topic sentence. In another 13% of the essays the writer does not summarize the material presented, but makes comments on the essay itself, expressing the hope, for example, that the project has been useful.

In more than 70% of the English essays, however, the writer takes the matter further. A few offer predictions about the future, some in unsettling terms ("Someday there will be an explosion."). Some draw implications from their own analysis ("They will have to keep up with young people . . . if they ever want to have a conversation with them.").

In approximately 40% of the essays, possible solutions are offered for the problem. These solutions are presented in counterfactual form, as in the sentence, "We would be able to understand each other better if we listened to each other with open minds," with the past tense forms "would" and "listened" used to create the counterfactual. Often the attempt to create the counterfactual form is not completely correct ("It would make it easier . . . if we both understand each other"), but the intention is clear, nonetheless. These writers use the counterfactual to speculate on the possible results of potential solutions, independent of any estimate regarding the likelihood of the proffered solutions being put into effect.

The Thai essays are very different in this respect. In 10% of the Thai essays there is no concluding section. The writer defines the relevant terms and describes the problem to his or her own satisfaction, and simply stops. In 25% of the Thai essays the concluding section, labeled "summary" or the like, is a simple restatement of the problem. Thus these student writers seem to place a strong emphasis on examining the problem at hand, but do not feel compelled to draw conclusions based on that examination.

Approximately 60% of the Thai texts do offer solutions for the problem as described in the text. Nearly all of these potential solutions are formed with the word *khuan* (should). Approximately one third of these essays simply advise appropriate action with no direct statement of the desired outcome ("Adults should have more time for teenagers."). The other two thirds of these essays advise appropriate action and then indicate the desired result or potential usefulness of the activity ("Teenagers should listen to the advice of their elders to have it available for future use."). But there is no indication in any of these essays that the writers are engaging in speculative thought. There does not seem to be any shift in the mode of analysis comparable to that made by the writers of the English essays who employed the counterfactual form.

The counterfactual is created in English by a special use of the tense system, and it is an essential part of abstract, speculative reasoning in English. Thai does not employ the concept of tense, so it is not surprising that Thai predicate structures are not put to any special use in this regard. What is significant, however, is that there is no trace whatever in these essays of an attempt by the writers to indicate that they are using a speculative mode of reasoning, or to suggest that the reader do so, either.

It is possible, of course, that the type of speculation signaled by the counterfactual is simply not appropriate in Thai reflective writing, and is used elsewhere, but this seems unlikely. The authors of this study can identify no linguistic devices by which Thai initiates or accomplishes the sort of detached and speculative reasoning associated with the English counterfactual form. The complete lack of anything resembling speculative counterfactual in the IEA essays suggests that this cognitive strategy is simply not used in reflective writing in Thai. Additional research will most likely show that it is not used in Thai at all.

SUMMARY

The essays provided for this study suggest several interesting points of contrast between native speakers of Thai and native speakers of American English in their attitudes toward language use, their concepts of essay structure, and their analytical styles. The present study assumes that the students, who wrote their compositions in the classroom, received at least implicit suggestions that they should write a formal essay of the type that they had studied previously in their classes. Those suggestions seem far stronger for the Thai students, and they seem to have paid more attention to them.

The authors of the Thai essays devote considerable energy to defining terms and to listing the various aspects of character and behavior that have bearing on the topic under discussion. They strive to give a balanced perspective, often offering reasons for the adult behaviors that they identify. Their conclusions are frequently offered as advice or suggestions for changes in behavior, along with the anticipated benefits to be derived from the change. The authors of the English essays do not offer definitions for the terms they use, and accept them as given. Their perspective is primarily from that of the teen, and seldom is any attempt made to justify the positions or actions of the adults. Conclusions are often offered in speculative counterfactual form, a type of reasoning that is not found in the Thai essays at all.

The Thai essays tend to be impersonal and formal, with very little slang or vocabulary that is normally associated only with speech. Some of the English compositions are also impersonal, but many are also very personal, with a conversational tone and much vocabulary that is normally associated more with speech than with writing. A number of the English essays that begin with impersonal terms do not sustain that type of usage and mix in terms that are normally associated with speech. Also, many of the English essays mix slang terms and terms that are associated with preadult speech styles with more formal written vocabulary, something that does not happen in the Thai compositions. These facts suggest that the Thai students may share a more sharply defined model of a reflective essay than do the students working in English, or they develop such a model at an earlier point in their training. It may also be that Thai speakers, attuned to levels of usage by the sociolinguistic constraints with which they live, come to be aware of the distinction between spoken and written forms at an earlier point and apply this to their writing.

These observations are based on a very small sample of writing, but the results suggest that a broader study would be of interest. It would be useful to study the writing of other age groups to determine how much the apparent uniformity in the Thai writing stems from classroom instruction about writing, and how much from the social constraints in which Thai students work. It would also be useful to pursue the question of the lack of the counterfactual in Thai, and the implications that this has for, among other fields, second-language teaching methodology.

REFERENCES

Bickner, R. (1986). *The catalog in ancient Thai poetry.* Unpublished manuscript, University of Wisconsin, Madison.

Bloom, A. (1981). *The linguistic shaping of thought.* Hillsdale, NJ: Lawrence Erlbaum.

Grima, J. (1978). *Categories of zero nominal reference and clausal structure in Thai.* Unpublished doctoral dissertation, University of Michigan, Ann Arbor.

IEA international study of achievement in written composition. Unpublished manuscript, University of Illinois, Curriculum Laboratory, Urbana.

Noss, R. (1964). *Thai reference grammar.* Washington, DC: Foreign Service Institute.

Peyasantiwong, P. (1981). *A study of final particles in conversational Thai.* Unpublished doctoral dissertation, University of Michigan, Ann Arbor.

Senanan, W. (1975). *The genesis of the novel in Thailand.* Bangkok: Thai Watana Panich.

Takala, S., Purves, A., & Buckmaster, A. (1982). On the interrelationships between language, perception, thought and culture and their relevance to the assessment of written composition. *Evaluation in Education, 5,* 317-342.

PART III

Transfer of Rhetorical Patterns in Second Language Learning

7

The Second Language Learner and Cultural Transfer in Narration

ANNA O. SÖTER

Until the emergence of the contrastive study of culturally and linguistically diverse rhetorical styles, we have viewed the errors made by ESL (English as a Second Language) students in their writing as linguistic ones and as caused by limited knowledge of the target language and its linguistic forms as well as by what was termed "interference" from the native language. Although Kaplan's (1966) study was preceded by the work of earlier linguists and anthropologists (Boas, 1911; Sapir, 1949, Whorf, 1956; Lado, 1957), it was the first major study that attempted to analyze how one's native thinking and discourse structures manifest themselves in the writing of ESL students. Influenced by the Sapir-Whorf hypothesis, Kaplan, in that study, argued that his subjects revealed evidence of culturally-influenced styles of thought development that emerge in their writing in ways that can be structurally and stylistically described.

Indeed, the notions that cultures express concepts and develop perceptions of the world and of relationships of various kinds in different ways are not new. What is new is the current attempt to integrate the study of languages and their uses in society in such a way as to reflect differences in cultural habits and differences in styles of expression in various contexts, including that of written text (Heath, 1983; Mathiot, 1979; Potter, 1981). Furthermore, contrastive rhetoric has extended its unit of analysis from that of linguistic elements to "discourse structures" or patterns of discourse, that is, beyond the word and sentence level.

177

Recent reports from the International Study of Achievement (IEA) in Written Composition (Purves, 1985a) reveal that although certain structural and stylistic commonalities may be shared across cultures in writing tasks, culturally specific features of discourse are nevertheless apparent in the writing products of students in that study. Until the IEA Study of Achievement in Written Composition and the study being described in this paper, written compositions of school-age children from diverse linguistic and cultural backgrounds have not been used in examining the rhetorical and stylistic differences for evidence of native linguistic, stylistic, and rhetorical influences.

The students described in this paper show evidence in their writing of native discourse (rhetorical) as well as linguistic influences of both oral and written kinds. This is not surprising if one recalls Heath's (1983) work with the Appalachian communities in which she clearly demonstrates that children from each of these communities bring to their schooling the discourse styles they have acquired as a part of their interaction with others in their communities. I am arguing, therefore, that the ways in which we express thought in writing are very strongly influenced by our experiences with discourse generally and written text specifically and the related conventions that govern each of these within our own social and cultural contexts.

In order to write effectively in a second language it appears that we must develop the schemata (Rumelhart, 1975) related to the discourse forms in that target language. Thus, the L2 writer (and one may argue the nonmainstream culture writer) has to become familiar not only with the linguistic forms of the language but also with the discourse patterns and conventions of that language. This is not a startling revelation. However, it appears that the influence of the native discourse forms is powerful enough to manifest itself in the product written in the target language (Kaplan, 1966) and, prior to the current research in the field of contrastive rhetoric, that influence has not been given a significant role in the writing of ESL students. One might suggest that the traditional focus on language learning, as distinct from discourse learning, implied that the ESL writer came to English writing without prior discourse schemata. Additionally, L2 writers come into the target language situation with their L1 (first language) knowledge of what is socially and culturally appropriate in terms of writer/reader roles and relationships; rhetorical and stylistic conventions that govern the use of various genres and modes within those genres; appropriate usage with related genres and modes (i.e., sociolinguistic knowledge); and knowledge about situational features or contextual features of written text. If we extend our consideration of the analysis of L2 written products to include aspects such as those described here, we may better understand why such writers can still produce what has been anecdotally described as wooden, stilted, foreignlike prose even though this prose may otherwise conform to standard forms of usage at the linguistic level. Strong support exists, therefore, for analyzing the writing of L2 writers from the perspective of the Cultural Context Model.

The model presents writers as part of an environment that influences them in all aspects of writing, both through schooling (the formal context) and through the whole community (the informal context). The process of influence is seen to be an interactive one: The writer writes in the context of his or her total community and with the norms and expectations in relation to written text acquired through schooling. Purposes, tasks, topics, and audiences are also an integral part of the sociocultural context. Thus, writers may choose topics and tasks but those topics and tasks may not necessarily occur in other cultures. Similarly, writers may select to write for particular audiences and have particular foci in mind for those audiences. However, these audiences are also a product of the same culture (although, it must be stressed that the more public the writing, the greater the likelihood that the product will be read by others in different cultures). By extension, the cognitive styles, the knowledge we have of the world, the content of our writing and thinking (schemata), the text and discourse styles, and the language systems and resources available to writers are as much products of the same culture as the writers themselves. More generally, the cultural context will influence writers through its definition of cognitive styles and the schemata acquired by its participants, through the conventions of text and discourse styles, and also through the range of linguistic and discourse resources available to create text (Kaplan, 1966; Scribner & Cole, 1981).

The view adopted in this chapter is that written discourse is a form of expression that is culturally defined and is thus describable through culturally agreed conventions. Fowler (1977, p. 125) expresses this more concretely when he states, "It [discourse] is . . . the system of conventions which makes possible the work and arrangements of words within the work. The systematic organization of society (including the 'rules' for writing) transcends and controls the individual, determining verbal patterns he or she can deploy or respond to. The writer can write meaningfully only within the possibilities provided by the systems of conventions which define the culture."

SETTING FOR THE STUDY

The data for the study were collected in Sydney, Australia, in the period February to May 1984. A total of 223 students in the study represented three language and cultural groups at Grades 6 and 11 levels of schooling from eight schools in the Sydney metropolitan region. These groups were Vietnamese, Arabic-speaking Lebanese, and native English-speaking students. From within the larger sample of 223 students, 26 volunteer students formed a focal group for which intensive analysis of the compositions was carried out. For these 26 students, additional data was also collected to provide more insight into the special literacy problems of the L2 writer in school contexts. A narrative task—a simple bedtime story—was used as the writing task and the focus for the analyses.

SUBJECTS AND THE TASK

Of the 223 students from two grades and three linguistic and cultural backgrounds (Arabic/Lebanese, Vietnamese, and English), the Vietnamese students had lived in Australia for a minimum of one year to a maximum of five years (the older students, in the main, had lived in Australia for 3 to 5 years, and the younger for 1 to 3 years). The Arabic students were all born in Australia, the one exception being a student who arrived in the country at the age of 3. However, all of these students first acquired their native tongue and then learned English when they reached school. Teachers of all students in the study ensured that those who participated were regarded as "adequately proficient writers" and had had a consistent record of writing in English in their schools, and had experience writing essay tasks within the normal time limits of a school period (i.e., 40 minutes).

THE TASK

One of the chief problems in setting common tasks for culturally and linguistically diverse groups is in finding common experience in the mode of writing selected as well as knowledge of the subject matter to be written about. Additional constraints on writing tasks, such as task and topic constraints (Baker, 1982; Crowhurst & Piche, 1979; Greenberg, 1982; Hoetker, 1982) may also cause variation in peformance by writers.

Narrative, therefore, appeared to be the most suitable choice as a genre for the diverse students in this study, since it is more likely that all of the students in the present study would have had experience with it, whether in oral or written form. Furthermore, the narrative is a socially evolved genre (Scribner, 1977), and such genres, according to Hymes (1974), may vary from culture to culture and from speech community to speech community. The students in both Grades 6 and 11 were given a narrative task—a bedtime story to a child younger than the writer (Little, 1975). The narrative is a form familiar to all children, and Little's index of difficulty of the task (moderately low level of difficulty) made the task a suitable one for a study that includes both native and nonnative writers. All students wrote the narrative in class, with the researcher present for a period of approximately 40 minutes.

METHODS OF ANALYSIS

All 223 compositions were rated using the IEA scoring scheme, which will be described in the following section. A total of 26 compositions (comprising a focal group for further data collection and in depth analysis), and an additional 19 randomly selected compositions from the total 223, were further analyzed for rhetorical and stylistic patterns. Space constraints limit the scope of this chapter and allow us to include only a detailed description of the main focus in analysis, the "storygraph," and the relationship of the quality ratings of the narratives to the patterns found in the storygraph.

The storygraph analysis was designed to determine gross structures of plot and story development, use of features such as setting and introduction of characters, amount of information allocated to

TABLE 7.1
Percentage of Total Words of Vocabulary Items in Each Group

Group	TWDS	V	N	PN	ADJ	ADV	CONJ	ART	PREP
NSE	3487	19.92	19.82	9.18	7.25	5.62	6.68	7.71	9.80
Arabic	3620	19.94	17.54	13.32	6.49	4.97	9.01	8.59	9.89
Vietnamese	3223	21.25	18.62	13.59	7.54	5.32	7.25	7.73	6.45

NOTE: Proper nouns and adjectives counted as nouns and adjectives; relative pronouns excluded—only personal, possessive, reflexive counted; adverbs and conjunctions—counted as such according to *function* in the context; prepositions—only those
counted which were *not* part of the verb unit (e.g. *pick up*); articles—include both
definite and indefinite articles; verbs—since propositional units (for storygram) are
based on verb units, these are the same number as propositional units.

description as distinct from plot information, and inclusion of
information that is not *typical* of English narratives. In addition, the
compositions of the 45 students were analyzed for word counts of
various lexico-grammatical types (nouns, verbs, adjectives, adverbs,
articles, pronouns, prepositions, and conjunctions, as well as total
word counts) to determine to what degree differences may be
attributed to the length of compositions, particular linguistic phenomena, and familarity with the use of English in written form.

VOCABULARY TYPES AND
LENGTH OF THE COMPOSITIONS

Little variation in the total word count (Table 7.1) was found
across the three groups. Variation in the percentage of various lexical
categories (principally, pronouns, conjunctions, and prepositions)
was found among the Vietnamese and Arabic students, which are, in
part, Ll (first language) effects. Grade 6 Arabic students show a
considerably higher percentage of coordinating conjunctions in their
stories, which may reflect Kaplan's (1966) finding of this linguistic
form as more common among the Arabic students in their writing.

QUALITY RATINGS OF THE COMPOSITIONS

The IEA (1983) holistic/analytic evaluation scheme was used to
rate the compositions according to how effectively they conformed

with English narrative conventions. The scheme (illustrated in Table 7.2) allows for the evaluation of writing that required raters to focus on a number of categories to the exclusion of others (as far as this is possible to do). For example, *mechanics* occupies a separate category, and it was felt that such a scale would therefore not disadvantage the nonnative students (NNS) as other scales may. The ratings for the narrative include the following main categories: A: Quality and Scope of Content; B: Organization and Presentation of Content; C: Style and Form; D: Mechanics; and E: The Affective Response of the Raters. A scale of 1 (Low) to 5 (High) was used for rating each of the items for each category. The criterion used for the scoring scheme was that developed by the IEA study (1983). The "ideal" narrative model was drawn from a variety of sources, among them Wilkinson, Barnsley, Hanna, and Swan (1980), Applebee (1978), and Vandergrift (1980). Thus a "good" bedtime story will generally have the conventional beginning, ("Once upon a time . . ."), a focus on action and event, one main character, and possibly an agent who brings about some kind of simple complication. The story will probably have a crisis or build up of action and will have an ending. In addition, the raters also considered the appropriateness of the style and content of the story, the audience having been specified as a child younger than the writer.

Three raters rated all 223 compositions. Two raters had had experience with the IEA scoring scheme and were trained ESL teachers, and one had had extensive experience in large-scale evaluation of compositions at the secondary school level. A training session in the use of the scoring scheme was carried out, particularly to draw the attention of the raters for the need to separate their evaluation of rhetorical structure and content from that of mechanics. The main goal of using such an evaluation was to discover how successfully the nonnative writers were perceived by the raters as observing the conventions of English narrative writing.

Results of the Ratings
of the Compositions

In the scoring scheme, items 1-10 consist of features related to narrative organization, technique, style, and mechanics. Items 11 and 12 show the affective responses of the raters to the compositions.

Using a covariance matrix and a reliability correlation matrix, the reliability of the raters was computed for each item (Table 7.2) in the five main categories. The unadjusted ratings given by each of the three raters on each item in the scoring scheme comprise the data used to determine the reliability coefficient. The range of reliability for all compositions on items 1-10 was from .75 to .88 and for items 11-12 from .63 to .69. The means and standard deviations on each item, according to total and focal groups and grade and language groups, are also shown in Table 7.2.

According to the range of means in the total and focal groups on each item, the focal group students generally appeared to write better stories than did other students in the total group (Table 7.2). In explanation of this pattern, attention is drawn to the fact that the focal group members were all volunteers, drawn from the total pool of subjects. Additional data were collected from these focal group students in the form of extensive interviews and questionnaires, as well as additional writing samples, in order to assist in the subsequent interpretation of the narrative data collected. The responses of these students in their interviews and questionnaires suggest that their higher quality ratings are a reflection of their greater interest and enthusiasm in carrying out the task. The results are grouped according to grade and language background.

The most significant items in relation to the subsequent analyses were those that dealt with the *development of the narrative situation or event (A1), the presentation of characters (A2), the focus on situation or event (B4), and the narrative structure (B5)*. When "mechanics" are separated out in evaluation, the nonnative students could score well despite their somewhat limited English proficiency. Lower scores on these items, however, reflect degrees to which the raters perceived the students' writing as conforming with English narrative conventions. The less proficient writers of English (whether L1 or L2) generally scored in the lower ranges in the "style" and "mechanics" categories. In general, the NS (native speakers of English) Grade 11 students, and the NS Grade 6 students, appear to understand the conventions of narrative writing as they have been exposed to them in reading and as they have been taught to observe them through writing experiences in the school. This assumption is supported by the data from the interviews and questionnaires of both the focal group students and their teachers. This also appears to be true for the Grade 11 Arabic students, all but one of whom were

TABLE 7.2
Means and Standard Deviations for Quality Ratings: Total and Focal Groups

Group			Category A			Category B			Category C		Category D		Category E		All Items
		Item 1	Item 2	Item 3	Item 4	Item 5	Item 6	Item 7	Item 8	Item 9	Item 10	Item 11	Item 12	
Total group															
Gr 11	mean	3.34	3.28	3.36	3.58	3.11	3.16	3.20	3.12	2.92	2.70	2.24	2.19	3.01
	SD	1.03	1.07	1.08	1.02	1.06	1.01	.97	.96	.93	.90	1.11	1.12	1.02
Gr 6	mean	2.30	2.07	2.14	2.43	2.00	2.03	2.04	2.02	1.80	1.69	1.56	1.56	1.97
	SD	1.03	1.05	1.07	1.15	1.01	.99	1.01	.98	.79	.71	.91	.88	.97
Focal group															
Gr 11	mean	3.95	3.72	3.87	3.79	3.38	3.59	3.49	3.56	3.15	2.82	2.28	2.23	3.32
	SD	.86	1.33	1.29	1.25	1.49	1.25	.95	.77	.85	.74	.59	.61	.95
Gr 6	mean	3.00	2.85	2.82	3.03	2.90	2.77	2.69	2.64	2.10	1.90	1.56	1.67	2.49
	SD	.84	.93	.92	1.07	1.03	1.04	1.00	.93	.82	.66	.39	.33	.77
FG English															
Gr 11	mean	4.50	4.50	4.75	4.50	4.50	4.42	4.00	4.17	3.75	3.25	2.83	2.75	3.99
	SD	.58	.58	.32	.58	.58	.50	.82	.69	.50	.50	.19	.32	.44
Gr 6	mean	3.27	3.27	3.07	3.53	3.13	3.13	3.27	3.07	2.53	2.07	1.87	1.80	2.83
	SD	.72	.72	.60	.84	.73	1.10	.83	.72	.90	.68	.18	.30	.64
FG Arabic															
Gr 11	mean	3.92	3.67	3.75	3.83	3.42	3.50	3.50	3.50	3.25	2.92	2.17	2.08	3.29
	SD	1.13	1.83	1.66	1.50	1.73	1.35	.88	.88	.96	.96	.43	.57	1.13

(continued)

TABLE 7.2 Continued

Group		Category A			Category B			Category C		Category D		Category E		All Items
		Item 1	Item 2	Item 3	Item 4	Item 5	Item 6	Item 7	Item 8	Item 9	Item 10	Item 11	Item 12	
Gr 6	mean	2.25	1.92	1.92	1.92	2.17	1.83	1.58	1.58	1.33	1.33	1.25	1.47	1.71
	SD	.88	.92	.92	.92	1.17	.88	.50	.50	.47	.47	.32	.32	.60
FG Vietnamese														
Gr 11	mean	3.53	3.13	3.27	3.20	2.47	3.00	3.07	3.13	2.60	2.40	1.93	1.93	2.81
	SD	.69	1.22	1.26	1.35	1.37	1.41	1.06	.51	.72	.60	.64	.64	.90
Gr 6	mean	3.42	3.25	3.42	3.50	3.33	3.25	3.08	3.17	2.33	2.25	1.50	1.75	2.85
	SD	.88	.92	.92	.92	1.17	.88	.50	.50	.47	.47	.32	.32	.51
Reliability coefficient		.83	.81	.80	.75	.78	.81	.85	.85	.88	.86	.63	.69	

educated in Australia, although the writing of this group also reveals some stylistic influences that cannot be clearly attributed to English narrative style.

Discussion of Results

A1: Presentation of events. Scores for the Grade 6 and 11 Vietnamese students in this category (dealing with presentation and development of the situation or event) were in the 2 to 4 range with the mean rating for this item being 3.53 on the 5-point scale. Apart from one student, the Grade 11 Arabic students scored in the 3 to 5 range in this category and the Grade 6 Arabic students in the 1 to 3 range. The latter appeared to be writing recounts (Martin & Rothery, 1980-81) or what Applebee (1978) has termed "unfocussed chains" rather than "true narratives" in which incidents are linked by centering and by chaining, indicating fuller control over the development of events (Applebee, 1978, p. 69). In contrast, the NS Grade 11 students scored in the 4 to 5 range, and the NS Grade 6 students in the 2 to 4 range, reflecting the raters' views that these students had generally met the criteria for narrative presentation of events.

A2: Presentation of character. The group that scored highest in this item was the NS Grade 11 group in the 4 to 5 range with the mean score for the item being 4.50. The Grade 6 Arabic group scored in the range of 1 to 3, the lowest for this item.

B4: Focus on topic, development of events. Other than the Grade 6 Arabic group all students in the other groups scored in the 2 to 5 range for this item, the overall means for the Focal Group Grade 6 students being 3.03 and 3.37 respectively. The NS Grade 11 students and one of the Arabic Grade 11 students scored mostly 4 and 5 on this item.

B5: Narrative structure. This item is perhaps the most important in that it relates most directly to the *storygraph analysis* and to the *stylistic analysis.* The range of scores gained reflects the structuring of the stories as analyzed in the storygraph. High scores reflect close conformity with a well-developed plot. In the focal group, the Grade 11 mean for this item was 3.38, and for the Grade 6 students, 2.90. The Grade 11 Vietnamese students scored in the 1 to 3 range. The pattern in these compositions was to have a lengthy introductory description (in effect, a story about a story) and many did not complete the story "proper." A typical rater response was that these compositions were close to being "off topic."

The results of the Grade 6 Vietnamese students were comparable with the NS students on this item, their range being 2 to 4 and their mean 3.33. Three of these students, however, wrote obvious derivatives of English stories (e.g., two variations of "Jack and the Beanstalk" and one of "Peter Rabbit"). All of these students had had regular exposure to English narratives since they began schooling in Australia and appear to have already become familiar with the conventions of "good story writing" in English. The high level of motivation to become "good English users" shown by the Grade 6 Vietnamese students may, in part, explain why they were so ready to totally adopt these stories. It is also rather self-evident but perhaps necessary to point out that the older students had also had a longer period of exposure to the rhetorical forms of their own culture and one would, therefore, expect to see more evidence of those forms in their English writing. Furthermore, the Grade 11 Vietnamese students had arrived in Australia as high school students and consequently were given less opportunity to write narrative forms in their subsequent schooling than were the Grade 6 Vietnamese students— narrative being a frequently used form in both writing and reading in elementary school, but not in secondary school.

All of the Grade 6 Arabic students scored in the 1 to 3 range for this item. Their teachers did not regard these students as being "good writers." All of the Grade 6 Arabic students received additional ESL instruction up to the time of data collection since they began school in kindergarten. However, their experiences with reading and writing in English are not extensive either in school or in the home as revealed in the interview and questionnaire data.

The NS Grade 11 students scored in the 3 to 5 range for this item. All have had extensive experience reading stories throughout childhood both in the home and in the school as have the Grade 6 NS students. The latter, however, scored in the 2 to 4 range. To some extent, this result is explained by the fact that the Grade 6 students tended to write forms of "recounts" as did the Grade 6 Arabic students. Their proficiency ratings in writing, as noted by their teachers, indicate that they are "middle-of-the range" students.

Students who did not complete their compositions were mostly in the Vietnamese group. Again, raters penalized such students by regarding their stories as unfinished. The Vietnamese students,

however, spent a great deal of time on the "setting" for the story, or as
termed in the storygraph, the "story about story." Their stories,
therefore, were not so much meandering as *evolving*, and the time
constraints we place on students in writing do not seem to *accommodate* their particular rhetorical style. When we consider their
stories in this light, the problem appears to lie with the conditions
under which students write rather than in the writers themselves.
Further discussion of the significance of this factor as an indication of
possible transfer of story-telling forms from the native culture will
follow in the discussion of the storygraph analysis and results.

STORYGRAPH ANALYSIS:
PLOTTING THE PLOT

Storygrammar methodology, although contemplated, was not
considered an appropriate approach for tracking the sequences in the
students' narratives. The method presupposes cultural hegemony of
rhetorical structure (Matsuyama, 1983) and has already been found to
be unsuitable for analyzing Japanese folklore in not being able to
capture either the surface or underlying structures of those tales.
However, certain aspects of the storygrammar approach were adapted
(e.g., the segmentation of information in the stories according to
"propositional units" as used by Warren, Nicholas, & Trabasso, 1979)
and subsequently applied. The term "storygraph" was coined by the
researcher to reflect the graphic nature of the analysis (see Figure 7.1).

Four categories comprise the storygraph (see Figure 7.1): story
about story, setting, scene, and plot. Each of these categories, and the
criteria for selection, is now further described before proceeding to
discuss how the stories were segmented according to the propositional
units of analysis.

Category A: Story About Story. This category refers to a story in
which the student has focused on him- or herself, or provided a
storyteller who is "outside" the actual tale, as well as to other
person(s) also "outside" the story and to whom the story is being told.
Details may include the reasons for telling the story, descriptions of
those who will be listening to the story and of their circumstances,
descriptions of the teller of the tale, the setting for telling the story,
occasional interpolations of the listeners in the telling of the tale and

their interaction with the teller of the tale. On occasion, the data revealed the "story about story" as being the story. That is, the frame tale is the tale. The signal always given by the writers in this study for moving out of this category is a typical "story-type" beginning, for example, "Once upon a time..."; "Once there was..."; "It was a cold night..." and so on. Dialogue between the teller of the tale and the listeners signals movement back and forth throughout the story event, to the frame category, for example, "Is she beautiful?" asked my brother, followed by "Yes, she is." (Student 041, Grade 11, Vietnamese).

Category B: Setting. For the purposes of this storygraph analysis, the setting and scene were separated. Setting may be a particular aspect of "scene" according to the definition by Hymes (1974) and Burke (1969). Setting in this analysis includes references made to place, time, and action in the story. It also includes the initial references to the appearances of characters in the story, but attributes of these characters are not included in this category. The kind of information appearing in this category is shown in the following examples:

"One day a greedy little old man : ... "

"Once upon a time in a far off African jungle. . . "

"Last year on Christmas Eve a little boy . . . "

Occasional references to time and space are made in the body of the stories, but in general such references appeared only at the beginning of the tales and functioned as locational (temporal and spatial) frames for the events and their development.

Category C: Scene. According to Hymes (1974), Burke (1969), and Saville-Troike (1982), "scene" consists of the total components of an event in a communicative context (Saville-Troike, 1982, p. 138). Among other things, "scene" incorporates setting, but its principal value as a category is that it captures the communicative aspects of the interaction among the participants in the stories, the thoughts and feelings of the characters, the attitude of the writer toward the characters and events (thus features that convey tone and point of view) as well as attributes of the characters and setting. Physical attributes of the setting are included if they contribute to the creation of mood or atmosphere (e.g., "a cold, dark room"). Emotional and psychological states of being are also included in the "scene" category. This is in accord with Hymes' (1974, pp. 55-56) definition of "scene" in which he suggests that it "designates the psychological setting or cultural definition of an occasion." Examples from students' stories are: "She've got a lovely sad eyes, a little nouse, and a long long hair." and "Poor Hugo, he felt all alone."

  Category D: Plot. Plot refers to the sequence of actions and events from the beginning to the end of the story. The story is literally "plotted" in this section from top to bottom and left to right on the chart. A new phase of action is termed "a turn," shown by a circled propositional unit. A "turn" may occur under the following conditions: A new participant appears in the story who is responsible for a change in the pattern of events or for initiating a new sequence of action; a change of location or setting occurs; a character changes focus from reflecting to acting or responding to the action of others; a new event is introduced by a new topic. The concept of a "turn" is adapted from that used in pragmatic discourse analysis (Sachs, Schegloff, & Jefferson, 1974; Saville-Troike, 1982) to incorporate the meaning given to it in dramatic literature (from the Greek word *tropos,* signifying a turn of direction or the introduction of a new event). In charting the plot, features such as climax and denouement are not marked in the storygraph nor is the kind of ending categorized. These features were dealt with in a detailed stylistic analysis reported elsewhere (Söter, 1986).

Segmentation of the
Stories: Propositional Units

  Adapted from the methods used by Stein and Glenn (1979) and Warren, Nicholas, and Trabasso (1979), propositional units proved to be suitable for dividing text of student writers into meaningful units and overcame the problems of ambiguous boundaries between sentences and sometimes of T-Units. For example, coordinating conjunctions, as used by the students (especially nonnative students), did not always seem to signal *coordination* in the conventional sense. It was not always clear from the data that "and" was used between clausal units, that it in fact signalled the commencement of another T-Unit.

  A description of how the propositional units were decided upon follows. A verb is the nucleus of a propositional unit. Where a verb phrase consisted of two verbs (e.g., *start to tell*) it was broken into two verbs with deleted arguments implied. In coding, propositional units may be "fused" (the main action being described is not completed by one unit alone). All propositional units are numbered from (1) as are sentences in which writers indicated these through punctuation. Propositional units may serve *multiple functions* in the text—that is, convey information related to character (scene) as well as plot or setting. This is shown as double coding. All propositional units were counted and proportions of units in any one section indicate in which sections writers concentrated their information. The plot line reveals where the story took a new turn and this is indicated by a circled propositional unit. For tracking propositional units, the plot line is shown in heavy broken lines, and the relationship between units within turns shown in light, unbroken lines that may zig-zag across the chart. Conventional trees, as used in storygrammars, were not used. Rather, the propositional units in the stories are placed beginning at the top of a chart moving from top to bottom at each "turn." A "turn" occurs where a new element or event is introduced.

A sample of text from a student's story illustrates the method of segmentation according to the principles described. The story segment is shown without correction or editing and has been divided into propositional units with the predicate and arguments shown in block letters following each unit. The first digit refers to the student's sentences and the second refers to the number of the propositional unit as it occurs in the text.

SAMPLE ANALYSIS: STUDENT 041: GRADE 11, VIETNAMESE

"The Magic Stick"

(1. 1)   That is the title of the story BE: TITLE OF STORY

(1. 2)   I think THINK: I

(1. 3)   I would tell to my brother at bedtime with the Magic Stick TELL: I, MY BROTHER, BEDTIME, MAGIC STICK

(1. 4)   I hope HOPE: I

(1. 5)   he will get into sleep easily GOT TO SLEEP: HE

(1. 6)   and a fairy dream would come to him COME (WOULD): DREAM, (TO) HIM

(1. 7)   and here is my voice BE: MY VOICE
(1. 8)   start (my voice implied) START: (MY VOICE)
(1. 9)   to tell the story (my voice implied) TELL: (MY VOICE), STORY
(1.10)   and my brother was already on the bed with the blue blankets
          upon his cheeks. BE: MY BROTHER, BED, BLUE BLANKETS,
          CHEEKS
(2.11)   Once upon a time, there was a king BE: ONCE A TIME, A KING

For the sake of analytic consistency, inferencing was restricted to a minimum. Adjectives, which were expressed as stative predicates (e.g., "she is beautiful"), were included as verbs. However, other adjectives (i.e., those that at the level of surface structure are prenominal modifiers, e.g., "a blue blanket"), were not transformed into predicates for the purpose of analysis.

The storygraph is not designed to describe all the details of the stylistic features of the students' compositions. Rather, it is a means of plotting the structural features of the story and thereby indicates *the structural patterns* that appear to characterize the writing of different groups of students. The primary functions of the storygraph are to indicate the sequence of story events through simple visual means and to allocate information in the stories to various "macro" categories that will reflect conventional story structure in English. As such, the approach offers a method of visually tracking the backward/forward movement of the plot and, because the categories themselves arise from the kinds of stories the students write in response to a task, the approach allows for additional categories to be added if these are warranted by the data.

General Findings and Discussion

The findings, based on percentage distributions of propositional units in the storygraphs (Table 7.3), may be summarized as follows. First, all three groups have stories that contain setting, attributes of setting, character, and action although the manner in which these are presented differs in varying degrees. Second, the three groups place different emphases on action and event, with the Vietnamese students appearing to be more concerned with presenting a context for their stories than either the Arabic or NS students. Third, when plot is present in the conventional sense, all of the stories show characteristic

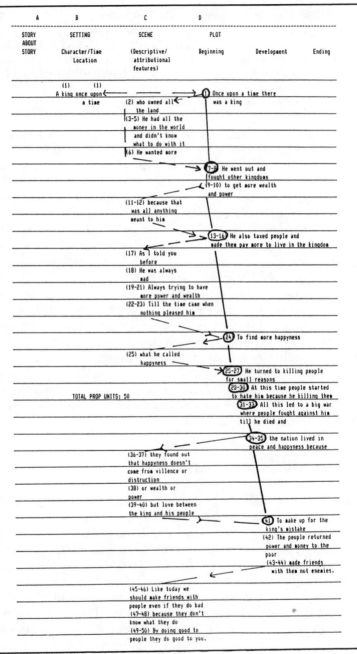

Figure 7.1 Sample Storygraph Analysis

beginnings (e.g., "Once upon a time . . .") and most have happy endings. The model stories referred to in the study (Robertson, 1968; two Vietnamese informants—a professional educated male now resident in the United States, and a linguistics graduate student) show some differences in this respect. Fourth, the Arabic students show a preference for using more detailed description (atributional features coded as "scene"). To what extent these writers were attempting to match new narrative patterns to old is a problematic question. Certainly the Grade 11 Arabic students wrote narratives that were more "English" in their structure, but close inspection of content reveals that a trend to descriptive digressiveness was apparent in their stories, but not in the Grade 11 NS group. Similarly, if not directly germane to a structural analysis, I should also point out that the content of several of the Grade 11 Arabic stories would not be regarded as appropriate for bedtime story purposes in contemporary western cultures.

The following samples are written by a Vietnamese Grade 11 student, a NS Grade 11 student, and an Arabic Grade 6 student, respectively. The story written by the Grade 11 Vietnamese student is representative of the group in that the opening third of the tale is a well-developed frame for another tale, with the writer also moving back and forth between the frame and the encompassed tale throughout the event. The NS story is similarly representative of that group in the focus on event and action so that the reader has a strong sense of forward movement in the plot. Finally, the Grade 6 Arabic tale was selected for its representativeness of that group's proclivity for recounts, although in this instance, not evidence of cultural difference.

Story 1: Grade 11 Vietnamese (a proficient student)

Daddy, daddy, I can't get to sleep, please daddy tell me a story, please.

No, Ricky, your eight years old and you should be able to get to sleep by yourself now.

C'mon daddy, just this one, please daddy.

Look son, this is the last time I ever tell you a story. i can't make one up every single deay when you can't get to sleep. I've got to get to sleep, too, you know. I've got to get up early tomorrow and every other sigle day, I've got to work hard to get money so you can live like a human being. Not like I was living! When I was your age I used to live in a room half as small as now are. There was four of us then. my father, Mother, brother and me. We used to live in Germany in those days. I didn't tell you about my older brother did I. His name was David. He was about six years older than me. I remember he used to take me fishing every day. I never used to go to school then. there was no school for that matter. See how lucky you are. Well, I remember one day when we went fishing, something very exciting happened. Whilst we were just lying there in the fresh open country, our rods were just laying in on the shore with the fishing line thrown out into the river just waiting for some unlucky fish to get sucked in.

Suddenly we heard a little noise, it was something coming through the forest. I tell you something, I was scared. But luckily my brother had his rifle. He told me to go hide behind a rock, so I did just that and waited.

All of a sudden, this thing came out of its hiding. It looked like a man but the funny thing abiyt ut was green. And another thing it danced everywhere. It had this funny little box that looked like some sort of sound machine, music came out of it, he was dancing everywhere, just then my brother fired his gun. It took off like a rocket. We nether saw it again. Ha, Ha, good night son.

Story 2: Grade 11 NS English Student

Once upon a time there was a little grey mouse. His mummy and daddy had gone away on a holiday and told the little grey mouse he had to stay at home and look after himself for a few days. The little grey mouse like this idea, as he had thought of lots of thing to do while his parents were away.

So as soon as the car had turned the corner he ran inside and started to prepare a party. He pulled out all the things his mother used when she was cooking and started to make a big birthday cake. As he turned on the stove there was a big "BANG" The stove had broken. So in order to have a cake for his party he took some money from his mothers room and bought a cake from the shop. the little grey mouse had forgotten that he was supsed to keep this money to buy his dinner with for the next few days.

At 6.00 o'clock all his friends had arrived, hundreds of them, and little grey mouse had everything ready. the little grey mouse's friends ate until they had eaten everything, listened to the music until someone broke the record player and played games till the house was very messy. Then when there was nothing more to do they all left. The little grey mouse was left to clean up.

It took the little grey mouse two days to clean up the mess, but this didn't worry him. He was worried about what his mother might say when she got home he was also very hungry as all his money went into buying the cake.

His mother returned and when she saw the broken equpiment she called the little grey mouse to her. The little grey mouse explained what had happened. His mother got very angry and he was sent to his room. He was also not allowed to have a party ever again and was made to work very hard to pay for the broken stove and the broken record player. The little grey mouse was very upset and never did anything else naughty while his parents were away instead he stayed at home and read books.

Story 3: Grade 6 Arabic Student

Once there was a prince he was riding his horse. Then he found a bottle. He picked it up. There was a beautiful princess. He took the cork off the top of the bottle then came a beautiful princess. She was magic. Then he told her that he wanted the best castle that there ever could be. Then in front of his eyes there was the castle. He ran as fast as he could go. He had millions of gold and millions of neckles [necklaces]. He was the richest prince in the world. Then princesses came all over the world to marry him. He didn't like them because they were jealous of him. He said that he would marry the magic princess because she wasn't jealous. then the next day he marry her and they lived happily for ever. Then the magic princess wasn't magic but he didn't care he just loved her.

Most strikingly, the NS group, irrespective of grade level, show a very consistent pattern for story telling (see Table 7.3). That is, little detail is evident to serve as introduction to the story, the plot is begun almost immediately, there is little digression to attributes of characters or setting, there is little evidence of reflection on action, and a clear forward movement of the sequence of events occurs. Of the three groups, the NS group showed the least divergence within the group itself in allocating information to the storygraph categories.

Table 7.3 illustrates the distribution of propositional units in the four categories for each of the groups and the relationship that these allocations appear to have with the quality ratings independently given to the compositions.

Similar patterns in story structure and content appeared among the NS group as a whole and the Grade 11 Arabic students. In

TABLE 7.3
Means (%) of Propositional Units in Storygraph Categories
for Each Group of Students Related to Average Range of
Quality Rating Scores on Selected Items

Group	Storygraph Categories				Narrative Rating Scores Average of Rater Scores			
	A	B	C	D	A1	A2	B1	B2
Vietnamese (T)	33.84	5.98	20.55	45.78				
Grade 6	26.34	6.58	17.60	54.88	3-4	2-4	2-4	2-4
Grade 11	42.42	5.60	23.92	35.36	1-4	1-3	1-4	1-3
Arabic (T)	15.45	5.31	17.61	68.62				
Grade 6	20.65	4.90	5.97	72.75	1-3	1-3	2-4	2-3
Grade 11	10.90	5.66	27.90	65.04	3-5	2-5	2-4	2-4
NS English (T)	3.27	7.32	16.20	81.82				
Grade 6	4.26	7.12	16.63	81.26	2-4	2-4	3-4	3-4
Grade 11	2.14	7.53	16.88	82.45	3-5	3-5	3-5	3-5

NOTE: Storygraph categories A, B, C, D represent "story about story"; setting; scene (description, attributes, states of mind); and, plot line. Categories for narrative rating scores, A1, A2, B1, B2, represent development of situation/event; presentation of characters; focus on topic; and development of narrative structure (including climax).

contrast, the Grade 6 and 11 Vietnamese students consistently showed a greater allocation of time and location for the *telling* of the story and a greater focus on the attributional features of characters (especially with respect to emotional and mental processes of characters). Three Grade 6 Vietnamese students did not follow this pattern and, as stated earlier in the discussion of quality ratings, these students wrote clear derivations of English type stories.

To some extent one may argue that the divergent patterns of most of the Vietnamese students and the Grade 6 Arabic students reflect their lack of familiarity with story-writing conventions in English as these are customarily taught to them in schools and, possibly, acquired through reading. However, in this sense, their structures do also indicate structures that may be derived from elsewhere (other models). Various Vietnamese narratives drawn on for the study reveal, as do Japanese stories (Matsuyama, 1983), that the Vietnamese stories appear to be less goal-oriented and hence less focused on plot than the typical English story. In the Vietnamese stories consulted and according to the Vietnamese informants, a greater emphasis appears to be placed on relationships among the participants in the telling of the story situation and on the inner states of characters within the story. The Vietnamese students in particular also drew more heavily on *dialogue* in their stories and the dialogue components did not include information that, in general, forwarded the action of the story but was reflective or attributive in nature.

The Grade 6 Arabic students were a problematic group in this study in that they were, on the whole, regarded as weaker writers and, through additional data collected for the focal group, appear to have had considerably less exposure to literary forms both in their native language and in English. Consequently, their stories do not, it seems, reflect so much a cultural influence in structure, as a limited proficiency with writing in general. The Grade 11 Arabic students, although having been exposed to English literary forms for most of their school lives, nevertheless appear to have more information in the attributional category (scene), which, according to the models of Arabic stories used as comparative sources, appears to be a feature of Arabic literary style.

THE RELATIONSHIP OF THE QUALITY RATINGS TO THE STORYGRAPH RESULTS

The Grade 11 NS students may be considered as indicating the English "narrative norm" group, these students having scored in the 4 to 5 range in the quality ratings. Where the raters gave higher scores for the specific narrative subcategories, they were, in effect, indicating their views that the stories were "good" narratives according to the English model.

The significance of the agreement between the analysis in the storygraph and the ratings lies in the following. When the writing of these students is checked; evaluated; and assessed by teachers in an English-speaking community, such as the one the students are members of, it will be responded to *in terms of the linguistic and literary norms of that community.* This means that narrative compositions will be judged as *good* or *bad* according to the accepted notions of narrative structure and development in that community. Students who do not conform to those norms will be less likely to be evaluated highly and this is, in fact, reflected in the ratings given to the students.

However, and more significantly, the rationale for such low ratings has been that students show poor organization, poor syntactic structure, and limited vocabulary (i.e., it is a "mechanics" oriented structure that we apply to student writing in general). Structure is admittedly considered, but again, this is in terms of what is *not done* rather than what is done. A storygraph analysis such as the one applied in this study indicates that ESL compositions may not "lack structure," but demonstrate "different structures." Stories in this study that were rated on the lower end of the scale were those that contained lengthy digressions, contained the category "story about story," as well as those that were, in the main, "recounts." Stories that scored on the upper end of the scale were those in which the writer clearly presented the situation and the characters involved, developed the situation along action-based lines, and concluded the situation in an appropriate way for younger children, that is, the "happy ending." The data suggest that in judging the writing of students from other cultures (and subcultures) and other linguistic backgrounds, we need to consider whether that writing reflects conformity to norms of other cultural communities or ignorance of writing norms in the adopted language and culture.

The additional analyses carried out on the data (a style vectors rating, a detailed stylistic analysis under the categories of plot, setting, characterization, point of view, and stylistic use of language, and a semantic analysis of verbs based on Chafe, 1970, and Longacre, 1976, 1983), are not included in this report of the study, but described in detail elsewhere (Söter, 1986). They are alluded to only to indicate that the findings in the storygraph are confirmable through more detailed stylistic and linguistic analysis and that these findings are clearly related to structural rhetorical patterns.

CONCLUSION

Making inferences about the influence of a particular culture (in this case Vietnamese and also Arabic) is a highly speculative task. Thompson (1965) in a study of Vietnamese grammar includes information as to Vietnamese styles of expression. However, he, as have others, points out that Vietnamese as a society has also been highly influenced by the Chinese language and culture. Stetkevych (1970),

Patai (1973), and Bakalla (1984) indicate similar problems for the
analyst in the writing of Arabic native speakers. Thus, to attribute
stylistic and rhetorical forms to particular sources is problematic, but
what has been ascertained is that the Vietnamese students and the
Arabic students do exhibit patterns of narration that are different in
various respects both from each other and from those of native
English writers.

In the process of identifying such patterns, we may further develop
our understanding of factors that create difficulties for ESL writers
beyond the lexico-grammatical systems employed. By examining
textual elements of narration we may better understand the sociocultural factors that are part of the writing activity, and, more
importantly, extend our view of ESL writers to include several new
perspectives. First, ESL writers are members of some culture or
society and bring various cultural experiences with them to their
writing and reading experiences. Second, as members of some culture
or society, ESL writers have been enculturated in particularly specific
ways with regard to language use in a variety of contexts and genres.
Third, as such members, ESL writers have also learned discourse
conventions of some other culture or society. Finally, as such
members, ESL writers may also encode meaning in ways that are
different from that of the target culture. More comprehensive
methods for the analysis of written as well as spoken language of ESL
writers is needed, however, to allow for consideration of the sociocultural aspects of writing, as well as the formal aspects of written
language. This study demonstrates that it is possible and fruitful to
use literary analysis and stylistics to analyze the written texts of
developing writers of diverse linguistic and cultural backgrounds
because these approaches also address sociolinguistic perspectives of
written language. One could argue that the degrees to which writers
observe rhetorical conventions in a particular cultural context may
reveal the extent to which writers are "acculturated" (i.e., socialized
into a target community). The method of analysis presented, while
not without problems, also offers teachers a way of presenting
comparative narrative discourse structures to ESL students, and the
concept of graphic illustration of text structure can be extended to
represent structures in other rhetorical modes.

One of the main limitations of the study is that the ESL students
were not able to write the compositions both in English and in their
native languages, although they had been offered the possibility of

doing so. Had they done so, clearer patterns of stylistic and rhetorical characteristics in the stories may have been observed. A further limitation occurs in the task dimensions. Time limits, while reflecting the real-school contexts for writing, prevented some of the Vietnamese students, in particular, from completing their narratives. Thus, unwittingly, further information about differences in writing styles may be excluded. Furthermore, in setting writing tasks, we may also confound task effects with writer effects. The present study specified an audience younger than the writer of the story, consequently, some students may have been encouraged to use "oral forms," which are more typical in the "bedtime story-telling situation."

Despite these limitations, the study has demonstrated some degree of influence of a student's prior knowledge of literacy and literary experiences on his or her current experiences and on his or her current writing performance. Such acknowledgment is already being accorded in the field of ESL reading (Carrell, 1983), but is yet to have its place in the field of ESL writing. In this respect, the field of contrastive rhetoric will contribute significantly to our understanding of the impact of the native language discourse patterns on writers learning a second language, and its discourse patterns.

REFERENCES

Applebee, A. (1978). *The child and story: Ages 2-17*. Chicago: University of Chicago Press.

Bakalla, M. (1984). *Arabic culture through its language and literature*. London: Kegan Paul International.

Baker, E. (1982). The specification of writing tasks. In A. Purves & S. Takala (Eds.), *An International perspective on the evaluation of written composition*. Oxford: Pergamon.

Boas, F. (1963). Language and culture. In J. A. Rycenga & J. Schwartz (Eds.), *Perspectives on language*. New York: Ronald Press. (Original work published 1911)

Boehm, L. (1979). Human values and the basics: Is there any choice? *College English, 40*(5), 505-511.

Burke, K. (1969). *A grammar of motives*. Berkeley: University of California.

Carrell, P. L. (1983). Three components of background knowledge in reading comprehension. *Language Learning, 33*(1), 183-246.

Chafe, W. L. (1970). *Meaning and the structure of language*. Chicago: University of Chicago Press.

Chafe, W. L. (1980). *The pear stories: Cognitive, cultural and linguistic aspects of narrative production*. Norwood, NJ: Ablex.

Chatman, S. (1978). *Story and discourse: Narrative structure in fiction and film.* Ithaca, NY: Cornell University Press.

Crowhurst, M., & Piche, G. (1979). Audience and mode of discourse effects on syntactic complexity in writing at two grade levels. *Research in the Teaching of English, 3,* 101-109.

Dehghanpisheh, E. (1978). Language development in Farsi and English: Implications for the second language learner. *IRAL, 16*(1), 45-61.

Duong Thanh Binh, Diller, A. M., & Sutherland, K. (1975). *A handbook for teachers of Vietnamese students: Hints for dealing with cultural differences in schools* (Vietnamese Refugee Education Series 3). Washington, DC: Center for Applied Linguistics.

Fowler, T. (1977). *Linguistics and the novel.* London: Methuen.

Goodenough, W. (1981). *Culture, language and society.* Menlo Park, CA: Benjamin/Cummins.

Greenberg, K. (1982). Some relationships between writing assignments and students' writing performance. *Writing Instructor, 1,* 7-13.

Grimshaw, A. D. (1973). Sociolinguistics. In I. Pool, W. Schramm, W. F. Frey, N. Maccoby, & E. B. Parker (Eds.), *Handbook of communication.* Chicago: Rand McNally.

Heath, S. B. (1982). Protean shapes in literacy events: Ever-shifting oral and literate traditions. In D. Tannen (Ed.), *Spoken and written language: Exploring orality and literacy.* Norwood, NJ: Ablex.

Heath, S. B. (1983). *Ways with words.* Cambridge: Cambridge University Press.

Hoetker, J. (1982). *Effects of essay topics on student writing: A review of the literature.* Tallahassee, FL: Department of Education.

Houghton, D., & Hoey, L. (1983). Linguistics and written discourse: Contrastive rhetorics. *ARAL, 3,* 2-21.

Hymes, D. (1974). *Foundations in sociolinguistics: An ethnographic approach.* Philadelphia: University of Pennsylvania Press.

IEA International Study of Written Composition (1983, November). Instrument/Questionnaire Series (IEA/WR). Unpublished manuscripts. University of Illinois, Curriculum Laboratory, Urbana.

Kaplan, R. (1966). Cultural thought patterns in intercultural education. *Language Learning, 16*(1-2) 1-20.

Kaplan, R. (1983). Contrastive rhetoric revisited. *ARAL, 3,* 138-152.

Lado, R. (1957). *Linguistics across cultures.* Ann Arbor: University of Michigan Press.

Lai, Nam Chen (1981). *Images of South East Asia in children's fiction.* Singapore: Singapore University Press.

Leech, L. (1976). *Culture and communication.* Cambridge: Cambridge University Press.

Little, G. (1975). *Form and function in the written language of sixteen year olds.* Unpublished thesis. School of Education, University of New South Wales, Sydney, Australia.

Longacre, R. E. (1976). *An anatomy of speech notions.* Lisse, The Netherlands: Peter de Ridder.

Longacre, R. E. (1983). *The grammar of discourse.* New York: Plenum.

Martin, J., & Rothery, J. (1980-1981). Writing project (Report Nos. 1-2). *Working papers in linguistics.* Sydney, Australia: University of Sydney, Department of Linguistics.

Mathiot, M. (1979). *Ethnolinguistics: Boas, Sapir and Whorf revisited.* The Hague: Mouton.

Matsuyama, U. K. (1983). Can story grammar speak Japanese? *The Reading Teacher, 36*(7), 666-669.

McClure, E., Mason, J., & Williams, J. (1983). Sociocultural variables in children's sequencing of stories. *Discourse Processes, 6,* 131-143.

Michaels, S. (1981). Sharing time: Children's narrative styles and differential access to literacy. *Language in Society, 10*(3), 423-442.

Patai, R. (1973). *The Arab mind.* New York: Scribner's.

Perrine, L. (1966). *Story and structure* (2nd ed.). New York: Harcourt Brace and World.

Potter, L. D. (1981). American Indian children and writing: An introduction to some issues. In B. Connell (Ed.), *The writing needs of linguistically different children.* (Proceedings at the Conference of SWRL Educational Research Development, Los Alamitos, CA.)

Purves, A. C. (1985a). *The IEA literature and composition studies and their elucidation of the nature and formation of interpretive and rhetorical communities.* Unpublished manuscript, University of Illinois, Urbana-Champaign.

Purves, A. C. (1985b). *Literacy, culture and community.* Unpublished manuscript, University of Illinois, Urbana-Champaign.

Purves, A., Söter, A., Takala, S., & Vähäpassi, A. (1984). Towards a domain-referenced system for classifying composition assignments. *Research in the Teaching of English 18*(4), 385-417.

Robertson, D. L. (1968). *Fairy tales from Vietnam.* New York: Dodd, Mead.

Rumelhart, D. (1975). Schemata: The building blocks of cognition. In R. Spiro, B. Bruce & W. Brewer (Eds.), *Theoretical issues in reading and comprehension.* Hillsdale, NJ: Lawrence Erlbaum.

Sapir, E. (1949). *Language, culture and personality* (D. G. Mandelbaum, Ed.). Berkeley: University of California Press.

Saville-Troike, M. (1982). *The ethnography of communication: An introduction.* Oxford: Basil Blackwell.

Schachter, J., & Rutherford, W. (1979). Discourse function and language transfer. *Working Papers in Bilingualism, 19,* 1-12.

Scribner, S. (1977). Modes of thinking and ways of speaking: Culture and logic reconsidered. In P. N. Laird-Johnson & P. Mason (Eds.), *Thinking: Readings in cognitive science.* Cambridge: Cambridge University Press.

Scribner, S., & Cole, M. (1981). *The psychology of literacy.* Boston: Harvard University Press.

Selinker, L., Todd Trimble, R. M., & Trimble, L. (1976). Presuppositional rhetorical information in ESL discourse. *TESOL, 10*(3), 281-290.

Söter, A. (1986). *Writing: A third language for second language learners. A cross-cultural discourse analysis of the writing of school children in Australia.* Unpublished doctoral dissertation, University of Illinois, Urbana-Champaign.

Spiro, R. (1980). Constructive process in prose comprehension recall. In R. J. Spiro, B. C. Bruce, & W. F. Brewer (Eds.), *Theoretical issues in reading comprehension.* Hillsdale, NJ: Lawrence Erlbaum.

Stein, N. L., & Glenn, C. C. (1979). An analysis of story comprehension of elementary school children. In R. Freedle (Ed.), *Advances in discourse processing* (Vol. 2). Norwood, NJ: Ablex.

Stetkevych, J. (1970). *The modern Arabic literacy language: Lexical and stylistic developments.* Chicago: University of Chicago Press.

Tannen, D. (1979). What's in a frame? Surface evidence for underlying expectations. In R. Freedle (Ed.), *New directions in discourse processing* (Vol. 2). New York: Ablex.

Thompson, L. C. (1965). *A Vietnamese grammar.* Seattle: University of Washington Press.

Thompson-Panos, K., & Thomas-Ruzic, M. (1983). The least you should know about Arabic: Implications for the ESL writing instructor. *TESOL, 15*(5), 5-13.

Thorndyke, P. (1977). Cognitive structures in comprehension and memory of narrative discourse. *Cognitive Psychology, 9*, 77-110.

Vandergrift, K. (1980). *Child and story: The literary connection.*

Warren, W., Nicholas, D. W., & Trabasso, T. (1979). Inferences in understanding narratives. In R. Freedle (Ed.), *Advances in discourse processing* (Vol. 2). Norwood, NJ: Ablex.

Whorf, B. L. (1940). Science and linguistics. *Technological Review, MIT, 42*, 229-231, 247-252. (Reprinted in S. I. Hayakawa, 1941, *Language in Action.* New York: Harcourt Brace.)

Whorf, B. L. (1956). *Language, thought and reality* (J. B. Carroll, Ed.). Cambridge: MIT Press.

Wilkinson, A., Barnsley, G., Hanna, P., & Swan, M. (1980). *Assessing language development.* Oxford: Oxford University Press.

8

Narrative Styles in the Writing of Thai and American Students

CHANTANEE INDRASUTA

The study I will present in this chapter is a part of my work on contrastive analysis of two languages and two cultures (Indrasuta, 1987). In this study two types of writing are compared. The first is a comparison of writing in two native languages, English and Thai, in order to find out the degree to which the discourse patterns, styles, and ways of using language are similar or different. The second is a comparison of writing by the same Thai group of writers in two languages, Thai and English, in order to examine to what extent writing in the second language reflects the influence of the native culture, that is to say, whether the Thais transfer the pattern of writing from the first language into the second language.

American and Thai students were chosen for the subjects of this study for many reasons. First, I was familiar with the educational setting in Thailand before coming to study in the United States. Second, most of the research in the Thai language and in English as a foreign language in Thailand has focused on linguistic analysis such as contrastive grammar and error analysis, but not on discourse analysis or on language in use. Third, there has been a large body of research on written discourse in English and in English as a second language (Connor, 1982; Connor & McGagg, 1983; Y. Kachru, 1982, 1985; Kaplan, 1966, 1982), which needs to be tried on other languages. Fourth, although a large body of research has been conducted on the comparison of various different first languages and first and second languages, none has been conducted with written discourse among three subject groups: in this case, writing in English by American students, writing in Thai by Thai students, and writing in English by Thai students.

SELECTION OF WRITING CORPUS

Writing in school was selected because it is a first step of writing in a language and does not vary as much as the work of professional writers who have their own styles. The selected groups of students from the highest class of secondary education in the two cultures can be seen as representative of writing in school at this level. At this stage, the students, who are about 16-17 years old, have learned the language to the degree that they can express themselves well and conventionally in a first and, perhaps, in a second language.

Narrative compositions were used in this study for many reasons. First, a narrative composition is the first type of composition that students learn in their native language, both Thai and English, because it is a familiar form based on a simple type of organization: sequential events described chronologically. Second, from the pilot study of the IEA Written Composition, which studied written compositions of the students at this level in Thailand and the United States in May 1984, it was found that both Thai and American students wrote narrative compositions better than argumentative or expository compositions. The reason for this may be owing to the lack of practice in those forms.

THE SOURCE COMPOSITIONS

The two subject groups, 30 students in each group, were selected at random from the final year students at a high school in Urbana, Illinois, and from a Thai secondary school in Bangkok, Thailand, because these two subject groups had the following characteristics in common: a homogeneous background, a well-educated upper-middle-class family, similar college-bound programs, classification as twelfth graders at the onset of data collection, and age ranging from 15.5 to 17.5 years.

The sample consists of three subject groups, and within each subject group there are two subgroups.

The three subject groups are defined as follows: "AM" means the 30 American Grade 12 students writing compositions in English; "TH" means the 30 Thai secondary school students (equivalent to

TABLE 8.1
Subject Grouping

Group	Student Number	Composition Number	Topic
AM 1	1 – 15	1.1 – 1.15	1
AM 2	16 – 30	2.1 – 2.15	2
TH 1	1 – 15	1.1 – 1.15	1
TH 2	16 – 30	2.1 – 2.15	2
TT 1	16 – 30	1.1 – 1.15	1
TT 2	1 – 15	2.1 – 1.15	2

Grade 12) writing compositions in English; "TT" means the same 30 Thai students writing compositions in Thai. Table 8.1 shows the three subject groups: AM, TH, and TT. Each group has two subsets: The first subset wrote a narrative composition on the topic "I Succeeded, At Last" (Topic 1), and the second subset wrote a narrative composition on the topic "I Made a Hard Decision" (Topic 2).

The two topics, "I Succeeded, At Last" and "I Made a Hard Decision" are comparable because both have a similar kind of conflict. According to Scott and Madden (1980, p. 6), most stories have one of two patterns of conflict. Either it is an accomplishment story, in which the protagonist tries against opposition to achieve some goal, or it is a decision story, in which a protagonist must choose between two things—two courses of action or two sets of values. Furthermore, the two topics were used among other topics in the narrative task in the IEA study of written composition, and the comparable quality of these topics has been verified by international scorers.

Two topics had to be used because each Thai student had to write two compositions, one in English and the other in Thai. If they had written the two compositions on the same topic, they might have written the two compositions exactly in the same way, or they might have translated the first to the second. The purpose of this study was not to compare the translation of the first language to the second language, but to compare the ability to write a well-formed text in both languages. Since the quality of the two topics is comparable, as mentioned above, the Thai students were split into two subgroups, 15 students in each subgroup. Each student wrote a narrative composition in one language on Topic 1 and the other composition in the other language on Topic 2, as shown in Table 8.1. For comparison across the topics, the American students were also split into two subgroups and wrote on one of the two topics.

Since the sample in this study is small, that is, 30 subjects in each group (a total of 90), results from statistical analyses, while significant, can result from one or two student compositions. The statistics, therefore, can only hint at tendencies of similarities and differences in the phenomena. Yet such tendencies can raise questions whether similarities and differences among the three subject groups result from linguistic or cultural causes.

DATA COLLECTION PROCEDURES

Two methods were used for specific purposes. First, the interviews of students, teachers, and experts in writing in the two cultures were conducted to investigate the functions and models of narrative in the two cultures. In addition, all students in this study, and the teachers of the classes selected, were asked to answer the questionnaires concerning their perception of the roles of narrative writing. The other method was the student writing of narrative compositions during 40 minutes of their usual class work. The data collected for this study consist of one narrative composition from the American students and two narrative compositions from the Thai students, one in Thai and the other in English. The basic purpose of the research design was to elicit data that revealed how the three subject groups write narrative texts. The description of the data was based on a system of objective factors that function together to form a narrative text. They are: (a) linguistic data (cohesive ties), (b) stylistic data (narrative components), and (c) discourse data (forms and functions of clauses).

ANALYTIC APPROACHES

The analysis of cohesion (Halliday & Hasan, 1976), which reveals the semantic and syntactic relationship within a text, was used for the linguistic analysis. Analysis at this level is mostly linguistic, that is, to count the types and numbers of cohesive ties used in the compositions of each subject group and compare the percentages of frequencies of each type across the three subject groups by using a statistical analysis (F-test). Differences might be expected in the use of cohesive ties in the two languages because of differences in the language systems. In addition, differences in writing by the second language writers from the native writers of the target language might be expected because of transfer from the first language to the second language.

The categories of cohesion were taken from the Summary Table in Halliday and Hasan's *Cohesion in English* (1976), which states that there are five categories of cohesive ties: reference, substitution, ellipsis, conjunction, and lexical cohesion. In this study, only reference, substitution, conjunction, and lexical cohesion were used. Also, owing to the different nature of data in this study, some other subcategories of cohesive ties were added. In addition, the researcher decided to use the inter-T-unit cohesive ties for many reasons. According to Hunt (1965), a T-unit refers to: (a) a simple sentence, (b) a complex sentence, and (c) coordinate clauses, which construct a compound sentence. The salient reasons are, for example, since a T-unit is a single set of grammatical structures, there is no need to analyze the relationship within a T-unit. Also, from Hunt's research (1965), it was found that a T-unit is particularly useful in the study of children's writing because children's writing has not been developed well enough to be analyzed by sentences. The writing in the second language of the Thai students can be considered as being in this category.

Anaphoric reference refers to the ties linking the current information to the preceding text. The cohesion lies in the continuity of the reference of which the identity is prominent. Three types of reference (personal reference, demonstrative reference, and comparative reference) were used in this study.

Substitution is the replacing of one item for another. Substitution is different from reference in that "substitution is a relation between linguistic items such as words or phrases, whereas reference is a relation between meaning" (Halliday & Hasan, 1976, p. 89).

Conjunctive ties are assigned to five categories: (a) additive (e.g., and, and also, or); (b) adversative (e.g., yet, only, but); (c) causal (e.g., so, then, therefore, consequently, because); (d) temporal (e.g., then, next, before, after); and (e) other continuative (e.g., now, of course, well, anyway) (Halliday & Hasan, 1976, p. 336). Because the basic unit of analysis is the T-unit, only the conjunctions that connect between

T-units are counted. Since the T-unit may include either simple or complex sentences, the subordinating conjunction within the T-unit is not counted.

"Lexical cohesive tie" refers to the relationship of vocabulary in the current T-unit to the previous T-units. There is a borderline between grammatical and lexical cohesion in the use of general nouns such as *mother* and *grandma*. If in the second T-unit, the reference *she* is used, it is counted as a pronominal reference, but if the word mother or grandma is used, it is counted as a same-item-lexical cohesive tie. The general principle of the lexical classification is reiteration, which is categorized by Halliday and Hasan (1976) as (a) same item, (b) synonym or near synonym or hyponym, (c) superordinate, (d) general item, and (e) collocation.

The second set of data is based on an analysis of narrative structure (Booth, 1983; Frye, 1957; Perrine, 1959) including the styles of the compositions in terms of the following factors: plot, conflict, setting, theme, character, scene, and figurative language. This part reveals how the writers planned to present their stories and most clearly points to cultural rather than to linguistic factors.

The description of criteria of the narrative structure is briefly described as follows. Plot is concerned with whether the sequence of incidents or events of which a story is composed occurs chronologically or achronologically. There are four primary kinds of conflicts depending on the type of the antagonist, which can be persons, things, conventions of society, or traits of the writer's own character. Setting is the physical background of the story and also the element of place and time. The integral setting is closely interwoven with character, action, and theme, while in the backdrop setting, time and place are not important. As for the theme, if the theme is stated openly and clearly, the story has an explicit theme; otherwise, it has an implicit theme. The character may change throughout the story (dynamic) or remain unchanged (static). The story may occur in the real world (real scene) or in the imaginative or projected world (projected scene). Finally, three main types of figures of speech—simile, metaphor, and personification—are considered as figurative language.

The 90 student compositions were analyzed using the categories of narrative components mentioned above. The judgment in the analysis depends on the presence or absence of certain features of those categories. The frequencies of each category in each type were counted and compared across the three subject groups by the use of a statistical analysis (chi-square).

The third data set, discourse analysis, reveals how the form and function of the segments in narrative composition act in accordance with models of rhetorical coherence. Two methods of analysis are used: an analysis of the organization of the composition and an analysis of form and function.

It is broadly accepted that a narrative composition should have at least five parts in its pattern of organization. They are: beginning or introduction, sequential action, complicating action, climax, and ending (Labov & Waletzky, 1967; van Dijk, 1977). The examination of each composition using percentages of the five parts reveals whether or not the three subject groups perceive a similar pattern of organization.

Next, based on the theories of narrative discourse (Chatman, 1978; Genette, 1980; Lyons, 1984; Wann, 1939), the story includes events and existents, and the narrative discourse ordinarily has some kind of chronological order of events. Thus, the written compositions were segmented into clauses with emphasis on the main verbs of the main clauses and of the subordinate clauses in order to determine what kind of events and existents were narrated. At this point, the determination of the categories of verbs is based on the linguistic theories of Chafe (1970) and of Longacre (1976). After the types of events and existents (henceforth referred to as form) were determined, the next step was to find out how all those forms were related to created rhetorical coherence. The relationship of forms (henceforth referred to as function) is based on the theories of semantic relationship of the T-units of Fahnestock (1983), Sloan (1983), and Winterowd (1970), and the theory of the semantic relationship within sentences of van Dijk (1977). The main functions in narrative are, for example, to form sequential chains, causal chains, psychological chains, moral chains, or the like, since a narrative discourse is for narrating something that occurs after some other thing, or for relating events to their causes and effects.

The 10 forms of clauses in the analysis of discourse are: (a) generalization, (b) comment, (c) action, (d) mental state, (e) dialogue, (f) description of action, (g) description of mental state, (h) description of character, (i) description of setting, and (j) description of thing. Generalization refers to the philosophical observation that describes the real universe. It conveys the logical truth and the empirical laws of human nature (Chatman, 1978). Comment includes interpretation, judgment, and self-consciousness (Chatman, 1978). The salient criteria of an action are: (a) the verb is either the action or the process-action verbs as described by Chafe (1970), and (b) the subject of the verbs must be human beings or animated things that are the main part of the plot—kernel action, as described by Chatman (1978) in the story. Description of action, which is the subset of action, has other characteristics besides the ones mentioned above. A mental state verb describes a mental act or a voluntary or involuntary internal occurrence or self-induced state on the part of all characters in the story. These include verbs, for example, think, remember, feel, dream, decide, love, see (Chafe, 1970; Longacre, 1976). When mental states occur in the past, they are parts of the sequential chain or causal chain of events, and the writer is describing how he or she felt in the past. When mental states occur while the writer is writing the composition, they indicate the feeling the writer expresses at the time of writing. The category "description of mental state" is used for the former case and "mental state" is used for the latter. The main characteristic of the other three types of description is that the verb has to be a state verb (e.g., to be) that describes characters, settings, and things. Descriptions of characters are used only for the antagonist and protagonist; description of setting describes the overall existence, whereas the description of things describes specific things.

Based on the theories of Fahnestock (1983), Halliday and Hasan (1976), Sloan (1983), van Dijk (1977) and Winterowd (1970), the following relationships among clauses (function) were used: (a) sequential (which covers forward, backward, simultaneous, and future), (b) causal (cause-effect), (c) causative, (d) consequential, (e) adversative, (f) alternative, (g) elaborative, (h) additive, (i) locative, (j) temporal, and (k) analogous.

As for the method of analysis, after each main verb in all clauses was categorized into one of the 10 forms, it was analyzed in terms of one of the 16 functions. The percentages of each form and function were compared across the three subject groups, using a statistical analysis (F-test).

SUMMARY OF THE FINDINGS

The three methods of analysis used in this study reveal both similarities and differences, all of which must be seen as tendencies, given the small size of the sample.

In the first method, the linguistic analysis of cohesive ties, differences in language systems play the most important role in the comparison of the two first languages, and transfer of conventional style is the cause of difference in the L2 writing of the TH group. Since there are more cases of similarities than differences in the use of cohesive ties, it seems that the first method of analysis, the analysis of syntactic and semantic relationships, reveals the least difference among the compositions of the three subject groups.

The second and third methods of analysis, the analysis of narrative components and discourse analysis, reveal more salient differences among the three subject groups than does the first method. In these latter cases, most of the differences in the two cultures appear to result from language use rather than language system. It was found that the TH group is more different from the AM group than from the TT group. It can therefore be concluded that the TT and TH groups follow the Thai conventional model of narrative, whereas the AM group follows the Western model.

Nature of Similarities of
the AM and TT Groups

Cohesive ties. The AM and TT groups share similarities in the use of four categories of cohesive ties: comparatively low use of substitution, medium use of conjunction, high use of same-item lexical cohesive ties, and medium use of complementary collocation (Table 8.2). This may be owing to the fact that both American English and Thai share some patterns of use of devices to unify the text cohesively.

Narrative components. Both groups (AM & TT) tend to use chronological order of plot, the person-against-self conflict, and both static and dynamic characters, all of which appear to be the common characteristics of personal narrative (Table 8.3).

Pattern of organization. Both groups show common patterns of narrative composition in the use of amount of discourse in each of the five sections: introduction, sequential action, complicating action, climax, and ending. For example, the largest section is the sequential action and complicating action, and the smallest section seems to be climax.

TABLE 8.2
Comparison of the Use of Cohesive Ties
Among the Three Subject Groups

Cohesive Ties	AM	TH	TT
Similarities:			
1. substitution	L	L	L
2. conjunction	M	M	M
3. same-item-lexical cohesive ties	H	H	H
4. complementary collocation	M	M	M
Differences:			
5. reference	H	M	L
6. lexical cohesive ties (except 3 and 4 above)	M	L	H
7. reference "I"	M	H	M

NOTE: H = high; M = medium; L = low.

TABLE 8.3
Comparison of the Use of the Components of Narrative
Among the Three Subject Groups

	AM	TH	TT
Similarities:			
plot	chronological	chronological	chronological
conflict	self	self	self
character	dynamic/static	dynamic/static	dynamic/static
Differences:			
setting	integral	backdrop	backdrop
theme	implicit	implicit	explicit
scene	real	real	projected
figurative	low	low	medium

Form and function. Both groups use equal amounts of descriptions of settings, characters, and things, which appear to provide necessary background to the stories. Also, a low use of dialogue and generalization are common in all groups, as these are not perceived as parts of the narrative structures. In addition, the low use of comment, action, and mental state in subordinate clauses are common in all groups, as they appear not to form part of the main plot.

Perception of the Function of
Narrative in Society and in School

From the interviews of teachers and students in both cultures in this study, they seemed to agree that narrative is to inform and to entertain.

The Nature of the Differences
of the AM and TT Groups

Cohesive ties. The AM and TT groups differ in the use of all types of reference except "I" and in all types of lexical cohesive ties except same-item and complementary collocation. The AM group tends toward higher use of the former and lower use of the latter (Table 8.2).

Narrative components. The AM and TT groups differ in the use of narrative components in four ways (Table 8.3). First, the AM group uses integral setting more often, whereas the TT group uses backdrop setting more often. Next, the AM group uses an implicit theme more often, whereas the TT group uses an explicit theme more often. In addition, the AM group uses more scenes of the real world, whereas the TT group uses more of a projected world. Finally, more members of the TT group use specifically figurative language than do those of the AM group.

Form and function. The major differences in narrative discourse of the two languages are the higher use of verbs of mental states and description of mental states to express the writers' thoughts in Thai, as opposed to the higher use of verbs of action to present the real actions in the stories of the American students. Also, the difference is shown in the higher use of comment by the AM group than by the TT group, which tends to use generalization (see Figures 8.1, 8.2, and 8.3).

Perception of the Function of
Narrative in Society and in School

The Thai students said they had more occasions to use narrative than did the American students. Besides informing and entertaining,

Code	Form	Function
		<u>Sequential chain:</u>
⬡	Generalization	bg = beginning
		f = forward
◯	Comment	b = backward
▽	Mental state (ms)	s = simultaneous
		ft = future
☐	Action (act)	<u>Causal chain:</u>
DIA	Dialogue (DIA)	ca = cause
		ef = effect
△ act	Description of action	cs = causative
		cq = consequential
		av = adversative
△ ms	Description of mental state	al = alternative
△ ch	Description of character	<u>Description:</u>
		lo = locative
		ad = additive
△ st	Description of setting	tp = temporal
		ana = analogous
△ th	Description of thing	ela = elaborative

Figure 8.1 Codes for the Analysis of Form and Function

Thai narratives are, traditionally, supposed to convey a meaningful purpose. Thus, the Thai students said they ought to conclude the compositions with a moral coda, and, in general, they did.

Nature of the TH Model

Cohesive ties. The TH group is different from both AM and TT groups in three cases: medium use of reference of all types, low use of

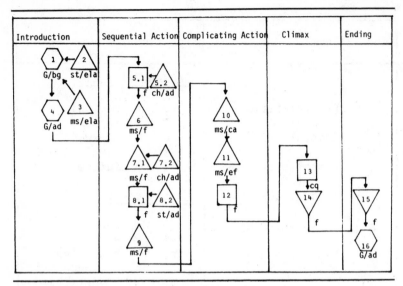

Figure 8.2   The TT Model of Personal Narrative

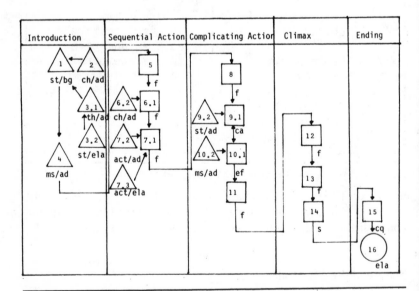

Figure 8.3   The AM Model of Personal Narrative

lexical cohesive ties (except same-item and complementary collocation), and high use of "I" (see Table 8.2).

Narrative components. The TH group seems to follow the TT
model more than the AM model in use of such narrative components
as backdrop setting, chronological order of plot, person-against-self
conflict, and types of scene and characters (see Table 8.3).

Form and function. The TH group seems to be more similar to the
TT group in the use of form and function, as there is only one case in
which the TH differs from the TT group, and that is in use of
description of mental states (addition) in subordinate clauses.

DISCUSSION

The two languages have some different grammatical structures
that cause differences in the respective language system. The use of
reference is an example of this; for instance, the absence of the article
"the" in Thai leads to a lower percentage of use of reference in the TT
group.

There is also a stylistic difference, perhaps related to language. The
Thai students used more highly figurative language, such as metaphor, simile, and personification, because analogy appears to be the
preferred way of describing things in Thai. On the contrary, the
American students in this study did not generally choose this type of
language.

At the same time, rhetoric, the user's knowledge of the language
system and the relation of that system to the context in which
language is used, comes into play. The students in this study
perceived the narrative "register" and its rhetoric as they had been
taught in their cultures. These registers differ in three respects: (a)
context of situation, (b) content, and (c) discourse.

"Context of situation" here means the situation in which narrative
functions in both cultures. From the interviews of teachers, experts,
and students in each culture, it is apparent that the people in the two
cultures perceive the context differently. In Thailand, narratives serve
a purpose other than entertainment; they are the vehicle for exposition
and instruction. What the Thai students considered appropriate
content for a personal narrative were real events that happened in
their lives, so if they thought there was no actual experience

appropriate to a personal narrative, they wrote that there was none. They did not create a story to entertain the readers, but to instruct. On the contrary, the American students said that they created stories to interest the readers, so the function of narrative discourse differs in the two groups.

In terms of discourse the five sections of macrostructure—intro-duction, sequential action, complicating action, climax, and end-ing—which make up the overall narrative discourse structure, are shared characteristics, since they distinguish a narrative discourse from other types of discourse. However, the microstructures of the discourse differ, as mentioned earlier, and result from convention in both languages.

The Thai culture is closely related to Buddhism since Buddhism has been part of Thai life for more than 700 years. The Thai use of setting and scene may be influenced by Buddhism, as Buddhism enhances the belief that Thais do not have control over the events in their lives. The use of backdrop setting in the TT compositions implies that Thai students do not consider setting as important as what is in their minds. What is important, however, is how those events affect their lives. This reason also contributes to the finding that the TT compositions deal more with internal struggle than with external struggle. In addition, the use of futuristic worlds in the projected scenes in the TT compositions implies that Thais believe in the continuity of life, and that they must pursue that futuristic way to fulfill this continuity. Finally, since religion has strong influences on the Thai way of life, the explicit moral theme is inevitable. What the Thai students wrote was for the purpose of giving or teaching moral values.

On the other hand, the interviews seem to reveal that Western culture tends to consider narrative as an instrument over which people have control. The American students plan plot, setting, scene, and theme in terms of cause and effect, and action and reaction. This is evident in the use of real world events more than projected events.

This difference is related to discourse (microstructure). Thai students used more mental states and descriptions of mental states, since they tended to observe actions as outsiders and look into their minds to determine what they felt or thought about the actions. Therefore, they tended to describe their mental states along with actions.

On the opposite side, the American students were not influenced by religious beliefs, and they used narrative as an instrument to present a story to captivate the readers' interest. They were not interested in whether or not the story actually happened in their real lives; their only concern was to make the story interesting. As a result, they used devices in narrative structure to create surprise and suspense through sequences of actions. This may explain why there are more actions in the AM compositions than in the TT and TH compositions.

The interviews of teachers and students support the idea that differences in the written compositions of the American and Thai students are also partly a result of schooling, which supports the conventions of a culture.

The Thai student writing in English shows two types of language learning effects: interlanguage (Selinker, 1972) and transfer (Jakobovits, 1970; B. Kachru, 1983). First, the Thai students show interlanguage when their writing is not similar to either the AM or the TT groups, such as in the use of the article "the." In this case they had to use the article, but it might not have been used as correctly as it was by the American group. Since the article "the" does not exist in Thai, the deviant use of it in the TH group is considered "interlanguage." In this study, "transfer" occurs when the Thai students convey a pattern or model of writing in Thai into writing in English as in the following cases. The use of nouns instead of pronouns according to the degree of formality shows transfer of Thai conventional style into writing in English. In addition, transfer of conventional discourse structure is shown when the Thai students wrote in the same way as they wrote in Thai; examples are frequencies of mental states and descriptions of mental states. Overall, the Thai students' written compositions in English are more similar to the Thai compositions than they are to the American compositions. Clearly they are between two cultural rhetorical models.

CONCLUSION

This study reveals both similarities and differences of narrative written discourse of the two cultures, and claims that the factors that influence the differences seem to be cultural factors rather than linguistic factors.

In the linguistic analysis, it was found that differences in linguistic systems are not the sole factors that cause the differences in written discourse of the two cultures. An example is the high use of reference by the AM group, but the low use of it by the TT group. A factor to be claimed is the different linguistic system, since the article "the" does not exist in Thai. However, one of the other factors that may be claimed is that the Thais prefer to use "noun" instead of "pronominal reference," according to the rules of language use.

With regard to discourse analysis, the cultural factors seem to be prominent. From the global viewpoint, people in the two cultures perceive the functions of narrative differently. The perception of entertaining and informing functions leads to a certain method of teaching and a specific expectation of American teachers. This in turn leads the American students to plan their compositions in a way that captivates the reader's interest, to have certain kinds of narrative components, and to select specific lexical items to serve those purposes. On the other hand, the function of narrative in the Thai culture influences the way of teaching and evaluating student writing. The Thai students, in order to fulfill the expectation of the teachers, have to choose appropriate content, follow the conventional rhetorical structure, and apply the appropriate choice of lexical items.

It is clearly seen that the topics being given influence the choice of register, in this case—narrative, which is influenced by convention in the culture. All of these influence the choice of components, the choice of rhetorical style, and the choice of words to describe the story.

The use of writing in L2 confirms this claim; that is, the similarities of the TT and TH groups in many ways imply that as the Thai students write in L2, they bring with them the appropriateness of language use and the conventional rhetorical style in their first language, because the students at this age have steadily been enculturated in their own culture.

APPENDIX 8.A
THE ANALYSIS OF FORMS AND FUNCTIONS

I SUCCEEDED, AT LAST

Everyone must have hope or dream. (T.1)/In other words, everyone must have dream (T.2)/and they must try to accomplish that dream. (T.3)/But not

*

everybody could get their dream. (T.4)/However, life cannot exist without hope. (T.5)/There is (6.1) a saying that "those who do not have (6.3) hope are the dead (6.2)" (T.6)/In my opinion, I think (7.1) that success in life does not mean (7.2) security in work and economic status. (T.7)/For me, success is the way to reach our goal. (T.8)/

I graduated from the College of Education, Chulalongkorn University. (T.9)/Then I travelled to a district in Maehongsorn Province to work as a teacher. (T.10)/I hoped (11.1) that I would be (11.2) a good teacher. (T.11)/When I arrived (12.2), I felt (12.1) the warm welcome. (T.12)/All villagers were waiting (13.1) smilingly and showing (13.2) confidence in me. (T.13)/All my tiredness has disappeared. (T.14)/When I stayed (15.2) here for a long time, I felt (15.1) lonely. (T.15)/Sometimes I felt hopeless. (T.16)/I thought of going back to Bangkok many times. (T.17)/But I had determined (18.1) that I had to do (18.2) it. (T.18)/Then when I endured (19.2) longer, I began to love (19.1) it. (T.19)/Life is full of hard work yet memorable. (T.20)/My homesick has gone (21.1) because I thought (21.2) that here was (21.3) my home. (T.21)/Everybody was my family. (T.22)/But this place is much different from my place. (T.23)/Here I can drink (24.1) cold water that runs (24.2) through gravels in the stream. (T.24)/But the place where I came (25.4) from I had to (25.1) use coin so that I got (25.2) drinking water whose taste is (25.3) not different from this water. (T.25)/I spent (26.1) time teaching until I forgot (26.2) how long I have been (26.3) here. (T.26)/However, I remembered (27.1) many years had gone by (27.2). (T.27)/

Tonight I received (28.1) a letter from a student whom I taught (28.2) in my first year. (T.28)/He had the opportunity to continue his study in Bangkok. (T.29)/He wrote (30.1) that that day he received (30.2) his degree from the King (T.30)/and he wanted to thank me. (T.31)/I walked out of my house. (T.32)/I felt (33.1) very happy that I could not described. (33.2) (T.33)/I walked along a winding path of a cart. (T.34)/The stars began to dwindle. (T.35)/All things in the world seemed to congratulate me. (T.36)/The wind seemed to whistle endlessly. (T.37)/The moon was laughing. (T.38)/Crickets were chirping. (T.39)/Bamboo boughs were beating repeatedly at one another like the sound of music. (T.40)/I laid (41.1) on the soil that I love (41.2). (T.41)/The tear began to come down my tough cheeks (T.42)/and I said (43.1) to myself, "At last, I succeeded (43.2)". (T.43)

I MADE A HARD DECISION

My shiny, bright red motor scooter did not know (1.1) that it was approaching (1.2) its doom and that it would soon become (1.3) a bent, bashed, discarded piece of dull metal. (T.1)/I was gaily riding my motor scooter down a one-lane, one-way street. (T.2)/Everything was great! (T.3)/I had good grades, (T.4)/summer vacation had just started, (T.5)/I was soon to begin a profitable summer job, (T.6)/and I would have the house to myself for a whole week! (T.7)/Everyone around me saw (8.1) my enormous grin, and smiled (8.2) in turn, although my smile was only directed (8.3) at the air in front of me. (T.8)/

Then everything happened at once. (T.9)/An enormous Mack truck (it seemed (11.1) all the more enormous because I was hunched (11.2) inside my tiny motor scooter) (T.11)/turned into the one-way street! (T.10)/As the lumbering truck thundered (12.2) and bounced (12.3) toward my obscure, faintly humming motor scooter, I thought (12.1) to myself, "Hey, Melinda. Don't you need to make a decision? And Fast?" (12.4) (T.12)/I was faced with two possibilities (T.13)/(there would have been (14.1) three if my motor scooter had (14.2) a rocket launcher). (T.14)/I could try to get past the truck, (T.15)/or I could ensure a safe life by crashing myself into one of the parked cars along each side of the road. (T.16)/Getting past the truck would be some feat; (T.17)/the truck and I would be shadowing each other's moves. (T.18)/Maybe it would look funny, (T.19)/but it was a matter of life and death! (T.20)/The other alternative was a bit easier. (T.21)/I had to do (22.1) no maneuvering, hardly any steering, and didn't have to rack my brains (22.2) just to slip past the truck. (T.22)/All I needed to do was crash myself into one of the parked cars, (T.23)/and then I wouldn't have to worry! (T.24)/Although it wasn't (25.2) an easy task, I decided (25.1) to crash myself into a car. (T.25)/All the while the Mack truck was slowly closing in on me. (T.26)/Before I turned away (27.2) to crash into a car, I made fleeting glimpse (27.1) of the truck driver. (T.27)/He wasn't holding his head in agony. (T.28)/Nor was he trying in desperation to steer away from me. (T.29)/His grin almost matched (30.1) the grin I had (30.2) before I saw (30.3) the truck. (T.30)/Well, the truck vroomed. (T.31)/I directed my motor scooter toward a parked Porsche 9211. (T.32)/If my motor scooter was to "die" (33.2), its life was to end (33.1) alongside one of its idols. (T.33)/My life flashed before me. (T.34)/What sarcasm my brain had it gave (35.1) me a view of my smiling face when I bought (35.2) my brand-new motor scooter! (T.35)/But soon the Porsche loomed forward. (T.36)/I remember (37.1), as I hit (37.2) the car, the air current from the passing truck. (T.37)/I thought (38.1), "That's a nice breeze (38.2). Where did it come from? (38.3)" (T.38)/I hit the car. (T.39)

I MADE A HARD DECISION

Somebody said (1.1), "There is (1.2) no friend in war and no friend in love". (T.1)/It's a hard decision to choose one between my love and my friends. (T.2)/I got this problem many months ago. (T.3)/I fell in love with my friend's girlfriend. (T.4)/I decided (5.1) to leave my friend and get along (5.2) with her. (T.5)/I knew (6.1) that I could do (6.2). (T.6)/But if I do (7.2) that I'll lose (7.1) my friend. (T.7)/Although he was not my best friend. (T.8)/So I didn't know what to do. (T.9)

I tried to make a decision about this (T.10)/but it's (11.1) hard one that I've ever met (11.2) before. (T.11)/So I've let the time choose it for me. (T.12)

I called her two times a day. (T.13)/I loved to call somebody. (T.14)/It's the best way to relax (T.15)/but I would be taken a time. (T.16)/Talking on the phone affects my study! (T.17)/I've spent two or three hours with a phone. (T.18)/I go home at 8:00 p.m. (19.1) and spend (19.2) two hours with a phone everyday. (T.19)/So the time that I started (20.2) my education is (20.1) about ten or ten-thirty every night. (T.20)/When I called (21.2) her, I felt (21.1) that I did (21.3) something wrong. (T.21)/I talked with her about this problem. (T.22)/I asked (23.1) her if I did (23.2) something wrong. (T.23)/She said, (24.1) "No!" (24.2)/She said (25.1) that it was (25.2) not my faults, (T.25)/I didn't treat my friend in a wrong way (T.26)/but I don't think so! (T.27)/

One thing you should know, (T.28)/it's (29.1) where my friend lives. (29.2) (T.29)/He lived in England near London. (T.30)/There wasn't much time for them to spend together (T.31)/but I don't want to take a chance in this position. (T.32)/

But now he came (33.1) back to Thailand so I must make (33.2) a decision. (T.33)/It's (34.1) a very hard decision that I've ever had (34.2). (T.34)/You know (35.1) what I decided (35.2)/. (T.35)/I decided to leave her (36.1) and be (36.2) like her friend, maybe her best friend! (T.36)/You know (37.1) why I decided (37.2) like this? (T.37)/I have two reasons, (T.38), one is for my friend, (T.39)/the other is for my life. (T.40)/I wrote this reason above. (T.41)/Do you know (42.1) what I got (42.2) after this decision? (T.42)/Oh! It's great. (T.43).

Although I lost (44.2) her but,
I saved (44.1) my friend (T.44)/and
I saved my live." (T.45)

REFERENCES

Booth, W. C. (1983). *The rhetoric of fiction* (2nd ed.). Chicago: University of Chicago Press.

Chafe, W. L. (1970). *Meaning and the structure of language.* Chicago: University of Chicago Press.

Chatman, S. (1978). *Story and discourse.* Ithaca, NY: Cornell University Press.

Connor, U. (1982). *A study of discourse features in ESL students' compositions: Cohesion and coherence*. Paper presented at the Fifth Annual Colloquium on Classroom Centered Research, TESOL 1982, Hawaii.

Connor, U., & McGagg, R. (1983). Cross-cultural differences and perceived quality in written paraphrasis of English expository prose. *Applied Linguistics, 4*(3), 259-268.

Fahnestock, J. (1983). Semantic and lexical coherence. *College Composition and Communication, 34*(4), 400-416.

Frye, N. (1957). *Anatomy of criticism*. Princeton, NJ: Princeton University Press.

Genette, G. (1980). *Narrative discourse, an essay in method*. Ithaca, NY: Cornell University Press.

Halliday, M.A.K., & Hasan, R. (1976). *Cohesion in English*. London: Longman.

Hunt, K. W. (1965). *Grammatical structures written at three grade levels* (Revised Report No. 3). Urbana, IL: National Council of Teachers of English.

Indrasuta, I. (1987). *A comparison of the written compositions of American and Thai students*. Unpublished doctoral dissertation, University of Illinois, Urbana-Champaign.

Jakobovits, L. (1970). *Foreign language learning*. Rowley, MA: Newbury House.

Kachru, B. B. (1983). *The Indianization of English: The English language in India*. Delhi: Oxford University Press.

Kachru, Y. (1982). Linguistics and written discourse in particular languages: Contrastive studies: English and Hindi. *Annual Review of Applied Linguistics, 3*, 50-69.

Kachru, Y. (1985, December). Discourse strategies, pragmatics and ESL: Where are we going? *RELC Journal, 16*(2).

Kaplan, R. (Ed.) (1982). *Annual review of applied linguistics* (Vol. 3). Rowley, MA: Newbury House.

Kaplan, R. B. (1966). Cultural thought patterns in intercultural education. *Language Learning, 16*(1-2), 1-20.

Labov, W., & Waletzky, J. (1967). Narrative analysis: Oral versions of personal experience. In J. Helm (Ed.), *Essays on the verbal and visual arts*. Seattle: University of Washington Press.

Longacre, R. E. (1976). *An anatomy of speech notions*. Lisse, The Netherlands: Peter de Ridder.

Lyons, R. (1984). *Autobiography: A reader for writers* (2nd ed.). New York: Oxford University Press.

Perrine, L. (1959). *Story and structure*. New York: Harcourt Brace.

Scott, V., & Madden, D. (1980). *Studies in the short story* (5th ed.). New York: Holt, Rinehart & Winston.

Selinker, L. (1972). Interlanguage. *IRAL, 10*, 201-231.

Sloan, G. (1983). Transitions: Relationships among T-units. *College Composition and Communication, 34*(4), 447-453.

van Dijk, T. A. (1977). *Text and context: Exploration in the semantics and pragmatics of discourse*. London: Longman.

Wann, L. (1939). *Century readings in the English essay*. New York: Appleton-Century-Crofts.

Winterowd, W. R. (1970). The grammar of cohesion. *College English, 31*, 828-835.

9

Cultural Differences in Writing and Reasoning Skills

SYBIL B. CARLSON

The research presented in this chapter approaches contrastive rhetoric from a different vantage point than other chapters in this volume. This orientation addresses an immediate, pragmatic situation—large-scale assessment of the writing proficiency of nonnative speakers of English within English-speaking communities in institutions of higher education in the United States and Canada. The major objective of the current study is to gain more information about the reasoning skills being tapped by the analytical measure of the Graduate Record Examinations (GRE) General Test by examining how performance on its constituent item types relate to alternative criteria. A second objective is to ascertain the extent to which additional information on examinees' analytical skills might be obtained by more detailed analyses of their writing performance.

The objectives of this research afforded the opportunity to design scoring schemes that reflect different perspectives of reasoning skills demonstrated in academic writing tasks. The schemes represent the criteria that are applied to written composition, ranging from general evaluations that invoke implicit cultural norms (holistic scores) to more specific identification of salient textual features (computer analyses).

By viewing writing samples from these different perspectives and, further, comparing these observations with one another and with scores on standardized tests, we were able to make more explicit the criteria applied in the evaluation of American academic prose. Not surprisingly, the preliminary findings indicate that more complex and specific evaluations of compositions may reveal more significant information regarding cross-cultural and individual differences in approaches to the production of effective papers. The design of this study and its findings are presented in a subsequent section.

PREVIOUS RESEARCH FOUNDATIONS

The current research builds on the results of two extensive studies that culminated in the addition of a writing sample to the Test of English as a Foreign Language (TOEFL). The first study, funded by the TOEFL program, consisted of a survey that enabled us to define writing competence situationally, and identify the kinds of writing tasks that native and nonnative undergraduate and graduate students would be expected to perform successfully when they enter post-secondary institutions in the United States and Canada (Bridgeman & Carlson, 1983).

The definition of competence in writing was restricted to the academic writing skills that demonstrate functionally based communicative competency—the ability to use language to communicate effectively within the specific context in which the communication takes place by conveying the ideas the writer intended to convey to the recipient of the communication (Canale, 1983; Canale & Swain, 1979; Munby, 1978; Walz, 1982). Because our situational context included the evaluation of the writing skills of nonnative speakers of English at the beginning of their educational training on this continent, this definition also incorporated the views of contrastive rhetoric. It was particularly important to recognize that writers from different cultures have learned rhetorical patterns (Kaplan, 1966, 1972, 1976, 1977, 1982) that may differ from patterns used in academic settings in the United States and that are reinforced by their educational experiences in their specific cultures (Purves, 1985, 1986). In addition, current investigations in the field have led us to appreciate that the definitions of effective writing are being modified and expanded to reflect more appropriately the differential task demands of writing in different situational contexts (Ruth & Murphy, 1987). With these perspectives, the writing performance of nonnative speakers as well as of native speakers cannot be evaluated in terms of traditional, possibly narrow criteria (Park, this volume). Instead, we recognize that ideas can be effectively communicated by combining the elements of language in diverse ways.

The results of the survey also indicated that no single writing topic was universally accepted by all academic disciplines surveyed. Two types of topics were perceived by respondents as distinctively different tasks.

One type of task asks the writer to compare and contrast and take a position (Compare/Contrast), while the other type asks the writer to describe and intepret a chart or graph (Chart/Graph). The two types of tasks were used in the subsequent and current research.

The second study (Carlson, Bridgemam, Camp, & Waanders, 1985), jointly funded by the GRE and TOEFL programs, investigated the relationship of writing performance on four writing samples written in English to scores on other measures (the GRE General Test, the TOEFL, and a multiple-choice test of writing ability). Overall, the results suggested that, with careful topic selection and adequate training of raters, writing samples can provide a reliable measure of the English language proficiency of nonnative speakers as well as of native speakers of English, and that direct measures of writing performance, although substantially correlated with multiple-choice measures such as the TOEFL and GRE General Test, contribute additional information regarding English language proficiency.

For the purposes of the TOEFL, this research suggested that holistic scoring would serve most appropriately for the time being, given the "state of the art" in our ability to deliver defensibly valid and reliable estimates of writing competence and the necessity for efficient and cost effective admissions testing.

The research also suggested further questions to investigate, leading to an exploratory study currently funded by the GRE Board for which the preliminary findings are reported in this chapter (Carlson & Powers, in progress).

THE CURRENT STUDY

In the previous study, one aspect that clearly distinguished levels of writing competence, apparent to the investigators and scorers in reading the writing samples, was the quality of the reasoning expressed in the papers. In the postsecondary contexts in which students write papers in order to communicate their ideas within a discipline, educators evaluate observable features of the written test in order to make judgments about the quality of student thought. This situation poses a practical measurement concern. Because academic grades are assigned on the basis of such judgments, and because these judgments reflect implicit cultural norms, this research focuses on making explicit the criteria that influence the judgments. Although this study is exploratory, based on somewhat restricted data and sample sizes, it is intended to stimulate further investigation. As described in the next section of this chapter, we attempted to develop a variety of scoring schemes that reflected the perceptions of different communities of readers regarding the reasoning skills that could be observed, reliably and with validity, in the written discourse of native and nonnative speakers of English. Ultimately, one or more elements of such schemes might contribute to our understanding of the differential performance of writers from different cultures and, possibly, toward effective approaches to feedback in instruction when writing skills are exercised.

The data for this study consist of 406 writing samples prepared by 203 students, primarily nonnative speakers of English (6 Arabic, 73 Chinese, 35 Spanish, 89 English) who had recently taken the GRE General Test for admission to institutions of higher education in the United States. The bulk of this data was collected for the previous TOEFL/GRE project, in which the writing samples were scored to reflect writing skills. Additional writing samples were collected from 80 native speakers of English who had recently taken the GRE General Test and who were in their first year of graduate education in the United States in order to supplement the sample of native speakers.

In using the term "reasoning skills," we do not assume that the writing sample data will provide information about the thinking processes applied by the writers, or that we can develop scores that describe sophisticated constructs such as analytic reasoning. We recognize that the processes involved in thinking and writing are investigated more legitimately through protocol analysis, or "think-aloud" studies. In addition, we understand that the quality of thinking can be inferred only indirectly when the product of that thinking is in written form, and that, in fact, poorly developed writing skills can mask an individual's ability to express thoughts verbally.

We did not approach this task by developing a hypothetical model of the complex factors that might contribute to writing that might be judged "different," but equivalently competent within a cross-cultural perspective. Instead, this research is exploratory, intended to obtain more information that may lead to hypotheses to be tested, and, eventually, to possible models to be tested that might be useful to the evaluation and instruction of writing. An accumulated body of research data might yield systematic patterns of relationships among the variables we have created and labeled, therefore contributing inferences made about the validity of the model(s) (American Psychological Association, 1984).

THE WRITING TASKS

On the basis of the findings of the writing survey study, two types of topics were selected to serve as complements to one another, particularly since the demands of each task would be expected to elicit different writing skills that are required in postsecondary academic writing. For the TOEFL/GRE study, writing samples written in response to four topics, two of each topic type (Compare/Contrast and Chart/Graph), were collected.

The results of the TOEFL/GRE study indicated that correlations among holistic scores were as high across topic types as within topic types.

This result suggests that (1) the different topics did not elicit qualitatively different writing performance, and/or (2) the readers maintained a comparable scale for evaluating the writing samples, despite performance fluctuations from topic to topic. These results should not be interpreted as evidence that papers written in response to any topic or topic type would yield equivalent scoring agreement. The correlations reflect the relative, rather than absolute, values of student scores (e.g., a student with a high score on one topic received a high score on the other topic). Since a holistic score summarizes an overall, general impression, different features of writing may have contributed to the same score for different individuals as well as for different tasks. Although readers could learn to internalize criteria for reliably evaluating writing samples within a specific context, it is likely that performance varies both in degree and kind, in response to different task demands. Because the single scores are likely to reflect different combinations of features, it is possible that important differences might be revealed if multiple scores are used.

Because the data analyses indicated that the holistic writing scores within and across topics were highly correlated, the writing samples obtained for the two contrasting topic types, Space and Farming, were used for further analyses in the current study. The Space prompt, a Compare/Contrast topic type, asked students to write an essay comparing the advantages and disadvantages of the exploration of outer space and to take a position. The Farming topic, a Chart/Graph topic type, presented three graphs (number of farms, size of farm population, average farm sizes) depicting changes in farming in the United States from 1940-1980.

The writers were asked to write a report that interpreted and interrelated the graphs and explained the conclusions reached from the information in the graphs, using the graphs to support the conclusions.

All writing samples were collected under controlled examination conditions with a 30-minute time limit per task. For the nonnative speakers, the papers were written during the afternoon of the same day the candidates took the TOEFL.

At the outset, we recognized that the papers, obtained for somewhat different purposes, had limitations but would serve the purposes of this exploratory study. Ideally, the demands of the writing tasks might have been different and more explicit. For example, the instructions to the student writers did not indicate that reasoning skills were to be evaluated. Also, the task demands might have been structured differently to elicit specific reasoning skills. Despite these drawbacks, the project staff and collaborators agreed that some reasoning skills could be identified since they contributed to the organization of the ideas developed in the papers. Another limitation was posed by the relatively small sample sizes, particularly if broken down by major field and native language groups. As a result, the data collected from the small subgroup of Arabic speakers were included only in the total-group analyses, and the score data were not analyzed by major fields.

THE SCORING SCHEMES

In order to provide the kinds of information that are needed to fulfill the purpose(s) of a writing assessment program, evaluators have developed a range of different scoring schemes. Holistic scoring in its various forms recognizes that the singular factors that constitute a piece of writing are elements that work together to make a total impression on the reader. Holistic scores, though, do not provide sufficient information for diagnostic purposes or for research that will lead us to a better understanding of the interplay of the numerous variables that influence and contribute to a definition of the writing skills being evaluated. As a result, many different scoring schemes have been devised in order to obtain multiple scores. Typically, these schemes tend to oversimplify and mechanize the evaluation task by adopting or inventing a proliferation of labels that reflect a particular reader perspective.

These labels do not necessarily reflect the perceptions of another community of readers who do not share the same perspective. The readers who share a common perspective may produce highly reliable judgments in evaluating writing samples, but the validity of the scores assigned to these labels is questionable unless readers who represent a different audience can agree with these judgments as well. Making a match between the expectations of the reader and the writer involves yet another complex interaction, since readers and writers have acquired their idiosyncratic approaches to defining competent performance, largely through educational experience within their particular cultures or subcultures.

For the current study, several experts in writing assessment and linguistics, with experience in research and instruction in reasoning/writing skills and in English as a second language (ESL), were convened for two days in May 1985 to discuss the objectives of the research and to formulate strategies for developing scoring schemes that would emphasize the reasoning skills that might be observed in the writing samples. Three of these schemes are named after their primary developers. The following scoring schemes were applied to the writing samples: the Purves/Söter scheme, the Moss scheme, the Reid holistic reasoning scheme, the holistic writing scheme, and the UNIX Writer's Workbench (WWB) system,[1] supplemented by Lawrence Frase's computer analyses.

The two holistic schemes represent approaches to evaluation for which the criteria being applied are least explicit. Although the readers used benchmark papers to maintain comparable standards, the benchmarks provide examples in which the integration of potentially different and discriminable features contribute to one numerical score. The Purves/Söter and Moss schemes attempt to evaluate several characteristics of the reasoning process demonstrated in written prose that might be identified by human judges. At the extreme of the range of scoring specificity, the WWB programs yield a considerable number of explicit features of the texts.

The Purves/Söter Scheme

Alan Purves and Anna Söter, then at the University of Illinois in Urbana-Champaign, conducted preliminary analyses of 20 representative writing samples for the Space and Farming writing topics. They adapted, modified, and extended Carroll's (1960) descriptive vectors of prose style, from which they derived 14 unipolar scales that were applied to the papers. A factor analysis yielded three factors that reflected content/thinking, organization, and style/tone as identifiable features of the essays. This work culminated in the development of the scoring scheme (Purves, 1985) used for both the Space and Farming papers in this study. Briefly, the scheme identifies the following features:

    (1) content/thinking
            (a) adequacy of information presented
            (b) richness of additional information
            (c) relationships drawn
            (d) inferences made
            (e) synthesis
            (f) evaluation
            (g) consideration of alternatives
    (2) organization
            (a) framing
            (b) grouping
            (c) unity
    (3) style/tone
            (a) objectivity
            (b) tentativeness
            (c) metalanguage

The specific aspects of each of the three major dimensions were evaluated separately, using a 1-5 scale with "1" as the lowest rating.

These features are further defined in greater detail; Anna Söter developed an even more extensive scoring guide, containing examples from the papers as well (Söter, 1985).

The Space and Farming writing samples were rated by four experts at the University of Illinois with knowledge and experience in the evaluation of English and ESL writing. They were trained in two sessions in which the criteria were discussed in relation to 10 samples per topic. During their evaluation of the full set of papers, the readers referred to a chart of categories and criteria. All four readers rated all papers for the Space topic. For the Farming topic, two different groups of two readers rated the odd-numbered papers and two readers rated the even-numbered papers.

Estimates of reader reliability of scores assigned to the separate categories within each dimension were quite low. These separate categories, however, are assumed to represent elements that contribute to and define each of the three major dimensions. Thus the separate subscores assigned by each reader were summed within each dimension, and reader reliability coefficients (alpha) were calculated for the three dimensions for each topic. The reader reliability estimates for the Space topic were considerably higher than for the Farming topic: content/thinking, .88; organization, .85; style/tone, .85. For the Farming topic, the reader reliabilities were as follows: content/thinking, .66; organization, .63; style/tone, .66. These reliability coefficients for the Space topic fall within a range that is acceptable in the evaluation of open-ended responses by human judges. For the Farming topic, however, the readers appeared to experience greater difficulty in making reliable judgments about the features of these papers. Because the reader reliability estimates were not abysmally low, but only lower than what is considered highly acceptable, the Farming scores were still included for the purposes of this study. These reliabilities would not be acceptable in any testing or other decision-making situation, but this topic still might provide some useful information in this exploration, as long as interpretations regarding the Farming data take into account the lower reliabilities of scores.

For the final analyses, the scores assigned by each reader, summed over each of the three dimensions for each of the two topics, were averaged in order to obtain one score per student for each dimension for each topic (a total of six scores per student).

The Moss Scheme

Pamela Moss, of the School of Education of the University of Pittsburgh and director of evaluation for the Critical Thinking Project of the Pittsburgh Public Schools, developed a scheme that builds on the work of Stephan Toulmin and his colleagues (1984). Toulmin uses the word "argument" in a broad sense to mean any claim and the reasons that support or justify it. He has described the features of all arguments as follows:

> The *claim* is the statement of one's ideas; *grounds* provide the foundation of evidence for the claim; *warrants* provide the rules, laws, formulae, or principles on which the grounds are based; *modal qualities* indicate the degree of certainty with which the argument is made; and *possible rebuttals* deal with circumstances where the argument or claim may break down. For the writing tasks in this research, advantages and disadvantages of space exploration, the statement of the writer's position, and the conclusions drawn from these elements were all considered to be claims. For Toulmin, these elements are generic to all arguments, but manifest themselves in different ways in different disciplines (Moss, personal communication, 1986).

With Toulmin's scheme as an approach to organizing data regarding reasoning skills, Moss read through sample papers in order to distill the ways in which these elements might be manifested in the discourse produced in response to the two topics. The scoring scheme she designed is intended to identify the elements relevant to thinking or reasoning and to ignore those aspects of the essays—focus, organization, irrelevancies, redundancies—that usually are taken into account when evaluating writing and may be differentially valued in different cultures.

Related but specific scoring schemes were developed for the two topics since reasoning skills were evidenced in different ways in response to the specific demands of each topic type. Also, the labels for the elements of the scheme were couched in more common terms, eliminating the need for readers to be familiar with the Toulmin approach. Essentially, readers were asked to list all claims made in the essays and then to evaluate each claim independently. Emphasis was placed on ideas in context rather than on the sequence of ideas in order to stress reasoning skills and not the writing skill of organization. Instead of evaluating the characteristics of the papers, readers indicated the presence (or absence) of the particular features, resulting in scores that reflected frequencies of occurrence. Five readers, all experts in the instruction and evaluation of English and ESL writing skills, spent five days scoring the papers using the Moss scheme. A full day per topic was required for the training of the readers by a project director. It involved working with sets of sample papers in order for each reader to arrive at internalized definitions of the reasoning skills in the scheme as they are evidenced in written discourse (e.g., to agree on the kinds of performance that indicate a "reasonable inference"). The tallies on the score sheets were compressed to reflect the major elements of reasoning skills that the scheme was designed to identify. Four scores were derived for the Space (Compare/Contrast) topic:

(1) claims
(2) support (justifications)—evidence and explanation
(3) qualifications/rebuttals
(4) integration—claims as grounds for subsequent claims

For the Farming (Chart/Graph) topic, six scores were derived, four scores that were parallel to the Space topic, and two scores (1 and 2) that are specific to the topic type:

(1) graph reading skills
(2) deduction skills
(3) claims
(4) justifications
(5) qualifications/rebuttals
(6) integration

The score derivations, excepting the two unique Farming scores, involved dividing the tallies for each score by the tallies reflecting the number of ideas in order to eliminate fluency in evaluating the quality of reasoning skills.

Estimates of reader reliability (Kuder-Richardson) for the Moss scheme were higher for the Farming topic than for the Space topic, the reverse of the trend for the reliability estimates for the Purves scheme.

For the Farming topic, the reliability coefficients were as follows: graph reading, .81; deductions, .62; claims, .71; justifications, .55; qualifications/rebuttals, .45; and integration, .30. It is interesting to note that the indicators of graph reading skills were easier for readers to identify (.81 reliability). As the elements of reasoning skills become more elusive and less concrete (e.g., qualifications/rebuttals and integrations), they were identified less reliably. Another reason for the lower reliability of these elements is that very few writing samples evidenced these higher-order reasoning skills; slight disagreements among readers regarding the small number of papers demonstrating a particular characteristic are likely to influence dramatically estimates of agreement. Given these low reliabilities, however, the integration score was eliminated from the Moss scheme analyses for the Farming topic.

Estimates of reader reliability for the Space topic were as follows: claims, .59; support, .61; integration, -.02; and qualifications, .51. The extremely low coefficients for integration again can be explained by the very small number of writers that evidenced this aspect of reasoning. The score for integration consequently was dropped from the analyses.

For the final analyses, the scores assigned by the two readers were averaged to obtain one score for each element of the Moss scoring scheme for each writer on each topic. As with the Purves/Soter scheme, scores with only moderate reader reliabilities were retained, but the reliabilities need to be taken into account when interpreting the data.

Reid Holistic Scoring Scheme

Joy Reid, associate professor in the Intensive English Program of the Department of English at Colorado State University, has considerable experience in ESL writing instruction and research, and in evaluating the compositions of ESL writers, both as a reader and in using the Writer's Workbench. Working with sample papers and with ETS writing assessment expert, Janet Waanders, she developed a broad rubric to guide readers who evaluated the papers holistically, with an emphasis on reasoning rather than on writing skills. The same readers who applied the Moss Scheme were trained to assign the general-impression scores by using benchmark papers that reflected the range of 1-6 score scale (with "1" as the lowest score). A holistic reasoning score was assigned by each of two readers per paper before the readers applied the Moss Scheme to the paper.

Although the overall rating of the papers may have partially influenced the readers' Moss evaluations, the readers felt that they perceived an overall rating on the first reading, regardless, and that the use of the Moss Scheme required a different kind of decision making in that the treatment is more analytical and did not involve judgments about degrees of quality or sequence.

Estimates of reader reliability (coefficient alpha) for both topics for the holistic reasoning scores were highly acceptable: .88 for the Space topic and .86 for the Farming topic. For the final analyses, the scores were averaged across the two readers, resulting in one holistic reasoning score per writer per topic.

Holistic Scoring of Writing Skills

A major portion of the writing samples had been holistically scored for the evaluation of writing skills for the TOEFL/GRE study. A full description of the scoring appears in the report of that research (Carlson et al., 1985). This method was duplicated in the scoring of the 80 additional papers per topic that were collected to supplement the writing samples for this study. These papers were read in less than one day by two readers, one an ESL writing expert, the other an English writing expert, who were trained by a chief reader. All three readers had participated as readers in the TOEFL/GRE study, and were trained with the same benchmark papers used previously in order to maintain the same standards. Each paper was read by two readers, who required less than one half day to evaluate the Space and Farming topics separately.

Estimates of reader reliability (coefficient alpha) for the holistic writing scores for both topics were acceptably high: .89 for the Space topic and .92 for the Farming topic. The scores were averaged over the two readers for the final analyses, yielding one holistic writing score per writer per topic.

Differential Reader Reliability Estimates for Language Groups

Of the four scoring schemes that required human judgments, the estimates of reader reliability differed for separate language groups and from the total sample estimates, without apparent systematicity, with the exception of estimates for the holistic reasoning scores. For the holistic reasoning scores, estimates of reader reliability were approximately equivalent, except that the reliability of the scores for the Chinese students for the Space topic were somewhat higher than for the other language groups. The reader reliability estimates for the holistic writing scores for all language groups but the English speakers fell within the same range. The reliability estimates for the English group undoubtedly were low because of restriction of range—their holistic writing scores were all very high. For the Purves/Söter scheme, the reader reliability estimates were lower than those for the other language groups for the content/thinking and organization scores for the Space topic and for organization scores for the Farming topic. Reliability estimates for both the English and Spanish groups were somewhat lower than those for the Chinese group for the content/thinking and style/tone scores for the Space topic. The reliability estimates for the Moss scheme were similarly and unsystematically variable for the different language groups. For the claims and qualifications scores for the Space topic, the reader reliability estimates for the Chinese were higher than for the other language groups, but lower for the support score. For the deductions, claims, and justifications scores for the Farming topic, the estimates were higher for the Spanish group.

The differential reliability estimates observed for these data should not be viewed as generalizable trends. The exploratory nature of the scoring schemes, the relatively small language group samples, and the task demands all probably contributed in undetermined ways to these differences. They are noted, however, because subsequent research should investigate whether reader reliability estimates differ by language group, and whether they do so systematically. Perhaps readers experience greater ease or difficulty in identifying and evaluating certain characteristics of written prose that may be influenced by the different approaches taken by writers from different cultures.

Writer's Workbench Textual Analyses

The UNIX Writer's Workbench (WWB) system, a computerized text analysis tool, was used in the TOEFL/GRE study to obtain detailed information about the features of the texts for a representative subsample of the writing samples. The data suggested that certain characteristics of writing that are attended to by a human reader are related to, and therefore are likely to have influenced, the evaluation (in this case, holistic evaluation) of a piece of writing. It is possible that readers are responding unconsciously to particular features of writing that affect their judgments. Thus we realized that the WWB programs could contribute to our understanding of the implicit criteria that are being applied in holistic scoring. Furthermore, we recognized that multiple scores assigned by human judges might yield additional insights about these criteria. Thus, in the current study, we extended the Workbench analyses to our newly designed scoring schemes.

The Writer's Workbench software programs at Colorado State University (CSU) were used to analyze all writing samples. A writing instructor was employed to type all papers for computer input. Her work was edited for fidelity to the actual papers, and the WWB output was obtained. In addition, Lawrence Frase, who contributed to the development of the Workbench programs at AT&T Bell Labs, provided advice and conducted other exploratory analyses.

The WWB programs incorporate expert knowledge from rhetoric and psychology, offer a variety of approaches to assessing writing skills, and are capable of being adjusted to the standards for a particular writing population (Cherry et al., 1983; Kiefer & Smith, 1984; Smith & Kiefer, 1982).

The CSU programs have been refined over several years to reflect the standards for academic writing at the college level (Reid & Findlay, 1986). The WWB output yields a considerable amount of data with which to describe the syntactic and semantic features of written prose in numerical or quantifiable forms. Many of these features were highly interdependent (e.g., number of words), infrequently observed in these data (e.g., compound-complex sentences), or unnecessarily specific; for our purposes, we focused on certain features that might provide information relevant to reasoning/writing skills. The number of features to be used in the analyses was further reduced on the basis of the intercorrelations of the features— features that were highly correlated, hence very interdependent, were reduced to one representative feature, and some features were eliminated if they were identified infrequently in this set of papers (see list in Table 9.1). For example, the percentage of shorter sentences

TABLE 9.1
Means and Standard Deviations of Variables in Analysis (N = 203)

Variables	Space Topic (29 variables)		Farming Topic (30 variables)	
	Mean	S.D.	Mean	S.D.
Holistic writing	4.23	1.57	4.34	1.58
Holistic reasoning	3.49	1.21	3.53	1.33
Purves/Söter Scheme				
content	18.44	4.80	17.72	4.94
organization	8.23	2.14	8.01	2.50
style and tone	7.56	2.12	7.70	1.99
Moss Scheme—Space				
claims	5.88	2.20	—	—
support	2.67	1.53	—	—
qualifications	.45	.54	—	—
Moss Scheme—Farming				
graph reading	—	—	3.70	1.36
deductions	—	—	.89	1.00
claims	—	—	2.70	1.21
justifications	—	—	1.63	1.13
qualifications	—	—	.15	.25
Writer's workbench variables				
number of suggestions	6.14	4.58	6.35	5.06
number of spelling errors	2.81	2.55	2.09	2.47
% vague words	6.71	2.54	5.22	2.67
number to check	2.50	1.77	2.07	1.66
average sentence length	21.10	6.69	22.11	7.50
% shorter sentences	27.40	14.49	28.12	13.34
% longer sentences	11.58	8.40	11.42	9.25
% to be verbs	81.14	11.86	75.21	18.74
% passive voice	11.32	9.09	11.56	10.46
% nominalizations	3.56	1.42	2.80	1.32
average word length	4.70	.31	4.65	.27
% content words	54.88	3.80	57.48	4.00
average length content words	6.20	.46	5.86	.67
% prepositions	11.00	2.42	13.33	3.35
% adjectives	15.07	3.14	17.60	3.60
% abstract	3.55	1.44	2.90	1.32

(continued)

TABLE 9.1 Continued

GRE General Test Scores	Mean	S.D.
Verbal		
sentence completion	6.99	3.85
discrete verbal	19.02	8.89
reading comprehension	11.95	5.60
Analytical reasoning		
analytical reasoning	21.25	6.61
logical reasoning	5.85	2.77

was eliminated in favor of the percentage of longer sentences and average sentence length. Many of these features are self-explanatory, and serve as generally agreed-upon indicators of good and less effective writing skills; more complete definitions appear in Reid and Findlay (1986) and the other WWB references. Those features most relevant to the data analyses in this chapter are described in the section reporting the results.

The efficiency and reliability of a computerized text analysis system, of course, are high in relation to human judges. Because the programs lack the human judgment needed to identify certain aspects of English prose, however, the programs are not 100% reliable. The parts of speech program, for example, is approximately 90% accurate; the identification of passive voice is 93% accurate (Cherry et al., 1983; Frase, in press). Also, the program that flags spelling errors is not always accurate. For this study, words that actually were not misspelled but were listed in the output as such were eliminated from the counts.

GRE Part Scores

The GRE General Test is composed of three major sections, verbal, quantitative, and analytical reasoning. Because the emphasis of the study was on verbal and reasoning skills, the quantitative scores were not included in the analyses. Separate part scores for the GRE General Test are not reported to candidates because their contribution to the instrument depends on the combination of the parts. For research purposes, though, we were able to calculate separate scores for the parts of the verbal and analytical reasoning sections. Three parts of the verbal section, sentence completion, discrete verbal, and reading comprehension assess different aspects of language skills. The two parts of the analytical reasoning section represent two important aspects of the reasoning process (Graduate Record Examinations Board, 1986). The analytical reasoning items assess the ability to understand a structure of arbitrary relationships, to deduce new information from the relationships given, and to assess the conditions used to establish the structure of relationships. The task demands of the Space topic, in contrast, require the writer to generate a structure of relationships and move beyond the brief structure that is supplied by the prompt. The Farming prompt, on the other hand, offers some structure that writers can use to organize the development of their ideas. The logical reasoning items assess the ability to understand, evaluate, and analyze arguments. Studies validating the analytical reasoning section have indicated that logical reasoning scores tend to be at least moderately or highly correlated with the verbal section scores, whereas the analytical reasoning scores tend to be correlated moderately with the quantitative section scores (Wilson, 1985).

RESULTS

Performance of the Separate Scoring Schemes

The Purves/Söter scheme. The scores for the three dimensions for each of the two topics were correlated (Table 9.2)[2] to determine the degree to which the dimensions are related. Within one topic type, the correlations among the three dimensions were very high, ranging from .90 to .93 for the Space topic and from .88 to .91 for the Farming topic.

Across topics, the correlations among the three dimensions were moderately high, ranging from .72 to .77. Thus within a topic, scores assigned to three dimensions appear to be highly interdependent; it would be difficult to justify a claim that any one of the dimensions is measuring something unique from the others. The higher correlations within a topic as opposed to across the two topics suggest that the readers reacted to the specific demands of the different topics when evaluating the papers.

The scores obtained for the three Purves/Söter dimensions also are highly correlated with the holistic writing scores. Correlations of the scores for the three Purves/Söter dimensions per topic with the scores for the Moss scheme yielded relatively low correlations, generally ranging from .22 to .57. The only correlations among these scores that were relatively high were the correlations of the three Purves/Söter scores for Space with the Moss claims score for Space (.71 to .72). The high correlations of the Purves/Söter scores with one another and with holistic writing scores suggests that written language ability heavily influences these scores, and that reasoning ability has not been isolated from writing ability. The considerably lower correlations with the Moss scores suggest that something other than writing ability has been identified with this scoring scheme.

The scores for the 13 separate elements per topic within the dimensions of the Purves/Söter scheme were factor analyzed as well. The varimax factor analysis resulted in a two-factor solution in which the two factors were defined by the two different writing tasks, Space and Farming. This analysis lent additional support to the unidimensionality of the three dimensions for scoring within one topic, and to the differentiation of the two tasks.

Finally, the Purves/Söter scores for the three dimensions for each topic were correlated with the GRE part scores. These correlations yielded the same pattern of relationships, at approximately the same levels, observed for the correlations of holistic writing scores with the GRE part scores (Table 9.2), reflecting the trend observed with other verbal data and these GRE part scores. The correlations of the holistic writing scores yielded similar patterns and values of relationships. These patterns of relationships underscore the assumption that the Purves/Söter scores are highly related to holistic scores of writing ability and moderately related to verbal ability scores. Although the three dimensions of the Purves/Söter scheme did not appear to be independent, the three scores per topic were retained for final analyses in order to further explore their relationships with Writer's Workbench variables.

The Moss scoring scheme. Correlations of the separate scores derived from the Moss scheme with one another indicated that the scores were relatively independent of one another (Table 9.2). The

TABLE 9.2
Correlations of Scoring Schemes and GRE Part Scores

Column groups: **GRE General Test** — GRE V (1 SC, 2 DV, 3 RC), GRE AR (4 AR = analyt R, 5 LR = logical R); **Purves/Soter Scheme** — Space (6 CT, 7 O, 8 ST), Farming (9 CT, 10 P, 11 ST); **Moss Scheme** — Space (12 C, 13 S, 14 Q), 15 G, Farming (16 D, 17 C, 18 J, 19 Q); **Holistic Schemes** — HR (20 S, 21 F), HW (22 S, 23 F).

Measure	SC 1	DV 2	RC 3	AR 4	LR 5	CT 6	O 7	ST 8	CT 9	P 10	ST 11	C 12	S 13	Q 14	G 15	D 16	C 17	J 18	Q 19	S 20	F 21	S 22	F 23
GRE V 1 sent comp																							
2 disc V	.81																						
3 read comp	.80	.77																					
GRE AR 4 analyt R	.39	.39	.43																				
5 logical R	.76	.68	.77	.48																			
Purves/Söter 6 cont/think	.67	.66	.72	.33	.62																		
7 organization	.69	.66	.71	.29	.62	.93																	
8 style & tone	.70	.69	.72	.33	.65	.91	.90																
Purves/Söter 9 cont/think	.64	.61	.68	.33	.59	.73	.74	.73															
10 organization	.62	.59	.66	.34	.61	.72	.73	.72	.91														
11 style & tone	.65	.64	.69	.34	.64	.76	.76	.77	.88	.88													
Moss 12 claims	.31	.35	.35		.28	.52	.52	.52	.37	.33	.36												
13 support	.55	.57	.58	.21	.43	.72	.71	.71	.58	.56	.57	.55											
14 qualification	.32	.38	.35		.22	.32	.33	.35	.31	.30	.30	.17*	.32										
15 graph	.25	.18*	.18*		.26	.26	.25	.24	.22	.31	.28	.26	.30										
Moss Farming 16 deduction	.40	.46	.42		.26	.24	.21	.21	.17*	.45	.26		.30	.28	.19								
17 claims	.35	.36	.40		.37	.41	.40	.41	.51	.51	.39	.22	.31			.64							
18 justification	.44	.41	.38		.30	.37	.38	.39	.57	.51	.41	.22	.31	.28	.17*	.19*							
19 qualification					.42	.42	.42	.39	.38	.41	.48	.18*											
Holistic reasoning 20 space	.68	.72	.70	.37	.60	.81	.81	.79	.69	.70	.70	.63	.77	.42	.24	.24	.43	.39	.41				
21 farming	.72	.69	.74	.41	.64	.74	.75	.75	.81	.80	.78	.35	.59	.34	.33	.25	.64	.61	.47	.74			
Holistic writing 22 space	.76	.74	.76	.35	.70	.82	.81	.80	.70	.71	.74	.44	.65	.34	.23	.27	.37	.34	.43	.80	.74		
23 farming	.72	.71	.76	.37	.69	.78	.76	.78	.78	.77	.79	.45	.60	.34	.30	.26	.48	.46	.39	.76	.82	.85	

NOTE: N = 203 . .001 level of significance.
*at .01 level.

two highest correlations, .55 for support with claims for the Space topic, and .64 for justifications (a form of support) with claims for the Farming topic indicate a necessarily dependent relationship, since support is offered for the claims being made. The correlations of Moss scores across the two topics also were low, another indication of the differential task demands of the topics. Generally, the correlations of the Moss scores with the holistic writing scores for both topics were low to moderate, ranging from .26 to .45, with the exception of the moderate correlations of the Moss support score for Space with the holistic writing score for Space (.65) and the holistic writing score for Farming (.60). Clearly, writing skills play some role in the ability to offer support for a claim.

Correlations of the Moss scores with the GRE General Test part scores resulted in low and moderate correlations. Thus it is possible (a question for further investigation) that the Moss scores reflect verbal skills to some extent, as would be expected, but also tap some other abilities. The correlations of the Moss scores with the GRE analytical reasoning part scores add to the confusion, however, since the Moss scores do not correlate differentially with the two parts of the analytical reasoning section and, in fact, are somewhat less highly correlated with these GRE scores (ranging from correlations of .20 to .43) than they are with the GRE verbal part scores. It is possible that the Moss scores, although related to verbal ability as would be expected, assess a different kind of reasoning skill than assessed by the analytical reasoning section of the GRE General Test.

The Reid holistic reasoning scores. Correlations of the holistic reasoning scores for Space and Farming were higher within topic (.80 for Space holistic reasoning with Space holistic writing and .82 for Farming holistic reasoning with Farming holistic writing) than across topics (.76 for Space holistic reasoning with Farming holistic writing and .74 for Farming holistic reasoning with Space holistic writing). Again, the data suggest the performance differences between the two topics. It is interesting to note, however, that the correlations of holistic writing scores for Space with Farming (.85) and the correlations of holistic reasoning scores for Space with Farming (.74) appear to indicate that holistic writing scores were still more highly related to each other than were the holistic reasoning scores. Because the holistic writing scores and the holistic reasoning scores are relatively highly correlated, the high interdependence of these scores should be taken into account when interpreting the final data analyses.

Finally, the correlations of the holistic reasoning scores further support the assumption that the holistic reasoning and writing scores are essentially interchangeable, since their correlations with the GRE verbal scores reflect nearly identical patterns and levels of relationships.

The Writer's Workbench analyses. The correlations of the WWB features with one another and with the scores yielded by the scoring schemes reflect some complex relationships beyond the purview of this chapter. It is interesting to note that, even though the different Workbench variables would be expected to be highly related, the variables we selected for the analyses do not reflect high correlations with one another for this sample of papers. The WWB thus provides a valuable investigative tool to enable researchers to define the labels they have assigned to features of written discourse. Because the sample size is small, and the number of intercorrelations so numerous, any attempt to generalize from this data would be spurious, in addition to the recognition that the reliabilities of some of the scores for two of the scoring schemes were not sufficiently high for this kind of analysis.

Varimax factor analyses of the 21 WWB scores for each topic yielded four factors that appear to be interpretable as well as relevant to the performance observed in the papers. The factors reported (eliminating loadings of lower than .30) again support the differences in performance that are elicited by the two topics, but also suggest that some similar features contributed to the writing skills demonstrated in both topics. Factor 1, for example, depends predominantly on content-related features, although average word length loads on this factor for Farming, and on Factor 2 for Space. Factor 2 seems to reflect sentence variety. Factor 3 again reflects some similarities across the two topics (average word length, average length of content words, percentage of nominalizations, a negative loading for percentage of vague words), but some differences in that additional features are reflected in performance on the Space topic (passive voice, "to be" verbs, number of possible confused homophones and word pairs to check, average sentence length, percentage of nominalizations). Factor 4 further distinguishes between the two topics in several ways: Passive voice contributed heavily to this factor for the Farming topic, but contributed moderately to Factor 3 of the space topic; the percentage of "to be" verbs contributed to Factor 4 for Farming and to Factor 3 for Space; fewer nominalizations contributed to Factor 4 for Space, but not for Farming (more nominalizations contributed to Factor 3 for both); and number of suggestions regarding possible diction problems contributed somewhat to Factor 4 for both topics. These data for the papers analyzed for the total sample of writers, representing the features of writing that can be used to describe performance on the two tasks, are relevant to the interpretations of the analyses for the different language groups, reported in the final results section.

Factor Analysis of All Variables

The data for all variables for each topic—writing and reasoning scores assigned by human judges, WWB features extracted from the papers, and GRE part scores—were factor analyzed. The varimax factor analyses should be interpreted with caution, but can be viewed as suggestive of future possibilities.

Some of the scores for the Purves/Söter and Moss scoring schemes were not highly reliable, and some of the scores do not appear to be independent of one another (holistic writing and holistic reasoning, the three Purves/Söter scores, and the Purves/Söter scores with holistic reasoning and writing), hence could be considered to be interchangeable to some extent. However, it is interesting to note that although the holistic writing and reasoning scores had separate but high loadings on Factor 1 for the Farming topic, the loading for the holistic writing score is considerably lower than the holistic reasoning score on Factor 1 for the Space topic. Again we can observe evidence for differential performance on the two topics is apparent.

Generally, without ignoring the specific differences between topics, Factor 1 appears to reflect verbal ability, as measured both directly by the writing samples and indirectly by the GRE General Test. The Purves/Söter, Moss, and holistic writing and reasoning scores all contribute to this factor. Factor 2 for the Space topic primarily reflects GRE verbal scores, with a small contribution from the highly correlated holistic reasoning, Purves/Söter style/tone, and holistic writing scores. Factor 2 for the Farming topic, however, is dominated by WWB and Moss variables. Factors 3, 4, and 5 are formed entirely from WWB variables, which again appear to be relatively independent of the other variables and suggest that the WWB variables contribute additional information about performance on the writing tasks. In general, Factors 3, 4, and 5 reflect WWB fluency, content, and sentence variety measures, respectively.

Comparisons of Language
Group Means

Regression analyses were conducted to predict the holistic writing scores and to predict part scores for the two parts of the analytical reasoning section of the GRE General Test from the full set of variables, both for the total group and for the separate language groups. Since the sample size for the Arabic language group was too small, these data contributed only to the analysis of total-group data. of scores obtained by the students from different native language groups (Tables 9.3 and 9.4). The patterns of scores for the holistic writing, holistic reasoning, and Purves/Söter schemes reflect the same general trends, in which the native speakers of English received higher scores than did the Spanish speakers, who obtained higher scores than the Chinese speakers (significant at $p = .001$ for these F ratios for 3, 199 df). These patterns are repeated for the Moss scheme scores, except that the mean scores for the Chinese and Spanish groups are considerably lower than the English group on the qualifications score ($F = 16.32$ for 3, 199 df at $p = .001$).

The WWB scores reveal greater differentiations that do not always favor the English group. Although the English speakers committed fewer spelling errors on the Space papers (significant at the .02 level), the Chinese also have fewer spelling errors on the Farming papers. For both the Space and Farming topics, the English papers exhibited a lower percentage of vagueness on the Farming papers (significant only at the .06 level) and the Chinese used considerably more vague words on the Space topic ($p = .001$). All groups, however, were relatively more similar (no significant differences) with respect to the use of abstract words and nominalizations (nominalized words) for both topics. The English papers contained considerably more ($p = .001$) potential problems with diction (number of suggestions) and confused homophones or word pairs (number to check) than the Chinese and Spanish papers—possibly because greater fluency is associated with greater potential for error. The English group used

TABLE 9.3

Means and Standard Deviations of Variables in Analysis
for the Three Language Groups, Space Topic

Variables	Chinese (N = 73)		English (N = 89)		Spanish (N = 35)	
	Mean	S.D.	Mean	S.D.	Mean	S.D.
Holistic writing	2.78	1.05	5.60	.69	3.70	1.10
Holistic reasoning	2.48	.79	4.47	.86	3.03	.61
Purves/Söter Scheme						
content	14.18	3.12	22.30	3.00	17.53	3.27
organization	6.40	1.55	9.92	1.28	7.65	1.53
style and tone	5.71	1.08	9.37	1.40	6.69	1.32
Moss Scheme						
claims	4.79	1.93	6.88	2.23	5.52	1.46
support	1.60	1.08	3.69	1.33	2.23	.97
qualifications	.24	.34	.70	.64	.22	.32
Writer's workbench variables						
number of suggestions	4.04	3.26	8.21	5.08	5.09	3.18
number of spelling errors	2.97	2.17	2.47	2.74	3.34	2.83
% vague words	8.24	2.92	5.59	1.83	6.56	1.69
number to check	1.50	1.29	3.38	1.80	2.34	1.49
average sentence length	18.66	7.61	21.90	4.81	23.96	7.27
% shorter sentences	23.28	16.37	28.13	11.40	34.23	15.09
% longer sentences	9.29	9.19	12.29	6.15	13.51	9.84
% to be verbs	77.18	12.33	84.22	10.40	80.97	11.59
% passive voice	6.11	6.81	15.26	8.76	11.83	8.65
% nominalizations	3.68	1.63	3.52	1.21	3.51	1.48
average word length	4.49	2.71	4.90	2.26	4.61	2.73
% content words	54.60	3.56	56.11	3.02	52.65	4.47
average length content words	5.88	4.02	6.48	3.23	6.18	4.39
% prepositions	9.26	2.28	11.99	1.59	11.72	2.60
% adjectives	14.53	2.85	16.20	2.84	13.54	3.47
% abstract	3.55	1.67	3.50	1.17	3.59	1.44

NOTE: GRE General Test Scores are included in Table 9.4.

the passive voice most frequently in both the Space and Farming papers ($p = .001$ for Space; $p = .04$ for Farming), whereas the Chinese used it the least in the Space papers and the Spanish, in the Farming papers.

TABLE 9.4
Means and Standard Deviations of Variables in Analysis
for the Three Language Groups, Farming Topic

Variables	Chinese (N = 73)		English (N = 89)		Spanish (N = 35)	
	Mean	S.D.	Mean	S.D.	Mean	S.D.
Holistic writing	2.92	1.04	5.78	.52	3.61	1.10
Holistic reasoning	2.49	.78	4.66	.84	2.81	.89
Purves/Söter Scheme						
content	13.58	3.00	21.67	3.50	16.29	3.14
organization	6.08	1.49	10.00	1.79	7.00	1.90
style and tone	5.97	1.16	9.35	1.28	6.99	1.34
Moss Scheme						
graph reading	3.51	1.30	4.02	1.16	3.30	1.77
deductions	.61	.72	1.22	1.17	.64	.82
claims	2.20	1.15	3.23	1.02	2.46	1.25
justifications	1.14	.88	2.14	1.16	1.34	.97
qualifications	.03	.10	.26	.30	.11	.18
Writer's workbench variables						
number of suggestions	3.49	3.29	9.00	5.31	5.60	3.63
number of spelling errors	1.79	1.79	1.82	2.46	3.49	3.25
% vague words	5.59	3.27	4.82	2.03	5.76	2.67
number to check	1.18	1.21	2.71	1.57	2.37	1.90
average sentence length	19.68	6.89	22.33	6.53	24.93	6.24
% shorter sentences	26.10	14.68	27.91	10.86	32.23	14.04
% longer sentences	10.22	9.11	11.21	8.12	14.83	10.87
% to be verbs	71.83	19.91	79.64	16.38	69.54	20.17
% passive voice	10.10	12.36	13.74	9.05	8.00	7.06
% nominalizations	2.96	1.30	2.53	1.25	3.17	1.44
average word length	4.55	2.60	4.78	2.23	4.51	2.50
% content words	57.99	3.87	58.34	3.53	54.37	3.50
average length content words	5.63	7.38	6.06	6.58	5.82	3.37
% prepositions	12.22	3.77	14.13	2.47	13.77	3.61
% adjectives	17.17	4.07	18.46	3.05	16.39	3.49
% abstract	3.15	1.40	2.67	1.22	2.93	1.39
GRE General Test Scores						
Verbal						
sentence completion	3.60	1.63	10.03	2.94	6.29	2.81
discrete verbal	11.18	4.87	25.87	6.64	18.29	5.69
reading comprehension	6.62	3.03	16.63	3.33	10.86	4.01

(continued)

TABLE 9.4 Continued

GRE General Test Scores	Chinese (N = 73)		English (N = 89)		Spanish (N = 35)	
	Mean	S.D.	Mean	S.D.	Mean	S.D.
Analytical reasoning						
analytical reasoning	19.89	6.09	24.02	6.15	17.26	5.99
logical reasoning	3.74	1.47	7.93	2.26	4.86	2.17

On the GRE General Test, the Chinese group scored the lowest, and the Spanish scored lower that the English speakers. The English group received higher scores on both parts of the analytical reasoning section, but the Chinese group obtained higher scores than the Spanish group on the analytical reasoning part and the Spanish group obtained higher scores than the Chinese group on the logical reasoning part. These scores may reflect the frequently observed higher relationship of scores on the analytical reasoning part with scores on the quantitative section and the higher relationship of scores on the logical reasoning part with scores on the verbal section. In general, Chinese nonnative speakers of English attend graduate The regression analyses should be interpreted in relation to the levels school in the United States in mathematical or scientific fields, and the Spanish speakers tend to be more highly verbal than the Chinese, hence these patterns of relationships.

Stepwise Regression Analyses for the Total Sample and Language Groups

Stepwise regression analyses[3] were conducted to predict the holistic writing scores (approximately equivalent to the holistic reasoning scores) from the 21 WWB variables before further reduction to 16 variables. For the total group, nine variables contributed to the prediction of holistic writing scores for both Space and Farming. The two predominant variables, number of words and average word length, indicate that overall fluency contributed to the quality of the holistic evaluations. (Since the "number of words" variable was highly correlated with other WWB features, it was eliminated from the final analyses; for the Space topic, the mean number of words for the papers in the total sample was 252.27, and for the Farming topic, 212.70.)

Some relatively predictable features influenced these holistic writing scores (e.g., fewer nominalizations and spelling errors). The prediction of scores for the language groups presents a somewhat different perspective in that slightly different stylistic features contribute to the holistic scores for the different groups and for the two different topics. Since these results served to describe the performances on this particular sample of data, we cannot draw any generalizable conclusions about the features of Spanish student writing, for example, until additional studies are conducted to support the findings.

Stepwise regression analyses also were conducted to predict the part scores (analytical reasoning and logical reasoning) for the GRE General Test from the 28 score variables obtained for the Space topic and the 29 score variables obtained for the Farming topic. For the total sample, scores on the verbal section of the GRE General Test, but not the scores on the analytical reasoning or logical reasoning parts, respectively, contributed heavily to the prediction of the logical reasoning and analytical reasoning parts, respectively. The scores from the scoring schemes contributed to a small degree (see the beta weights) to these predictions.

For the different native language groups, the analytical reasoning and logical reasoning scores were predicted predominantly by other GRE verbal scores, but scores from the scoring schemes contributed more substantially to the predictions. For the Spanish sample, whose analytical reasoning scores were lower than those of other groups, the prediction of their analytical reasoning scores required few steps in the analyses; the prediction of their logical reasoning scores included the holistic writing scores. (Note that the Purves/Söter scores, correlated approximately in the low .70s, may be essentially interchangeable in these analyses.) The stepwise regressions for the English sample are decidedly more prosaic—other GRE verbal scores contribute considerably to the predictions.

For the Chinese sample, whose logical reasoning scores were lower than those of the other groups, fewer variables contributed to the prediction of their analytical reasoning scores than to their logical reasoning scores. Their analytical reasoning scores are not predicted by other GRE scores but instead by scores obtained from the different

scoring schemes and the WWB analyses (the beta weights and correlations were very low, however). The logical reasoning scores for the
Chinese sample were predicted by seven variables for each topic,
dominated by GRE verbal scores, but also by scores from the scoring
schemes and WWB. Again, interesting language group and across-
topic differences were observed—a finding that requires replication,
of course, to be generalizable.

SUMMARY OF RESULTS

Overall, the mean scores for the four scoring schemes and GRE
General Test part scores were higher for the English group than for
the Spanish group, which were higher than for the Chinese group.
The WWB programs provided greater differentiation among the
language groups, since papers written by each of the groups could be
described by quite different combinations of Workbench features.

For the Space topic, the Chinese papers contained more vague
words but less passive voice and fewer potential usage problems, short
sentences, "to be" verbs, content words, and prepositions. The
Spanish papers for the Space topic presented more spelling errors,
somewhat more sentence variety, and fewer adjectives. The English
papers contained more potential usage problems, "to be" verbs,
passive voice, content words, and adjectives.

For the Farming topic, the Chinese papers presented fewer
potential usage problems, spelling errors (than the Spanish), prepositions, and less sentence variety. The Spanish papers exhibited more
spelling errors, more vague words (than the English), greater sentence
variety, and less passive voice. The English papers for the Farming
topic contained considerably more diction problems, "to be" verbs,
passive voice, content words, and adjectives.

For both topics, all three language groups appeared to be relatively
similar with respect to number of nominalizations, word length, and
abstractness. The native speakers of English used the passive voice
more frequently in their Space and Farming papers, and also
exhibited more instances in which diction and confused homophones
or word pairs may have been problematic. Perhaps the greater fluency
of the English students resulted in more variety and risk-taking,
whereas nonnative speakers of English tended to constrain their

writing by using syntax and vocabulary that are "safe." The observed mean differences were reinforced by the stepwise regression analyses, which indicated that different variables contributed to the prediction of holistic writing (and reasoning) scores and scores on the two parts of the GRE analytical reasoning sections for the three language groups. Somewhat different variables contributed to the predictions for the two different writing tasks as well.

CONCLUSIONS

This investigation, by placing emphasis on the methodology, demonstrated the value of comparing observations using several measures, and in a number of different ways (descriptive statistics, correlations, factor analyses, regression analyses) in order to understand better the interrelationships of the features of written discourse to thinking and writing skills as viewed from different measurement perspectives. The limitations of the study do not permit us to generalize, but the study can serve as a basis for further work. Overall, we observed the following:

- The reliability of scoring schemes applied by human judges can vary considerably, depending on the features of writing the readers are able to identify in sample of actual performance that can vary with the task and native language group. Some of the more important features of writing and thinking skills are the most difficult to identify with reliability, perhaps because they are less frequently demonstrated in papers and are more difficult to define for reader consensus when samples of writing are being evaluated.
- Scores based on the Purves/Söter scheme, despite the strenuous attempts of the developers and readers to separate scores from writing skills, were highly related to, therefore confounded by, verbal ability.
- The Moss scheme, in which verbal fluency was extracted from the scores, attempted to identify some higher-order reasoning skills that appeared to occur infrequently, thus leading to low estimates of reader reliability. Some of the more reliable scores, however, appeared to be independent of verbal ability, yet were not highly related to the part scores for the analytical reasoning section of the GRE General Test. It is possible that these scores tapped reasoning skills that are not assessed by the GRE, but further research is needed to determine what these scores mean and whether they represent important developed abilities.

- The Writer's Workbench provides measures that identify features of written discourse that are relatively independent and provides information about the characteristics of text. The WWB has the potential to supply diagnostic feedback in writing instruction, as is being pursued at Colorado State University and elsewhere. It might also serve, with more research, as a tool for equating prompts for open-ended assessment by generating evidence that the prompts elicit the same features and ranges of performance.
- The data support the contention that different task demands elicit different kinds of writing performance, and that the writing performance of students representing different first-language groups varies in complex ways in response to these tasks as well.

Several experts in the field contributed considerable effort to attempt to identify significant features that might serve as indicators of effective reasoning skills in written discourse. This kind of exploration, despite its uncontrollable limitations, is essential to this line of inquiry. What we have learned, it is hoped, will contribute to further extensions of some of the more promising directions that were pursued:

- Different communities of readers who can generally agree on the features of writing that evidence effective reasoning skills bring different approaches, labels, and definitions to the observation of these skills. The interrelationships within and among the different scoring schemes provide information about what we might be evaluating as well as the degree to which these skills are evaluated independently of other skills with which they are, perhaps, inextricably confounded. We need to collect more data to determine to what extent performance differences in text are a function of tasks and scoring methods, or of actual differences in developed abilities.
- The reasoning skills that are deemed to represent important, high-level abilities are difficult to identify with reliability and validity. One of the reasons for this difficulty is that such higher-order skills did not appear as frequently as would be expected in the papers written by graduate-level students. This problem may have been a function of the writing task demands and/or might be observed in student writing in general.
- In addition to the differential performance that is elicited in response to different task demands, students who have been trained in academic writing in different cultures may have different perceptions of performance expectations. Within the context of academic writing in the United States, it is possible that nonnative speakers of English, in the early stages of adapting to our expectations, still reflect strong disposi-

tions to write as they were trained to write (and think) in their cultures. At some intermediate point in their educational experiences in the United States, their writing may exhibit a combination of cultural influences that vary in effectiveness. Finally, we might expect that academic training in the United States would lead toward more westernized approaches, with a caveat—against what standards is it appropriate to evaluate effective academic writing? These standards are not sufficiently explicit, and vary, depending on the contexts—major fields, types of writing tasks, and whether or not the students who return to their native countries will need to make accommodations when writing in English within their native cultures.

These observations lead to an even more basic question—do the features observed in written discourse contribute differentially to the quality of writing, depending on the different types and contexts of writing, and are any of these features generalizable across types and contexts? Thus we continue to face and investigate a challenging dilemma, to clarify and communicate consistently the expectation of readers, writers, and interpreters of evaluations of written discourse.

NOTES

1. Trademark of AT & T.
2. All correlations reported are at the .01 or .001 levels of significance.
3. In all regression analyses, all variables contributing to the predictions were at least moderately reliable.

REFERENCES

American Psychological Association. (1984, February). *Joint technical standards for educational and psychological testing* (4th draft). Washington, DC: American Psychological Association, Office of Scientific Affairs.

Bridgeman, B., & Carlson, S. (1983). *Survey of academic writing tasks required of graduate and undergraduate foreign students* (ETS Research Report. No. 1983-18). Princeton, NJ: Educational Testing Service.

Canale, M. (1983). On some dimensions of language proficiency. In J. W. Oller, Jr. (Ed.), *Issues in language testing research* (chapter 20). Rowley, MA: Newbury House.

Canale, M., & Swain, M. (1979). *Communicative approaches to second language teaching and testing.* Ontario: Ontario Ministry of Education.

Carlson, S. B., & Bridgeman, B. (1986). Testing ESL student writers. In K. L. Greenberg, H. Wiener, & R. A. Donovan (Eds.), *Writing assessment: Issues and strategies.* New York: Longman.

Carlson, S. B., & Powers, D. (in press). *Relationships of thinking and writing skills to GRE analytical ability scores* (Report to the GRE Research Committee). Princeton, NJ: Educational Testing Service.

Carlson, S. B., Bridgeman, B., Camp, R., & Waanders, J. (1985). *Relationship of admission test scores to writing performance of native and nonnative speakers of English* (TOEFL Research Report. No. 19). Princeton, NJ: Educational Testing Service.

Carroll, J. A. (1960). Vectors of prose style. In T. A. Sebeok (Ed.), *Style in language* (pp. 283-292). Cambridge, MA and New York: Technology Press/John Wiley.

Cherry, L. L., Fox, M. L., Frase, L. T., Gingrich, P. S., Keenan, S. A., & Macdonald, N. H. (1983, May/June). Computer aids for test analysis. *Bell Laboratories Record.*

Cummins, J. (1983). Language proficiency and academic achievement. In J. W. Oller, Jr. (Ed.), *Issues in language testing research.* Rowley, MA: Newbury House.

Frase, L. T. (in press). Computer analysis of written materials. In D. Reinking (Ed.), *Computers and reading: Issues for theory and practice.* New York: Teachers College Press.

Frase, L. T., Kiefer, K. E., Smith, C. R., & Fox, M. L. (1985) Theory and practice in computer-aided composition. In S. W. Freedman (Ed.), *The acquisition of written language.* Norwood, NJ: Ablex.

GRE guide to the use of the Graduate Record Examinations program, 1986-87 (1986). Princeton, NJ: Educational Testing Service.

Kaplan, R. B. (1966). Cultural thought patterns in inter-cultural education. *Language Learning, 16,* 1-20.

Kaplan, R. B. (1972). The anatomy of rhetoric: Prolegomena to a functional theory of rhetoric. In *Language and the teacher: A series in applied linguistics* (Vol. 8). Philadelphia: Center for Curriculum Development.

Kaplan, R. B. (1976). A further note on contrastive rhetoric. *Communication Quarterly, 14*(2), 12-19.

Kaplan, R. B. (1977). Contrastive rhetoric: Some hypotheses. *ITL, 39-40,* 61-72.

Kaplan, R. B. (1982). Contrastive rhetoric: Some implications for the writing process. In I. Pringle, A. Freedman, & J. Yalden (Eds.), *Learning to write: First language, second language.* London:Longman.

Kiefer, K. E., & Smith, C. R. (1984). Textual analysis with computers: Tests of Bell Laboratories' computer software. *Research in the Teaching of English, 17*(3), 201-214.

Munby, J. (1978). *Communicative syllabus design.* Cambridge: Cambridge University Press.

Park, Y. M. (1986). *The influence of task upon writing performance,* Unpublished doctoral dissertation, University of Illinois at Urbana-Champaign.

Purves, A. C. (1985). *Framework for scoring: GRE/TOEFL.* Unpublished manuscript, University of Illinois at Urbana-Champaign, Curriculum Laboratory.

Purves, A. C. (1986). Rhetorical communities, the international student, and basic writing. *Journal of Basic Writing, 5*(1).

Purves, A. C., Söter, A., Takala, S., & Vähäpassi, A. (1984). Towards a domain-referenced system for classifying composition assignments. *Research in the Teaching of English, 18,* 385-409.

Reid, S., & Findlay, G. (1986). Writer's Workbench analysis of holistically scored essays. *Computers and Composition, 3*(2), 6-32.

Ruth, L., & Murphy, S. (1987). *Designing writing tasks for the assessment of writing.* New York: Ablex.

Smith, C. R., & Kiefer, K. (1982, April). *Writer's Workbench: Computers and writing instruction.* Paper presented at the Future of Literacy Conference, University of Maryland, Baltimore.

Söter, A. (1985). *GRE/TOEFL scoring criteria.* Unpublished manuscript, University of Illinois at Urbana-Champaign, Curriculum Laboratory.

Toulmin, S., Rieke, R., & Janik, A. (1984). *An introduction to reasoning* (2nd ed.) New York: Macmillan.

Walz, J. C. (1982). *Error correction techniques for the foreign language classroom.* Washington, DC: Center for Applied Linguistics.

Wilson, K. M. (1985). *The relationship of GRE General Test item-type part scores to undergraduate grades* (GRE Professional Report, No. 81-22P). Princeton, NJ: Educational Testing Service.

10

Academic and Ethnic Background as Factors Affecting Writing Performance

YOUNG MOK PARK

The purpose of this chapter is to follow up aspects of Carlson's study reported in this volume. More specifically, this study investigates:

(a) whether the different assignments testing college-level students affect judged performance;
(b) whether the assignment variables interact with different writer groups such as a student's major field and native language on the performance of writing;
(c) whether the different scoring scales leads to different interpretations of the effect of the assignment variables on the writing performance.

This report presents some data related to the first and third questions but concentrates on the second.

The original writing sample in this study consists of 424 essays written by 212 upper level college students. The sample includes 96 native speakers and 116 nonnative speakers of English (Carlson, Bridgeman, Camp & Waanders, 1985). In addition to the writing sample, the following information was available: the student's native language, major field, GRE scores, and holistic (general impression) score for the two different topics. (Use of the data was granted by the Educational Testing Service [ETS]).

From the original ETS data, 96 student writing samples were selected for this study—among these were 24 students, native speakers of English, with a major in a hard science; 24 students, native speakers of English, with a social science major in a hard science; and 24

TABLE 10.1
Topic Comparison in Relation to the
Elements of Writing Assignment

	"Space" Topic	"Farm" Topic
instruction type	topic and content	topic and content
stimulus (information type)	one paragraph with general information	one paragraph with specific information using graphs
cognitive demand	invent/generate/evaluate	invent/generate/evaluate
purpose	to convince/inform	to inform/convince
audience	unspecified (general)	unspecified (general)
mode	argument/exposition	argument/exposition

students, native speakers of Chinese, with a social science major. Since each student wrote two essays on two different topics, the total number of writing samples for this study is 192.

Characteristics of the essay topic. Each student wrote two essays on two different topics. For the "Space" topic, students were required to compare and contrast the advantages of space exploration and to take a position. In the "Farm" topic, students were required to interpret the relationships among three graphs showing the change in farming patterns over a period of 40 years in the United States. These two topics are distinctive in regard to the type of information provided in the assignment (see Table 10.1).

Quality of the Essays. Three different kinds of scoring methods were used: analytic score, holistic score, and syntactic characteristics. The analytic scores were generated by four raters using Purves's analytic scoring scheme as described by Carlson. For the "Space" topic, four raters rated all essays, whereas for the "Farm" topic, two raters rated the odd numbered essays, and another pair of raters rated the even numbered essays. To minimize the rater effect on the comparison of the two topics, the average scores of the two rater groups' rating for both the "Space" topic and the "Farm" topic were used in the investigation of the topic effect on students' writing performance. The interrater reliability estimates were consistent (interrater reliability coefficient alpha for "Space" topic = .90, and for "Farm" topic = .84). Consequently, it is assumed that the rater variable does not significantly affect the quality measure of these writing samples when the average score is used as the quality measure of the writing sample.

The holistic scores were generated on a six-point scale. In the holistic scoring method, the raters independently rated students' essays by evaluating where the paper fits within the range of essays written for the given assignment. The raters were trained to read the essay quickly and to score it as a whole without considering the several dimensions of writing skill (Breland & Griswold, 1981). The interrater reliabilities were consistent (interrater reliability coefficient alpha for "Space" topic = .81, and for "Farm" topic = .87).

In addition to the analytic scores and general impression scores, two kinds of syntactic characteristic measures—length of elaboration measures and syntactic complexity measures—were used as dependent variables. For the length of elaboration measures, the total number of words, total number of T-units, total number of free modifiers (openers, interrupters, and closers) were counted, using several reference materials (Christensen, 1968; Christensen & Christensen, 1978; Dixon, 1970; Hunt, 1970, 1977; O'Hare, 1973; Tibbetts & Tibbetts, 1984; Wolk, 1970). For the syntactic complexity measures, the mean T-unit length and the ratio of free modifiers (ratio of openers, interrupters, and closers) were counted. The T-unit (a group of words that constitute a main clause in addition to all subordinate clauses attached to it) and the ratio of free modifiers were used for determining syntactic complexity or maturity in English because it is widely accepted that the mean T-unit length increases with maturity and a mature style has a relatively high frequency of free modifiers, especially in the final position (Christensen, 1968; Christensen & Christensen, 1978; Hunt, 1977). According to Wolk (1970), the initial free modifier (opener) includes all words, phrases, and clauses that precede the noun phrase that serves as the subject. The medial free modifier (interrupter) is set off by punctuation and should occur neither initially nor finally. The final free modifier (closer) is set off by punctuation, and appears after the last word of the bound predicate.

SUMMARY OF RESULTS

The principal results of the investigation for the topic effects are summarized in conjunction with the three major questions of this study. (For a full account of the results, see Park, 1986.)

Task differences. Significant topic effects were found in the elaboration-length measures, the analytic content/thinking scores, and the holistic scores. However, in the syntactic complexity measures and all the analytic scores except the content/thinking scores, the topic effects were not significant. The following is a brief summary of the findings on the topic effects (in order of significance):

(1) The students generated significantly longer elaboration for the writing task with general information provided (the "Space" writing task) than for the writing task with narrowly defined specific information provided (the "Farm" writing task).

(2) The essays for the "Space" task received significantly higher scores in the analytic content/thinking main criteria than the essays for the "Farm" task. Of the seven subcriteria of the content/thinking dimension, significant topic effects were found in richness of information, evaluation, and alternatives.

(3) The essays for the "Space" task received significantly lower scores in the holistic rating than the essays for the "Farm" task.

(4) In the syntactic-complexity measures, the essays for the "Space" task were similar to the essays for the "Farm" task.

(5) In the analytic organization, style/tone, and total analytic scores, both sets of essays received almost the same level of ratings.

The interaction of topic, language, and major. The major findings related to the interaction effect of the native-language groups (NL) and topics, the interaction effect of the academic-major groups (MG) and topics, the interaction effect of the analytic main criteria and topics, and the interaction effect of the scoring methods and topics are as follows:

(1) The NL × topic interaction effects were significant only in the two elaboration-length measures: the total number of words and the number of words in free modifiers. This result indicates that the native-English language group used a significantly larger number of words for the "Space" task than for the "Farm" task; whereas, the native-Chinese language group used a similar number of words for both the tasks.

(2) However, in the syntactic complexity measures, all the analytic scores, and the holistic scores, the NL × topic interaction effects were not significant, indicating that the topic effects are parallel across the two different native-language groups.

(3) The MG × topic interaction effect was significant only in the holistic scores. This indicates that the hard-science major group received significantly higher scores on the "Farm" task than on the "Space" task, whereas the holistic scores of the social-science major group were not significantly different in the two different writing tasks.

(4) The nonsignificant MG × topic interaction effects in the writing skill measures, except the holistic scores, indicate that different academic backgrounds do not significantly affect writing performance (in elaboration-length, syntactic complexity, and analytic scores) for the two writing tasks.

(5) The interaction effect of the three analytic main criteria and topic was significant. This result indicates that the content/thinking score is significantly higher than the style/tone score in the "Space" task; whereas, in the "Farm" task, the style/tone score is significantly higher than the content/thinking score.

(6) The interaction effect of the two scoring methods and topics was significant, indicating that the essays for the "Space" task are rated highly by the analytic scoring method; whereas, the essays for the "Farm" task are rated highly by the holistic scoring method.

Task effects. The most significant effect of the topic was found in the elaboration-length variables. This result supports the notion that the amount of elaboration in writing may be related to the information types. For example, in the "Space" topic (general information provided), writers can draw information from their own knowledge and experience on the advantages and disadvantages of space exploration; whereas, in the "Farm" topic (specific information provided), writers have to rely heavily on the specific information given in the assignment. Therefore, the results suggest that a writing task requiring writers to draw more upon their previous knowledge facilitates more elaboration as measured by the total number of words and number of words in free modifiers. This result indicates that the findings of the learning and memory research on reading comprehension can be applicable to writing research. Several researchers (Anderson & Reader, 1978; Benton & Blohm, 1986; Bransford, Franks, Morris, & Stein, 1978; Stein & Bransford, 1979) reported that reading comprehension tasks requiring subjects to draw on previous knowledge resulted in higher levels of text recalls than did reading comprehension tasks not requiring extensive use of previous knowledge.

The nonsignificant effect of the information types on the syntactic

complexity variables supports several researchers' findings that the
T-unit length and the ratio of free modifiers are stable indices of
syntactic complexity and maturity (Christensen, 1968; Christensen &
Christensen, 1978; Hunt, 1965, 1983; Wolk, 1970). Some researchers
(Crowhurst & Piche, 1979; O'Donnell, 1976; Watson, 1983) reported
that syntactic complexity in written composition is significantly
affected by different discourse modes and different intended audience
variables. However, the results of this study provide evidence that the
syntactic complexity measures (T-unit length and ratio of free
modifiers) are stable across different types of writing tasks within the
same discourse mode and audience.

The significant effect of the information types on the analytic
content/thinking scores suggests that the general writing task
obligates students to produce more extensive information, more
explicit judgments, and more alternative views of thinking than the
specific writing task. The nonsignificant effects of the information
types on the analytic organization and style/tone scores suggest that
the different information types do not significantly affect judgments
of the organization of the essay and of the degree to which style
matches the conventions of academic English. This result indicates
that the latter two analytic criteria are not sensitive to the information
types provided in an assignment.

Why do the information types significantly affect the analytic
content/thinking scores but not the analytic organization scores and
the style/tone scores? One reason may be that the content/thinking
criterion focuses on declarative knowledge (knowledge of facts or
ideas); whereas, the organization and style/tone criteria focus on
procedural knowledge (automatized knowledge of how to do something). The significant topic effect on the holistic scores contrasts
with the topic effect on the analytic scores. The holistic scores for the
specific writing task are significantly higher than for the general
writing task, whereas the analytic scores for the specific writing task
are lower than the general writing task. One of the problems in
interpreting the above results has to do with the characteristics of the
holistic scoring method. The major function of the holistic scoring
method is to separate the better performers from the poor performers
by rank ordering the essays; hence the holistic scores provide little
information about the "intrinsic" quality (Hirsch, 1977, p. 189) of an
individual student's writing.

However, one of the reasons for this difference can be explained by the results of the investigation of relationship between the holistic scores and the syntactic characteristic variables and the relationship between the holistic scores and the analytic subcriteria scores. Holistic scoring focuses less on essay length variables compared to the analytic scoring, although the essays on the general writing task are significantly longer than the essays on the specific writing task. This means that holistic scoring focuses less on the number of ideas (more expensive ideas and alternative views of thinking) than the analytic scoring. The holistic scores correlate more highly with the analytic organization subcriteria (the unity subcriteria for the general writing task and the framing subcriteria for the specific writing task) than with the analytic content/thinking subcriteria. In addition, the holistic scoring method used in this study considered mechanical errors of students' essays, whereas the analytic scoring method used in this study did not deal with mechanical errors.

The language and academic major group differences. In exploring the differences between the two language groups and the two major groups in more detail, certain findings emerge. In terms of the sentence level scores, the significant NL main effect shows that the native-Chinese language group produces a less complex style of written discourse than does the native-English language group.

The significant NL main effect suggests that the native-English group uses a significantly higher ratio of free modifiers and closers than does the native-Chinese group. This finding also supports Christensen's (1968) claim that a large percentage of free modifiers is the mark of the skillful writer. One interesting result is the significant interaction effect of NL × MG × topic. Because of the small sample size of this study, the result is not generalizable. As shown in Figure 10.1, in the native-English group, the hard-science major group students use a higher percentage of free modifiers in the "Farm" topic than in the "Space" topic, whereas in the native-Chinese group, the hard-science major group students use a higher percentage of free modifiers in the "Space" topic than in the "Farm" topic. This result may indicate that the use of free modifiers can be affected by students' academic background, which may, in turn, affect interest or prior experiences with the task.

Holistic scores. Table 10.2 presents the mean and standard deviation of the holistic scores for each group and for the total group. The means of the "Space" topic holistic scores are lower than those of the "Farm" topic in the total group and for each of the native-

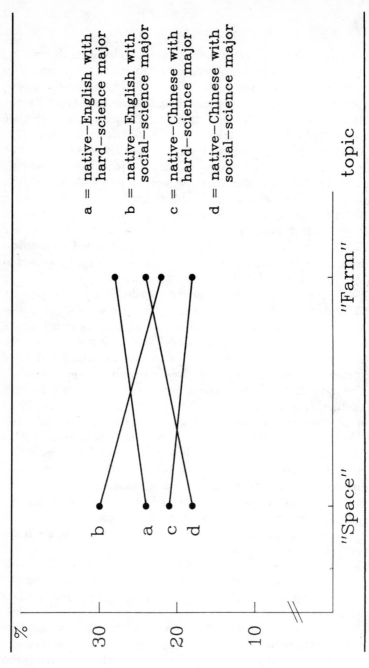

Figure 10.1 NL × MG × Topic Interaction Effect for Percentage of Words in Free Modifiers

TABLE 10.2
Mean and Standard Deviation of Holistic Scores

Group	"Space" Topic		"Farm" Topic	
total group	4.27	(1.55)	4.46	(1.55)
native-English group	5.52	(.76)	5.79	(.50)
native-Chinese group	3.02	(1.05)	3.13	(1.01)
hard-science group	4.04	(1.54)	4.41	(1.40)
social-science group	4.50	(1.55)	4.51	(1.71)

language group and major group. This result is clearly different from that of the analytic score in which there were no significant differences. In the major group, the mean of the social-science group is higher than the mean score of the hard-science group.

The results of the investigation for the topic effects on the holistic score provide the following four major points:

(1) The holistic scores are significantly affected by the different types of topics. Students received significantly higher scores for the "Farm" topic than they did for the "Space" topic, and the significant topic effect is clearer in the native-English language group.
(2) The pattern of topic effect on the holistic scores contrasts with the topic effect on the analytic score. The analytic score of the "Space" topic is generally higher than the "Farm" topic score; however, the holistic score for the "Space" topic is significantly lower than the "Farm" topic score.
(3) The two major groups' holistic scores are significantly affected by the two different topic types. The holistic score difference between the two topics is significant in the hard- science group, whereas the difference is not significant in the social-science group. This result indicates that the holistic scores can be affected by students' academic background, interest, and experiences to the given topic.
(4) The two native-language groups' essay quality scores are significantly affected by the two different scoring methods. The difference between the two groups' scores are more significant when their essays are rated by the holistic scoring method.

The results of an ANOVA show a significant topic main effect ($F = 5.66$ df $= 1,92$ p $= .0194$), NL main effect ($F = 284.70$ df $= 1,92$ p $= .0001$), and MG $\times$ topic interaction effect ($F = 5.07$ df $= 1,92$ p $= .0267$) for the holistic scores. However, MG main effect ($F = 3.26$ df $= 1,92$ p $= .0741$), NL $\times$ topic interaction effect ($F = .93$ df $= 1,92$ p $= .3372$), and NL $\times$ MG $\times$ topic interaction effect ($F = .69$ df $= 1,92$ p $= .4351$) are not significant. The significant topic effect indicates that when the quality rating is conducted by a holistic scoring method, the quality of student essays can be significantly affected by the different topics in regard to the types of information provided in the assignments. The significant MG × topic interaction effect indicates that the hard-science major group students receive a significantly higher holistic score on the "Farm" topic than on the "Space" topic; while the holistic scores of the social-science major group students are not significantly different across different types of topics. They received slightly higher scores for the "Farm" topic than they did for the "Space" topic.

The above results may be further clarified by the characteristics of the holistic scoring method itself. In the holistic scoring method, student essays are rated globally according to what the student has been able to perform compared with what the other students have been able to perform. The major function of the holistic scoring method is to separate the better performers from the poor performers by rank ordering the essays; hence holistic scoring provides little information about the quality of an individual student's writing against a specified criterion.

Such a conclusion does not diminish the fact that native-language teachers appear to judge more harshly students who are not speakers of that language and students who are in a discipline quite distinct from that of the teachers, particularly when the students are asked to write a composition on a topic that draws on their general knowledge. It may be the case that students in the sciences have more practice with the more "limited" task and thus appear to master it. Based on raters' holistic judgments, however, the contrast between languages may be supplemented by a contrast between disciplines, which are themselves rhetorical communities.

REFERENCES

Anderson, J. R., & Reader, L.M. (1978). An elaborative processing. In L. S. Cermak & F.I.M. Craik (Eds.), *Levels of processing and human memory* (pp. 385-405). Hillsdale, NJ: Lawrence Erlbaum.

Benton, S. L., & Blohm, P. J. (1986). Effect of question type and position on measures of conceptual elaboration in writing. *Research in the Teaching of English, 20,* 98-108.

Bransford, J. D., Franks, J. J., Morris, C. D., & Stein, B. S. (1978). Some general constraints on learning and memory research. In L. S. Cermak & P.I.M. Craik

(Eds.), *Levels of processing and human memory* (pp. 331-354). Hillsdale, NJ: Lawrence Erlbaum.

Breland, H. M., & Griswold, P. A. (1981). *Group comparisons for basic skill measures* (Report No. 81-6). New York: College Entrance Examination Board.

Breland, H. M. (1983). *The direct assessment of writing skill: A measurement review* (Report No. 83-6). New York: College Entrance Examination Board.

Bridgeman, B., & Carlson, S. B. (1984). Survey of academic writing tasks. *Written Communication, 1*, 247-280.

Brossell, G. (1983). Rhetorical specification in essay examination topics. *College English, 45*, 165-173.

Bruce, B., Collins, A., Rubin, A. D., & Gentner, D. (1983). *Three perspectives on writing* (Reading Education Report No. 41). Champaign: University of Illinois, Center for the Study of Reading.

Carlson, S. B., Bridgeman, B., Camp, R., & Waanders, J. (1985). *Relationship of admission test scores to writing performance of native and nonnative speakers of English* (Research Report No. 19). Princeton, NJ: Educational Testing Service.

Christensen, F. (1968). *The Christensen rhetoric program.* New York: Harper.

Christensen, F., & Christensen, B. (1978). *Notes toward a new rhetoric.* New York: Harper.

Crowhurst, M. (1980). Syntactic complexity and teachers' quality ratings narrations and arguments. *Research in the Teaching of English, 14*, 223-231.

Crowhurst, M., & Piche, G. L. (1979). Audience and mode of discourse effects on syntactic complexity in writing at two grade levels. *Research in the Teaching of English, 13*, 101-109.

Dixon, E. (1970). *Index of syntactic maturity* (Dixon-Hunt-Christensen). (ERIC Document Reproduction Service No. ED 091 748).

Greenberg, K. L. (1981). The effect of variations in essay questions on the writing performance of CUNY freshmen (Research Monograph Series No. 1). New York: City University of New York.

Greenberg, K. L. (1986). The development and validation of the TOFEL writing test: A discourse of TOFEL research reports 15 and 19. *TESOL Quarterly, 20*, 531-544.

Hirsch, E. D., Jr. (1977). *The philosophy of composition.* Chicago: University of Chicago Press.

Hoetker, J. (1982). Essay examination topics and students' writing.*College Composition and Communication, 33*, 377-391.

Hunt, K. W. (1965). *Grammatical structures written at three grade levels.* Champaign, IL: National Council of Teachers of English.

Hunt, K. W. (1970). *Syntactic maturity in school children and adults.* (Society for Research in Child Development Monograph No. 134). Chicago: University of Chicago.

Hunt, K. W. (1977). Early blooming and late blooming syntactic structures. In C. R. Cooper and L. Odell (Eds.) *Evaluating writing: Describing, measuring, judging* (pp. 91-104). Urbana, IL: National Council of Teachers of English.

Hunt, K. W. (1983). Sentence combining and the teaching of English. In M. Martlew (Ed.), *The psychology of written language* (pp. 99-125). New York: John Wiley.

Meredith, V. M. and Williams, P. L. (1984). Issues in direct writing assessment: Problem identification and control. *Educational Measurement: Issues and practice, 3*, 11-35.

O'Donnell, R. C. (1976). A critique of some indices of syntactic maturity. *Research in the Teaching of English, 10,* 31-38.

O'Hare, F. (1973) *Sentence combining: Improving student writing without formal grammar instruction.* Urbana, IL: National Council of Teachers of English.

Park, Y. M. (1986). *The influence of task upon writing performance.* Unpublished doctoral dissertation, University of Illinois at Urbana-Champaign.

Purves, A. C. (1985). *Framework for scoring: GRE/TOEFL.* Unpublished manuscript, University of Illinois at Urbana-Champaign, Curriculum Laboratory.

Purves, A. C., Söter, A., Takala, S., & Vähäpassi, A. (1984). Towards a domain-referenced system for classifying composition assignments. *Research in the Teaching of English, 18,* 385-409.

Söter, A. (1985). *GRE/TOEFL scoring criteria.* Unpublished manuscript, University of Illinois at Urbana-Champaign, Curriculum Laboratory.

Stein, B. B., & Bransford, J. D. (1979). Constraints on effective elaboration: Effects of precision and subject generation. *Journal of Verbal Learning and Verbal Behavior, 18,* 769-777.

Tibbetts, A. M., & Tibbetts, C. (1984). *Strategies of rhetoric with handbook* (4th ed.). Glenview, IL: Scott, Foresman.

Vähäpassi, A. (1982). On the specification of the domain of school writing. *Evaluation in Education: An International Review,* Series 5, pp. 265-289.

Watson, C. (1983). Syntactic changes: Writing development and the rhetorical context. In M. Martlew (Ed.), *The psychology of written language* (pp. 127-139). New York: John Wiley.

Wolk, A. (1970). The relative importance of the final free modifier: A quantitative analysis. *Research in the Teaching of English, 4,* 59-68.

PART IV
Summing Up

11

Contrastive Rhetoric and Second Language Learning: Notes Toward a Theory of Contrastive Rhetoric

ROBERT B. KAPLAN

Text and discourse linguists believe . . . that we must learn to describe textual and discoursal forces and principles if we are to understand how individual sentences work and why they look the way they do. In this sense, text and discourse linguistics are apt to surround, engulf, and absorb traditional sentence linguistics. And once this happens, terms such as "text linguistics" or "discourse linguistics" become redundant because all linguistics will always reckon with text and discourse. Such ultimate successes of text and discourse linguistics might, paradoxically, lead to their presiding over their own liquidation. (Enkvist, 1957, p. 27)

Given the increasing interest in text linguistics, of which contrastive rhetoric is probably a subset, and given the rise of schools of thought dedicated respectively to the intense study of oral text or of written text, this may not be a particularly auspicious time to produce a general statement about contrastive rhetoric—a kind of text analysis that has floated on the periphery of more formal linguistic studies for nearly a quarter of a century. The only possible excuse for doing so lies in the opportunity to offer a somewhat different point of view.

THE HISTORY OF CONTRASTIVE RHETORIC

Contrastive rhetoric, unlike other more formal approaches to text analysis, has not striven for predictive adequacy, but has had a

primary concern for descriptive accuracy.[1] It had its origins in pedagogical necessity. In the early 1960s, some ESL teachers gradually
became aware that the audio-lingual method (ALM)—then all the
rage—was not an adequate pedagogical approach to serve the needs
of foreign students studying in colleges and universities in the United
States. It was evident that such students needed, most urgently, to
improve their performance in reading (because they were faced with
extensive assignments involving extremely technical material) and in
writing (because they were faced with the immediate obligation to
produce term papers and theses/dissertations and to respond to essay
examinations). ALM not only was unsuited to these objectives, it was
actually counterproductive because it recognized no difference between speaking and writing and because its stress on sentence
grammar precluded attention to text structure. It is readily observable
that students with excellent control of sentence structure are not
necessarily able to compose text; it is further observable that students
who can parse every sentence in a text cannot necessarily summarize
its content. Something else was needed.

At the time, it seemed perfectly reasonable to look at the texts that
students produced, and to try to determine where their production
deviated from that of native speakers (writers). In order to do that, it
was necessary to have a baseline set of data descriptive of the
production of text by native speakers. And an obvious place to look
for such baseline data seemed to lie in the work being done in English
as a mother tongue education. This source provided two kinds of
information: On the one hand, it provided a large number of
pedagogical models for the teaching of composition to native
speakers in the form of handbooks; on the other hand, it provided a
very small number of research models because most handbooks traced
their origins to a small number of theoretical sources. In the early
1960s, research in rhetoric and composition was somewhat limited;
most writing programs were heavily involved in the teaching of
grammar, and many of the available "rhetoric" textbooks were
largely oriented to the fairly traditional approaches to composition
that had been in use in schools in this country for the preceding half
century (see Brooks & Warren, 1958).

The most interesting innovative model available was the one being
evolved by Christensen in his notion of generative rhetoric (1963)[2]
while a number of other useful ideas were coming out of the so-called
new-rhetoric movement. Some of these models and ideas were
applicable to the problem demonstrated by nonnative speakers of

English, and were applied by ESL teachers, but the models had to be modified and adjusted to applications in a linguistic area for which they were not intended.

Early Analytic Study

Because I was then the administrator of what was, for the time, a large and relatively important ESL program, I had the opportunity to observe a substantial number of compositions written in English by native speakers of a variety of languages other than English. The papers were written by students with evidently inadequate control of English; they were written over a relatively short time (within a few weeks in the same semester—so differences in teaching time were irrelevant), and they were written under essentially identical class-room conditions. This corpus demonstrated that there were problems that seemed to be unique to speakers of particular languages. The kinds of problems investigated were not simply grammatical or surface matters, that is, differences in spelling (e.g., *harbor* for *harbour*) or differences in lexicon (e.g., *petrol* for *gas*) were not given much attention. Rather, attention was focused on what were thought by me to be underlying differences.[3] The observations conducted over a large number of texts were reinforced by the experience of composition teachers; experienced ESL teachers were able to tell with astonishing accuracy what the native-language of a writer was by simply reading the text produced by that writer (independent, of course, of clues given in the text, e.g., the name of a city, of a well-known person). The evidence suggested that there must be regularities in the English writing of nonnative English learners from particular language backgrounds that could be observed and codified to provide teaching content and strategy for ESL writing courses. It also suggested that there were regularities in the English writing of native speakers of English and that there were regularities in the differences between the writing of native speakers and nonnative speakers. At this stage in the evolution of contrastive rhetoric there was no great interest in understanding the origins of the matters under study, rather, the interest was primarily in finding solutions to an immediate pedagogical problem. It is therefore relatively easy to explain why the earliest studies in contrastive rhetoric were focused entirely on the English writing of non-English

speaking students. This focus, in turn, helps to explain why some of
the notions look, from the vantage point of the present, naive and
oversimplified, ignoring, for example, emic/etic[4] considerations.
What was being sought—in the then still popular paradigm of
contrastive studies[5]—was some clear-cut unambiguous difference
between English and any other given language, the notion being that
such a clear-cut difference might provide the basis for pedagogical
approaches that would solve—within the normative academic space
of one or two semesters—the writing problems of speakers of other
languages trying to learn to function in written English in the
peculiar constraints of tertiary-level education in the United States.

Whether it had theoretical validity or not, the notion obviously
had a wide popular appeal. (The distribution of languages studied
was a direct reflection of the distribution of international students in
U.S. tertiary education.)[6] The general appeal of the notion led rather
quickly to the development of textbooks incorporating the basic
concepts (see Bander, 1971).

CONTRASTIVE RHETORIC AND TEXT ANALYSIS

Despite the fact that it arose from a pedagogical motive, contrastive
rhetoric belongs to the basic tradition of text analysis. The larger
tradition is of course much older, having its roots in Prague School
Linguistics and in the Firthian influence in Britain. There were,
however, important differences between the research tradition in
European text-linguistics and the immediate and pragmatic objectives of contrastive rhetoric. These differences, as well as the various
lines of connection, are well summarized in Houghton and Hoey
(1983). While contrastive rhetoric initially was largely an American
development, it was not compatible with either general or applied
linguistic traditions in the United States. There, as early as 1933,
Bloomfield had begun to insist that serious linguistics would be
limited to structures no larger than the sentence (although he did
admit the possibility of "dependent sentences"). The evolution of
transformational-generative grammar (particularly in its earlier
models) further served to focus attention on the sentence and to
inhibit studies of intersentential relationships. Additionally, the
differentiation in the transformational-generative paradigm between

deep and surface structure, and the emphasis on the analysis of deep structure proved essentially antithetical to contrastive rhetoric, which must be concerned with relationships manifested at the surface. The neo-Whorfian underlying assumptions of contrastive rhetoric have served further to differentiate it from other approaches, particularly in the United States. In the more recent past, however, the assumptions of the larger tradition and of contrastive rhetoric have become more and more compatible, and it will be useful to look at some notions from the larger tradition that have been incorporated into contrastive rhetoric.

In the larger tradition, it has been fairly clearly established that a text is not merely an exploded sentence, that a text is a complex multidimensional structure, and that the dimensions involved include at least syntactic, semantic, and discoursal feature—elements of cohesion (see Halliday & Hasan, 1976) and coherence—as well as considerations of schematic structure (see Carrell, 1984a, 1984b, 1984c; Meyer, 1975a, 1975b, 1977, 1982), of audience, and of the sociolinguistic functions of a given text (see Widdowson, 1984). At the same time, a growing interest from the pedagogical side in the teaching of English for special purpose—particularly in the teaching of English for science and technology—has drawn attention to the relationship between certain textual types and certain syntactic and semantic features (see Dubois, 1982; Heslot, 1982; Huckin & Olsen, 1980, 1981; Sellers, 1982; Trimble & Trimble, 1985; West, 1980). Still another research strand (see Biber, 1984a, 1984b; Grabe, 1984, 1986; Neu, 1985) has begun to demonstrate a clear linguistic difference between typical written and spoken text, and therefore has suggested that reading and writing require a set of quite separate pedagogical approaches (see, Dubin, Eskey, & Grabe, 1986). There is also a growing input from artificial intelligence studies and from psycholinguistics in terms of the role of short-term and long-term memory in encoding and decoding (see Caramazza & McCloskey, 1981). All of these strands have had an impact on the evolution of contrastive rhetoric both as a research paradigm (see Connor, 1986) and as a useful tool for teachers (see Rankin, 1985).

Contrastive rhetoric has never pretended to be a teaching *system*, rather it has claimed to be able to contribute to pedagogical systems that have a concern with reading and writing. It has been incompatible with such approaches as ALM (which has a heavy emphasis on spoken language and which is still strongly represented in actual practice) and with the more recent "humanistic" approaches (e.g., Silent Way, Community Language Learning, Suggestopedia—which have no visible basis in language theory but represent the views of strong, charismatic methodologists—and the Natural Approach. See Gattegno, 1972; Curran, 1976; Lozanov, 1979; Krashen & Terrell, 1983). European methodologists interested in the notional/functional syllabus[7] (see Munby, 1978) have not been concerned with reading and writing as such, nor have they given much attention to the more advanced levels; thus they have paid scant attention to contrastive rhetoric. The more recent concern with "communicative approaches"[8] has given primary attention to reading and writing and has resulted in a renewed interest in contrastive rhetoric and in other varieties of text analysis (see Quinn, 1985).

WHAT EVIDENCE CONTRASTIVE
RHETORIC EXAMINES

Underlying this complex interconnection between contrastive rhetoric and more broadly conceived text-analytic approaches are a number of ideas that need to be explored. Over a long period of time, the teaching of writing has been largely concerned with the text produced by the learner—with a *product*. More recent research (e.g., Flower, 1979; Hairston, 1982; Knoblauch & Brannon, 1984) has suggested that writing is a series of cognitive processes, and that the primary task in the classroom is the teaching of a method of internal discovery. However, any consideration of the vast variety of potential writing activities suggests that the process/product distinction may not be applied usefully to every writing act.

A Taxonomy of Writing Types

Perhaps a taxonomy of writing activities may help to clarify this point. In the real world (and to a lesser degree in the school world) individuals who profess to literacy engage in a wide variety of writing activities, ranging from the creation of shopping lists and laundry lists, to calendar entries, to notes to the milkman (e.g., of the sort that say, "2 quarts today"), to the creation of poems and—yes—even student essays. It may be useful to divide this broad range of writing tasks into three basic types: writing without composing, writing through composing in which the essential purpose is reporting of some sort, and writing through composing in which the composing process itself functions as a heuristic act. Even these main categories can be further subdivided, in general, into categories in which the motivation and inspiration derive from within the writer, as opposed to categories in which the content of the writing is externally dictated. Writing without composing includes such acts as list making (which is perhaps internally motivated), but it also includes that writing activity that has become pervasive in many societies around the world—form filling. In form filling, the composing, such as it is, is dictated to a significant degree by the form being filled rather than by any organizational structure deriving from the writer. The form filler has to be familiar with the societal conventions of form-filling—has to know that a slot requiring *name* is asking for the full name (family name, given name, middle name) provided in an order prescribed by cultural convention (e.g., Mao Tse Tung versus John Q. Public, but Public, John Q., for those societies that make a fetish of arranging names in alphabetical order), or has to know that a slot inquiring about sex is asking for a biological gender description rather than an indication of preference or frequency. But it is the form that controls the information (a fact regrettably overlooked with amazing frequency by designers of forms). Writing without composing also involves such real world acts as taking dictation (whereby the "dictator" provides the composing and the "dictatee" serves merely as a transcriber, perhaps adding minor technical editing along the way) and doing basic translation (whereby the translator is merely transcribing a text composed by someone else in one language into another language; e.g., défense de fumer = no smoking). This latter set of activities—form-filling, taking dictation, doing translation—is one in which the motivation, the content, the form, the inspiration are all extrinsic. The whole range of activities that may be called writing without composing constitutes a very large set, including far more types than have been enumerated above, and represents a set that accounts for a very high proportion of actual writing time for most literate people in most societies.

Writing through composing for the purpose of reporting is perhaps the next most widely distributed type. It subsumes much memo and letter writing, much of the work of scientists of various persuasions (ranging from physicians' patient records, to reports of medical clinical research, to reports from the chemical or pharmaceutical laboratory), and much of the article writing activity of a variety of social scientists (an activity in which empirical observations are recorded in support of an existing hypothesis and organized under an existing paradigm). It is more difficult in this category to draw clear lines between intrinsic and extrinsic motivation, though it is fairly clear that the activities can be described as composing because the content, at least, is provided by the writer. The form may be dictated by the conventions of an academic discipline or by the requirements of a journal publisher or a data repository.

There is, of course, a whole field—journalism—that engages in an activity designated as reporting, but it is not crystal clear that the activity of journalists is always unambiguously "reporting." If one looks at the content of a newspaper, it should be immediately clear that only a small percentage of the content can be called "reporting." Some substantial fraction of the space in a newspaper is filled with advertising—both in the form of the traditional larger ads bought by various retailers to call attention to their goods and services, and in the form of classified ads that range from invitations to announcements to the sale of goods and services. Beyond that, there are various pieces called features (which are not necessarily written to convey information in the narrow sense but are intended to create a mood or to portray a character), editorials, and letters to the editor, or to Ann Landers (which are intended to convey an opinion), cartoons (which are intended to amuse—and, perhaps, sometimes to instruct), and a variety of other special sections (e.g., travel sections, business sections—which, at least in the paper I read regularly, consist largely of long tabular lists of stock and bond transactions, currency fluctuations, and commodities market reports—and sports sections— which so far defy definition). Indeed, the amount of unadulterated reportage is relatively small, but such reportage would, in and of itself, certainly count in this category. This longish aside is intended in this definition both to include the only category of writing that self-consciously calls itself "reporting" and to exclude the large variety of other kinds of writing (both writing without composing— most obviously in stock-market reports or team standings—and writing through composing in which the writing process functions as a heuristic act). To a somewhat different degree, the same things may be said for magazine reportage. Books that aspire to that designation, of course, fall into a variety of categories. Some legitimately are instances of reporting, but many go well beyond reporting in the sense it is being used here—for example, *The Alexandria Quartet* can hardly be defined as pure reporting.

Writing through composing, in which the composing process functions as a heuristic act, is the rarest of the writing types practiced by literate individuals. It includes the creation of novels and short stories, of poems and plays, of theoretical and philosophical treatises by scholars, and—curiously—of the kinds of essays school children are most commonly asked to write. (It has struck me as odd that the educational system uses as its major pedagogic device a form so rarely occurring in the real world, and that the educational system largely ignores the forms that have far greater frequency and productivity.) The essays students write, however, can be differentiated from the work of creative artists and scholars with respect to motivation. Speech act theorists have long recognized the somewhat peculiar nature of academic discourse. Searle (1969, p. 66), for example, observes:

> There are two types of questions, a) real questions, b) exam questions. In real questions S[peaker] wants to know (find out) the answer; in exam questions S[peaker] wants to know if H[earer] knows.

But Searle does not discuss the distinction between the two types of responses. The response to the "exam question" is what Perelman (1986) describes as "institutional-based discourse." But even in institutional- based discourse (as well as in other types subsumed in this category of *writing through composing*) one must presume that the motivation is, in part at least, intrinsic, and that the writer has some responsibility for the form and the content. The differentiation in this category is one of degree. Obviously, when a student is told to write comparison and contrast as a rhetorical exercise, the writer has less control over form than he or she would have in a condition in which the writer chooses a particular rhetorical strategy in order to achieve a desired effect. In this type of writing, process considerations become much more significant; in this type of writing, the solitary author who strives to discover and communicate personal meaning becomes a much more believable construct. This view, however, takes little account of the fact that most writing constitutes a social activity in which purposes and constraints are externally dictated.

Shared Universes of Knowledge

Indeed, this summary taxonomy of writing types must be seen in the light of two other major factors: audience and a not yet well described set of culturally prescribed constraints. Obviously, writing is generally addressed to some audience. When one composes a shopping list, the audience is oneself; that observation is validated by the fact that when a basic shopping list is turned over to another person, it has to be annotated. When my wife composes a shopping list and then is, for some reason, prevented from doing the shopping herself, she often passes the list along to me. For me, she has to annotate the item milk to "2 half-gallons of 2% low-fat milk with a shelf-date as far in the future as possible." This annotation represents knowledge that she possesses but that I do not necessarily possess because our universes of knowledge are not precisely coterminous. As it is obvious that a shopping list is most commonly addressed to oneself, it is equally obvious that, for other writing types, there is a vast potential pool of audiences. Again, it seems to be possible to construct a small number of broad categories. In addition to oneself, a writer may address: one known other (as in a personal letter), one unknown other (as in some types of business letters), a group of known others (as in some types of sermons), or, a group of unknown others (as in this chapter). The size of the group of known or unknown is a consideration (because the larger the group, the lower the probability that the writer and the reader share a universe of common knowledge). And that is precisely why the question of audience constitutes a significant factor. When one writes to oneself, the universe of knowledge is absolutely coterminous; when one deals with a single known other, there is a high probability that, even if the universes of knowledge are not exactly coterminous, the universes of knowledge are at least well understood, but when one deals with large groups the probability of shared universes of knowledge diminishes in direct proportion to the size of audience. The question of shared universes of knowledge helps to determine possible presuppositions and to define structural/functional strategies.

There are, of course, other considerations that influence writers with respect to the audience they choose to address (and readers with respect to what they read). Clearly, the relative sociopolitical levels of reader and writer would have some important influence, as would the relative power status. A superior writing to an inferior, as in a memo for example, would demonstrate different textual features than would an inferior writing to a superior (see Pytlik, 1982). These sociolinguistic differences, while they are indeed important, are of lower significance here because they are more or less universal. Power relationships, for example, though they may evoke different realizations of the strong and weak positions, occur in all societies. There are, obviously, very important differences across linguistic communities, but this whole chapter tries to deal with that issue; the term *contrastive rhetoric* implies a contrast across languages and across cultures.

Furthermore, given that the act of writing severely constrains the information feedback loop, awareness of audience is critical in determining how to circumvent problems arising from that lack. In oral discourse a dense feedback loop normally exists, consisting of a whole range of kinesic and proxemic signals together with a whole range of verbal signals; speakers signal each other through intonation, eye contact, gesture, posture, encouraging vocal signs, spatial relations, and the like. None of these feedback mechanisms exist in the written system (except to the extent that punctuation may be regarded as a weak reflection of the intonation system). Only in such forms as the personal letter is there any sort of feedback loop, and even there, the feedback loop is significantly attenuated by time and distance.

Cultural Factors

The set of cultural factors is much more difficult to define, largely because no paradigm yet exists that could incorporate such information. It is possible to subdivide the cultural factors into two interlocking systems—one deriving from the total ambient environment, from the community of speakers of which the writer is a member (and thus one that at least in some senses implicates the linguistic system), the other deriving from the cultural conventions that surround the act of writing. While the problem has not yet been carefully studied, it is possible to claim that the three broad types of writing (writing without composing, writing through composing for the purpose of reporting, and writing through composing in which the composing act becomes a heuristic act) are differently distributed (having different functions and different frequencies) in different cultural settings. The fables of Aesop (though now preserved in various written guises) were intended for a particular function when they were initially created, and it is possible that in some "modern" societies the function is now served through a different mechanism. It is also observable that the functions of Aesop's fables, however defined, are rather different from the functions of a chemistry textbook. And there are different definitions of the social group to whom various functions belong; indeed, there is even a question of what is meant by "belonging" (Western societies have complex rules governing the notions of copyright and plagiarism, whereas other societies operate on the assumption that imitation is the greatest form of flattery—and of scholarly activity).

But quite beyond that, there are to be considered the localized conventions that surround the physical appearance of text on the page—such relatively trivial matters as the indentation (or non-indentation) of the first lines of paragraphs, the placement of punctuation in relation to the surrounding words, the matter of relative size of margins, and the like. In Chinese printed text, for example—perhaps because Chinese characters are assigned equal visual space—punctuation is equidistant from the characters on both sides, whereas in English punctuation is snugged up to the left side of the space (e.g., *English:* /word, word/ *Chinese:* /word , word/). The appearance of a text on the page constitutes a critical factor in its acceptability. Speakers of Arabic, writing in English, tend to use the edges of a page as margins, thereby inciting the enmity of English language teachers who grade their scripts. Another example occurs with respect to permitted ways to end a text line—to the uses of hyphenation and to the question of whether punctuation occurs at the end of a given line or at the beginning of the next line—rules that are in the process of change in English right now as a result of the increasing use of word processors.

These several considerations—the writing types, the issue of audience, and the issue of culturally defined conventions affecting both the frequency and distribution of types and on the functions and appearance of text—suggest that writing should be taught; that writing will not simply be acquired. Contrastive rhetoric strives to determine which of the several functions exists in a particular language as compared with English, and how a particular function would be used in a given language. Contrastive rhetoric strives to determine which of the several functions exists in a particular language as compared with English, and how a particular function would be used in a given language. For example, if one compares a newspaper from a Third-World country—the Philippines, to choose virtually at random—it is clear that the types of stories differ significantly from what is to be found in the *London, Los Angeles,* or *New York Times,* and that difference is not attributable solely to differences in resources. The notion that writing is acquired, on the contrary, requires the assumption that the types of writing and the essential distribution of types would not vary significantly across languages.

Spoken Versus Written Language

If indeed writing must be taught (while spoken language may be assumed to be acquired), there must be some distinction between oral and written language. Historically, spoken language is part of the genetic baggage of all human beings—it is built into the DNA, and indeed it has become a defining characteristic of the species and of the range of normalcy within the species. All human beings have spoken language, and they have had it for a very long time, even in evolutionary terms. But written language is relatively new; it is, at best, only a few thousand years old, and it is not universally distributed in the species. The possession of literacy is not a defining characteristic for normalcy in the species—though some educators would like it to become one. Henry Trueba (1986), for example, calls attention to the desire to use written competence as a defining characteristic:

> Issues. . . regarding "language handicaps" and "linguistic under-achievement" are social phenomena that surface in the form of linguistic deviance and are then "interpreted by the experts." The traditional assessment of concept formation is based on the assumption that, if a child does not demonstrate in an appropriate linguistic form that s/he recognizes a concept and its relationships in those domains "all normal children" know, the child is handicapped. A perfectly normal child who has just arrived from a linguistically, socially, or culturally different [environment], by not being able to produce in . . . written text the expected linguistic forms, becomes ipso facto "abnormal" in the eyes of the educator. (p. 45)

Most applied linguists now accept the notion that all human children are born with a natural, biologically conditioned predisposition to acquire spoken language, that all it takes to trigger that predisposition is the presence of a linguistic environment, and that such acquisition is essentially impervious to teaching. Written language constitutes a different sort of problem. The written language has been added to the human inventory through a set of postbiological evolutionary steps; that is not in any sense to diminish the importance of writing (at least in some cultures), nor is it intended in any sense to diminish the importance of written language. Rather, the point is merely that the two derive from different origins.

> At least some of the characteristics of writing can be seen as different realizations of features common to all discourse. Both speaking and writing are interaction processes that mediate in two ways. One way is that they serve to bring the states of mind (to use a very general formulation) of addressor and addressee into convergence. The other is that they serve to relate abstract knowledge with real instances; convergence requires each participant to negotiate the meanings of particular expressions by invoking conventional frames of reference in respect to their systematic knowledge of language and their schematic knowledge of reality. This mediation, then, is at the same time interpersonal/communicative and intrapersonal/conceptual. In the spoken discourse of conversation these mediating processes are enacted by reciprocal exchange so that communicative outcomes emerge contingently as collaborative elements. In writing, these processes are nonreciprocally enacted so that the responsibility for structuring the discourse rests with only one participant (the writer) who will, therefore, tend to place greater reliance on an assumed shared knowledge of the frames of reference and rhetorical arrangements that characterize different text types (Widdowson, 1984, p. 50).

Written language is used for communication, for negotiation of meaning; it constitutes part of the discourse process. Some work in discourse analysis has tended to focus on the spoken language, on the speech acts involved in conversations and on the more general notion involving the understanding of the ways talk is managed. This focus can be explained in terms of linguistic orthodoxy, which takes the primacy of speech for granted. In teaching, some of the same focus can be observed, for example in the idea that communicative language teaching concerns only the ability to talk. There seems to be a presumption that written language is somehow not authentic communication. In recent years, the idea of the primacy of speech has been challenged. While there are some extreme views of the matter (as, for example, some deconstructionist thinkers), what seems important is the concept that writing is a mode of language use, not merely an alternative medium, and that as such it is different from speech, it can be studied in its own right, and it is not necessary to hold a view of the primacy of either mode in order to study language.

Process and Product

Contrastive rhetoric is a way of studying language—albeit with attention to the product rather than the process—based on the belief that the analysis of text can lead to a better understanding of how language works. Contrastive rhetoric is not a *methodology* for teaching, though some of its findings can be (and indeed have been) applied to the teaching process since its inception.

While contrastive rhetoric is focused on the finished text—the product—or on some product along the way between idea and finished text,[9] it does not and cannot ignore the process of composing. Given that academic writing instruction at the secondary and tertiary levels is generally directed at "institutional based rhetoric," and given that most second-language programs at those levels have as an objective the inculcation of skill in "institutional based rhetoric," the question remains whether it is reasonable to expect large numbers of individuals to produce writing through composing in which the composing process functions as a heuristic act. The question is appropriate both in terms of the fact that such writing is relatively rare in virtually all cultures and in terms of the fact that such writing may be totally absent as a mode in some cultures. As Ostler (1987) points out, for example, among some Arabic speakers text structure exhibits a strong preference for Koranic style—for the notion that text represents, in some important way, THE TRUTH, and that, consequently, it is unlikely that text can be used as a heuristic process for the writer, since text has the primary function of producing an elaborate sense of harmony and balance in and through the language. To put it in a slightly different way, one could say that the primary focus of writing in Arabic rests on the *language* of a text, not on its

propositional structure. The distinction implied here is an important
one. In pedagogic terms, it is unlikely that a learner can acquire a text
type that has no reality for him or her; thus there is another argument
for teaching composing. The argument is not for teaching only the
form of this text type; rather the argument implies that both the form
and the ideological process through which one arrives at the form
need to be taught—that is, that both the process and the product
deserve serious consideration, that one cannot be ignored in favor of
the other.

Logic

In English, the ideological process subsumes a way of dealing with
propositional content—of conceptualizing what is called "logic"
(not in an absolute mathematical sense, but in a cultural sense), and
of managing the systems of cohesion and coherence through which
this logic is reflected in text. But these activities are, at least to some
extent, culturally prescribed. As Wilkerson (1986) points out, the
development of writing education in the United States reflects a
combination of two traditions: Aristotelian (based on syllogistic
reasoning) and Galilean (based on hierarchical taxonomies) sys-
tematizations. The traditional school rhetorics, from the middle of
the eighteenth century well into the twentieth, "in keeping with
the prevalent materialistic philosophy and its associated essentially
technologically world view... " (Berlin 1984, p. 9), placed great value
on clarity and precision in the framework of a rigorously logical
system (see the school rhetorics based on the work of George
Campbell and Hugh Blair). In the United States, in contrast to the
Arabic situation suggested earlier, the focus in writing, for generations of students, has been on the *structure* of propositions; it has
only incidentally given attention to the *language* of the text.
Wilkerson notes a very different tradition in Japanese. It would be
possible, in a reductionist sense, to place the responsibility for these
differences squarely on the educational systems (as Mohan & Lo,
1985, have done), assuming that educational systems are responsible
for the preservation and promulgation of preferred rhetorical types,
but that would be an oversimplification. Educational systems do not
serve as the intellectual frontline of most cultures, rather, they reflect
thought as they reflect more deeply embedded cultural preferences.

Role of Educational Systems

Interesting problems occur, by way of example, when educational systems are imposed on cultures of which they are not an integral part, as happened in the cases of American Samoa and Puerto Rico (and as happened for a brief time in post-World War II Japan) with respect to a U. S. based school rhetoric, or as happened in Hong Kong with respect to a British school rhetoric. While it is difficult to predict with accuracy what will ultimately emerge from such an imposition, some evidence has been accumulated by Santana-Seda (1974) and Santiago (1968) for Puerto Rico and by the Hong Kong Examinations Authority (1986, pp. 86-94) that what emerges is a form not representative of the "received" rhetoric of either of the input languages. Contrastive rhetoric has been concerned with such questions as these, trying to shed light on what learners bring with them from their own cultures and how what they bring interacts with what they encounter when they undertake to compose in English.

Writer Responsibility
Versus Reader Responsibility

The problems outlined above do not constitute the only points of rhetorical conflict between cultures. In the citation from Widdowson (1984), the following statement occurs:

> The responsibility for structuring discourse rests with only one participant [in written discourse] (the writer) who will . . . tend to place greater reliance on an assumed shared knowledge.

This statement raises two very interesting points of contrast: how much responsibility does the writer in fact assume, and what sort of shared knowledge can in fact be assumed to exist in a situation in which a writer is composing in a language not his or her own? Hinds (1986) proposes a typology of language based on relative reader/writer responsibility. He classifies Japanese as a reader-responsible language, English as a writer-responsible language, and Chinese (Mandarin) as a language in transition from reader-responsibility to writer-responsibility. This question of relative responsibility affects on the propositional structure of text; readers in a reader-responsible

language expect to supply some significant portion of the propositional structure, while readers in a writer-responsible language
expect that most of the propositional structure will be provided by the
writer. The *BBC World News* (while a scripted oral text) provides an
example of writer-responsible text—the news is introduced with a
clearly identified outline of the main points to be covered; that
introduction is followed by a detailed exposition of each of the
outlined main points in the order presented, and the news ends with a
summary of the main points, again in the same order. This structure
suggests that the writer assumes very heavy responsibility and that the
presumption of shared knowledge is severely constrained; Japanese
texts are very differently organized, placing heavy responsibility on
the reader to understand what is said, and assuming a very high
degree of shared knowledge (Hinds, 1986 provides an interesting
example).

Topic Marking

Contrastive rhetoric issues also involve grammatical issues as they
affect the structure of discourse, not merely the structure of isolated
sentences. In certain languages, for example, grammatical subjects
are redesignated by subject marking particles; such particles, however,
may also serve as topic designators (in which topic is a discourse
function rather than a sentential function). Tsao (1983) has looked at
the functions of the particle *ba* in Mandarin as topic marker, and
Hinds (1979, 1983a, 1983b) has looked at the particles *wa* and *ga* in
Japanese in a similar context. There has also been research that looks
at the frequency and distribution of various sentential types in
discourse patterns (Dubois, 1982; Guzman Lagos, 1983; Heslot, 1982;
Huckin & Olsen, 1980; Josifek, 1983; Latorre, 1983; Maldonado &
Guzman, 1984; Reichman-Adar, 1984; Trimble & Trimble, 1982, 1985;
West, 1980; Williams, 1983), these being drawn largely from the
English-for-Special-Purposes literature. And there has been research
that looks at the relationship between grammatical functions and
discourse types (Biber, 1984a, 1984b; Grabe, 1984, 1986; Neu, 1985;
Rottweiler, 1984). This newer research has also had pedagogic
realizations in textbooks (e.g., Kaplan & Shaw, 1983).

TEACHING ISSUES

These examples illustrate the kind of evidence sought in contrastive rhetoric. Of course, the point of searching for such evidence is to facilitate the teaching of composing in the second-language classroom. The intent is not to provide a pedagogic method, but to provide a body of knowledge concerning what is involved in writing various types of texts for various types of audiences in various types of culturally constrained settings. In sum, contrastive rhetoric has encouraged attention to the following issues in the teaching of writing (and reading):

- knowledge of the morphosyntax of the target language, not at the sentential but at the intersentential level;
- knowledge of the writing conventions of the target language both in the sense of frequency and distribution of types and in the sense of text appearance;
- knowledge of audience characteristics and audience expectations in the target culture; and
- knowledge of the subject under discussion.

These are, clearly, product concerns. While the primary emphasis has been on the composition rather than on the mental processes through which the composition is generated, those processes have not been, and cannot be, ignored. Exclusive attention to the product is the result of a number of basic misunderstandings.

Syntax

Teachers, for example, often assume that morphosyntactic information can be taught in a vacuum; the result of such an assumption is not a writing class but a grammar class. There can be no objection in principle to the teaching of grammar per se, but it is a fallacy to confuse the teaching of grammar with the teaching of writing. Accumulated research evidence suggests that grammatical knowledge alone is necessary but not sufficient to the teaching of writing. Indeed, morphosyntactic knowledge is prerequisite to composing; learners who write syntactic mazes[10] cannot give sufficient attention to text features. Morphosyntactic features, on the other hand, are probably sufficient for writing without composing. Once composing becomes involved, mere morphosyntactic knowledge is insufficient. Native speakers have in their repertoire a large number of clause-moving and clause-embedding strategies. Morphosyntactic instruction certainly can inculcate a selected subset of these strategies, but it cannot at the present time select those strategies that have the highest frequency, the widest distribution, and the greatest productivity, nor can morphosyntactic instruction inculcate the sociolinguistic information that necessarily governs choices among those strategies. The point, however, is that students who do not have control of basic clause-generating strategies are not prepared to deal with clause-movement strategies, and are certainly not prepared to deal with the sociolinguistic constraints on those strategies; thus morphosyntactic control is prerequisite to learning to compose. At the same time, the sociolinguistic constraints are not solely a function of product focus; sociolinguistic choices are made in the process of composing.

Conventions

The matter of writing conventions, discussed briefly above, is perhaps, more even than syntactic accuracy and spelling, part of the popular conception of literacy. Writing conventions are often dismissed by teachers as too obvious to need attention or as beneath notice for teachers of serious composition. Yet, in the contrastive situation, there is no reason to assume that the nonnative English speaker will be aware of this set of conventions in English, or that the learner will be able to acquire these conventions for him- or herself.

Audience and Assumptions

The matter of audience awareness is also crucial to writing success because it defines the possible assumptions concerning the extent of shared knowledge and the possible strategies to be used in determining how to avoid problems caused by the absence of a feedback loop. Inexperienced writers—literate youngsters in their L1, L2 learners, and others (whether inexperience is a function of inexperience of "institutional based discourse" in any language, or whether it is a function of inexperience in estimating knowledge shared with an audience) often tend to choose themselves as audience—an assumption that permits the problem of shared knowledge to be avoided, since the universe of knowledge of the writer is coterminous with that of the writer-as-audience. It is difficult for inexperienced writers to project themselves into another persona and to make assumptions about noncoterminous universes of knowledge. The artificiality of the writing class only complicates the issue by interposing the real audience (the teacher) between the writer and any assumption of audience he or she may choose to make. In this condition, there is no viable strategy the learner can employ, since, by definition, the teacher has a larger universe of knowledge than does the learner. The matter of audience is clearly in the process domain, since decisions about shared knowledge must be made in the composing process before the product exists.

Subject Knowledge

The matter of subject knowledge is somewhat out of the hands of the composition teacher (unless the subject is composition itself); the learner brings subject knowledge with him or her (except perhaps in the extremely artificial situation in which a composition class does collective research). The universe of knowledge that the learner brings with him- or herself into the classroom includes "world knowledge" (a culturally constrained universe) and technical knowledge (deriving from external resources—e.g., another course, library reading, experimental work in a laboratory—at work in the secondary and tertiary academic environment). The matter of subject knowledge also belongs to the process domain, since choices about what segments of the universe of knowledge will be used in relation to what particular audience and what particular writing objective must be made before product preparation begins. (The definition of process used here is not a standard one in the sense that it is relatively little concerned with the psychology of self-discovery.)

Contrastive rhetoric, then, works backwards, by trying to understand composing processes through looking at products both in the target language (by trying to understand the strategies and presuppositions used in that language to accomplish certain rhetorical objectives and strategies) and in the students' other language(s) (by trying to understand what strategies and presuppositions they bring with them, what strategies and presuppositions cooccur in the target language, and what strategies and presuppositions may create tensions with the target language).

Pedagogical Objectives

The pedagogical objectives of contrastive rhetoric may be summarized in the following 10 points:

(1) To make the teacher of composition aware that:
- (a) Different composing conventions do exist in different cultures and that these different conventions need to be addressed in teaching composing; the fact that a student is able to compose in one language does not mean the student can compose in any other language.
- (b) Certain grammatical features function at the level of discourse; the fact that a student has control only of sentential syntax does not mean the student can generate text.
- (c) There is a relative distribution of reader/writer responsibility in different cultural systems and that this distribution affects assumptions about audience and about shared knowledge (see discussion of Hinds, 1986, above); the fact that a student understands audience in one language system does not mean the student understands audience in any other language system.
- (d) A composition is a product arrived at through a process; the fact that the student may generate one relatively successful text does not the process.
- (e) Morphosyntactic[11] competence is prerequisite to writing; the fact that a student can understand the structure of individual sentences in a language does not mean the student can understand the structure of cohesion and coherence in text in that language.

(2) To make the student of composition aware that:
- (a) Audience must be defined before composition can be undertaken; the assumption that the audience is the writer is not always valid.
- (b) There are a number of different writing acts—writing without composing, writing through composing in which the essential purpose is reporting, and writing through composing in which the composing process functions as a heuristic act—and that each of these requires different strategies; the fact that a student is capable of writing in one language does not mean the student is aware of the frequency and distribution of writing tasks in any other language.
- (c) There exists a set of text conventions that the student is expected to be able to manage; the fact that the student knows the

conventions of his or her own writing system does not mean the student understands the conventions employed in the target language.

(d) In order to compose anything, the student must have, and be able to bring to bear on the composing task, a universe of knowledge, including both "world knowledge" and technical knowledge of the subject; the fact that a student has opinions about a given topic does not mean the student knows the subject well enough to write about it.

(e) Writing is a social phenomenon—a technique for negotiating meaning with some other identifiable set of human beings—which requires far more than a minimal control of syntactic and lexical items in the target language.

CONCLUSION

It would be absurd to claim that these 10 points are solely and exclusively the outcome of research specifically bearing the contrastive rhetoric label. Text analysis is in the air, and outcomes derive from a whole variety of research paradigms. What can be suggested, as the opening quotation from Enkvist says, is that the whole structure of linguistic inquiry is shifting to a concern with text. Granted that contrastive rhetoric (like most other research designs) is still constrained by the absence of a rigorous paradigm (and by other considerations like the emic/etic problem, the difficulty of comparing text forms in one language against text forms in another, and the conflicting claims concerning the universality of text structures), the fact remains that the realities of teaching cannot be put aside until all the problems are solved. Whatever its contributions to research, contrastive rhetoric has influenced the teaching of ESL composition (as an aspect of second language learning), it is to be hoped for the better.

What has been described and discussed here is not a rigorous model for text analysis nor a method for teaching writing, but an algorithm for understanding the structure of text contrastively—which may, in time, lead to a paradigm for analysis or a method for pedagogy. This algorithm offers the somewhat different point of view promised at the start.

NOTES

1. Linguistic theory currently seeks to produce models that have predictive validity; that is, models are supposed to predict possible structures. Chomsky's transformational/generative model was expected to predict all, and only, the possible syntactic structures of English. In an earlier time, linguistic models were designed merely to describe the structures of a language; for example, structuralist linguistics aimed to describe and catalogue all the structures of English. By analogy, one might say that the purpose of the OED is to describe (and define) the words of English as they exist; by contrast, a detailed linguistic study of phonological rules and semantic structures might be able to predict the way in which new words might be formed in English.

2. Christensen had been my teacher when I was a graduate student at the University of Southern California and, together with some of his other graduate students, I had worked on some of the analyses that were to become the data for the articulation of his ideas, in the article cited and elsewhere, later.

3. The first place in which this matter was addressed was the 1966 article "Cultural Thought Patterns in Intercultural Education," (*Language Learning, 16*,(1-2), 1-20). The problem has been additionally addressed in a large number of articles over the past 20 years, but the best general references are the 1971 book *The Anatomy of Rhetoric* (Philadelphia: Center for Curriculum Development) and the 1983 article "An Introduction to the Study of Written Texts: The 'Discourse Compact,'" (in R. B. Kaplan, R. L. Jones, & G. R. Tucker (Eds.), *Annual Review of Applied Linguistics*, Vol. III, pp. 138-151. Rowley, MA: Newbury House).

4. The terms *emic* and *etic* were coined by Pike in 1954 (see Pike 1967). More recently, he offers the following definition:

> Every repeatable or identifiable unit of human experience has a range of variation within it, or in the human's perception or experience or imagination of it. . . . The stance varies, and the sensations with it, even when the flowing river remains the same or the table is still a table. The persistence of units seen via their identificational-contrastive features, along with variableness in these units, forces us to a theoretical position for all of rational behavior (not just linguistics). Such a persistent, perceptual unit is termed an *emic* one . . . —an entity seen as the "same" from the perspective of the internal logic of the containing system, as if it were unchanging even when the outside analyst perceives that change. (Meanwhile, the term *etic* . . . labels the point of view of the outsider as he tries to penetrate a system alien to him; and it also labels some component of an emic unit, or some variant of it, or some preliminary guess at the presence of internal emic units, as seen either by the alien observer or as seen by the internal observer when somehow he becomes explicitly aware of such variants through teaching or techniques provided by outsiders.) (1982, xii)

5. It was the partial dependence on the paradigm of contrastive linguistics that gave rise to the word contrastive in the designation "contrastive rhetoric."

6. The article "Cultural Thought Patterns in Intercultural Education," for

example, has been criticized for failing to comment on the writing of speakers of European languages; the fact is that, at the particular moment in the history of foreign-student flows to U. S. tertiary education, there were relatively few speakers of European languages other than Spanish in the population (i.e., 11% of the sample analyzed in that article consisted of Spanish speakers, and there were three speakers of French, two speakers of Italian, and no speakers of, for example, Croatian, Danish, Dutch, Finnish, German, Hungarian, Norwegian, Polish, Serbian, Swedish, or any of the Slavic languages of the Soviet Union). Furthermore, the available demographic data did not specify the native language of individuals, but identified them by the kind of passport they held; thus, assumptions had to be made about native language in some cases. Finally, the makeup of the population forced a rather artificial categorization of the population, putting together in an undifferentiated group, speakers of, for example, Chinese, Japanese, and Korean—groups among which subsequent study has shown significant differences exist.

   7. Notional/functional syllabi represent an approach to language teaching in which the basic subject of instruction is neither grammatical nor situational but is predicated on the kinds of activities speakers are likely to perform.

> The term . . . function represents a semantic category that identifies individual purpose in using language. Function names are typically given as gerundive nouns (e.g., offering help, accepting), thereby emphasizing their role as units of language-as-action. They have been grouped according to the nature of their purpose. . . . The term notion also represents a semantic category, but it is a unit of language-as-reference; i.e., it concerns what we talk about rather than what we talk for. General notions are defined as those that cut across many different types of language use (e.g., location, sequence, class, cause and effect), and are called . . . semantico-grammatical categories, thereby reflecting their direct connection with realization systems. Specific notions are those deriving from a particular topic of language-use and being realized not by a linguistic category but by a limited range of possible exponents. Functions and notions are both components of . . . "meaning potential"; i. e., what the language user can mean. They are semantic options concerning what the language user can do within any social or purely personal context of situation, and they are realized by sets of linguistic options selected on the basis of languaging competence. (Barnett 1981, p. 45)

   8. Communicative approaches arose in reaction to the structural approaches popular earlier in the second half of this century; if one can date the period of structuralist influence from c. 1945 to c. 1965, then it is possible to claim that communicative approaches have occupied the time since 1965, and perhaps most influentially since 1975. They may be contrasted in the following ways:

Structural Approaches	Communicative Approaches
Focus of learning is on language as a structured system of grammatical patterns.	Focus is on communication

Structural Approaches	Communicative Approaches
Language items are selected on linguistic criteria alone.	Language items are selected on the basis of what the learner needs to know to get something done using language.
Language items are sequenced on linguistic grounds.	Sequencing is determined by meaning and need.
The aim is to cover the whole language system in linear progression.	The aim is to cover only what the learner needs at each stage of development.
A language is seen as a unified entity with fixed grammatical patterns and a core of basic words.	The variety of language is accepted; it is seen to be determined by the character of particular communicative contexts.
Language used tends to be formal and bookish.	Language is genuine "everyday" language; texts are supposed to be "authentic."
Objective is to have learners produce formally correct sentences.	Objective is to have learners communicate effectively.
Reading and writing tend to be emphasized.	Spoken interactions between people are seen as at least as important as reading and writing.
Tends to be teacher-centered.	Tends to be learner-centered.
Sees incorrect utterances as deviations from the norm to be corrected.	Accepts the notion of "interlanguage"— partially correct and/or incomplete utterances—as a necessary developmental stage.

9. The notion product is not as simple as it seems. Proponents of the "process approach" concentrate on the composing activity by working on revisions that occur before a "final" draft is prepared; proponents of the "product approach" stress the importance of rewriting the submitted draft after it has been commented upon by the teacher. The fact is that both approaches recognize the instability of a given draft. A major difference between the two approaches comes down largely only to the question of the point at which the teacher can safely intervene.

10. Recent research among students learning English as a foreign language in the People's Republic of China, for example, suggests that a significant number of "sentences" written by this population are literal translations of Mandarin structures, which can be deciphered only by bilingual Mandarin/English speakers who have the ability to back-translate such structures.

11. The term morphosyntax refers to the grammar of a language; indeed, traditionally, grammar has been seen as having two components—morphology and syntax—in which morphology deals with the internal structure of words while syntax deals with the ordering of words in sentences. In most contemporary grammars, the two are seen as linked and as operating from the basis of discoverable rules. However, in contemporary grammars, morphology is not concerned with word forms per se, but

with morphemes, which are basic irreducible units of language that may be coterminous with, or larger than, or smaller than words. If one accepts Halliday's conceptualization (Halliday & Hasan, 1976), it is clear that cohesive devices are at base morphosyntactic (or lexico-grammatical). Coherence is less clearly morphosyntactic, though there are morphosyntactic considerations that to some extent govern the logico-semantic nature of coherence. It is argued here that a learner must have basic competence in the grammar of the language before he or she can be concerned with composing; or to put it another way, despite the fact that a learner may be working at composing, if he or she does not have minimal control of the grammar, the communication gets lost in syntactic mazes, inappropriate syntactic and/or morphological choices, resulting in inappropriate focus, topicalization, thematization, and so on, and/or other substantial grammar-based misconstrual. The point applies to second/foreign-language learners more than to native speakers, though it would seem that victims of certain aphasias affecting grammatical control might serve as examples of the need for morphosyntactic control as a precondition to composing (i.e., to writing beyond the level of writing without composing).

REFERENCES

Bander, R. G. (1971). *American English Rhetoric*. New York: Holt, Rinehart and Winston.

Barnett, J. (1981). Notional/functional approaches. In R. B. Kaplan, R. L. Jones, & G. R. Tucker (Eds.), *Annual Review of Applied Linguistics* (Vol. I, pp. 43-57). Rowley, MA: Newbury House.

Berlin, J. A. (1984). *Writing instruction in nineteenth century American colleges*. Carbondale: Southern Illinois University Press.

Biber, D. (1984a). *A model of textual relations within the written and spoken modes*. Unpublished doctoral dissertation, University of Southern California.

Biber, D. (1984b, November). *A textual comparison of British and American writing*. Paper presented at NWAVE XIII, Philadelphia.

Brooks, C., & Warren, R. P. (1958). *Modern rhetoric*. New York: Harcourt Brace.

Caramazza, A., & McCloskey, M. (1981). Theory and problems in psycho-linguistics. In R. B. Kaplan, R. L. Jones, & G. R. Tucker (Eds.), *Annual review of applied linguistics* (Vol. I, pp. 71-90). Rowley, MA: Newbury House.

Carrell, P. L. (1984a). Evidence of a formal schema in second language comprehension. *Language Learning, 34*(2), 87-112.

Carrell, P. L. (1984b). The effects of rhetorical organization in ESL readers. *TESOL Quarterly, 18*(3), 441-469.

Carrell, P. L. (1984c, March). Some causes of text-boundedness and schema interface in ESL reading. Paper presented at the 18th Annual TESOL Conference, Houston.

Christensen, F. (1963). A generative rhetoric of the sentence. *CCC, 14*, 155-161.

Connor, U. (1987). Argumentative patterns in student essays: Cross-cultural differences. In U. Connor & R. B. Kaplan (Eds.), *Writing across languages: Analysis of L2 Text* (pp. 57-71). Reading, MA: Addison-Wesley.

302

Summing Up

Curran, C. (1976). *Counseling-learning in Second Languages.* Apple River, WI: Apple River.

Dubin, F., Eskey, D. E., & Grabe, W. (Eds.). (1986). *Teaching Second Language Reading for Academic Purposes.* Reading, MA: Addison-Wesley.

Dubois, B. L. (1982). The construction of noun phrases in biomedical journal articles. In J. Hoedt et al. (Eds.), *Pragmatics in LSP* (pp. 49-67). Copenhagen: School of Economics.

Enkvist, N. E. (1957). Text linguistics for the applier: An orientation. In U. Connor & R. B. Kaplan (Eds.), *Writing across Languages: Analysis of L2 Text* (pp. 23-43). Reading, MA: Addison-Wesley.

Flower, L. (1979). Writer-based prose: A cognitive basis for problems in writing. *College English, 41,* 19-37.

Gattegno, C. (1972). *Teaching Foreign Languages in Schools: The Silent Way.* New York: Educational Solutions.

Grabe, W. (1984). *Towards defining expository prose within a theory of text construction.* Unpublished doctoral dissertation, University of Southern California.

Grabe, W. (1987). Contrastive rhetoric and text-type research. In U. Connor & R. B. Kaplan (Eds.), *Writing across Languages: Analysis of L2 Text.* (pp. 115-137). Reading, MA: Addison-Wesley.

Guzman Lagos, C. A. (1983). *Statistical analysis of the forms and functions of the noun phrase in the written English of science and technology.* Unpublished doctoral dissertation, University of Texas.

Hairston, M. (1982). The winds of change: Thomas Kuhn and the revolution in the teaching of writing. *CCC, 33,* 76-88.

Halliday, M.A.K., & Hasan, R. (1976). *Cohesion in English.* London: Longman.

Heslot, J. (1982). Tense and other indexical markers in the typology of scientific texts in English. In J. Hoedt et al. (Eds.), *Pragmatics and LSP.* (pp. 83-103). Copenhagen: School of Economics.

Hinds, J. (1979). Organizational patterns in discourse. In T. Givon (Ed.), *Syntax and Semantics 12: Discourse and Syntax.* (pp. 135-157). New York: Academic Press.

Hinds, J. (1983a). Contrastive Rhetoric: Japanese and English. *Text, 3*(2), 183-195.

Hinds, J. (1983b). Linguistic and written discourse in particular languages. Contrastive studies: English and Japanese. In R. B. Kaplan, R. L. Jones, & G. R. Tucker (Eds.), *Annual review of applied linguistics* (Vol. III, pp. 78-84). Rowley, MA: Newbury House.

Hinds, J. (1986). Reader versus writer responsibility: A new typology. In U. Connor & R. B. Kaplan (Eds.), *Writing across Languages: Analysis of L2 Text.* (pp. 141-152). Reading, MA: Addison-Wesley.

Hong Kong Examinations Authority. (1986). *The work of the Hong Kong examinations authority 1977-1986.* Hong Kong: Author.

Houghton, D., & Hoey, M. (1983). Linguistics and written discourse: Contrastive rhetorics. In R. B. Kaplan, R. L. Jones, & G. R. Tucker (Eds.), *Annual Review of Applied Linguistics, III.* (pp. 2-22). Rowley, MA: Newbury House.

Huckin, T. N., & Olsen, L. A. (1980). Noun compounding in EST. (Material circulated at the Conference on Teaching Scientific and Technical English to Non-Native Speakers of English.) Ann Arbor: University of Michigan.

Huckin, T. N., & Olsen, L. A. (1981). Teaching the use of the article in EST. In L. Selinker, E. Tarone, & V. Hanzeli (Eds.), *English for academic and technical purposes: Studies in honor of Louis Trimble.* (pp. 165-192). Rowley, MA: Newbury House.

Josifek, J. L. (1983). *Toward a descriptive analysis and ESP pedagogy of infinitival and gerundive complements to nouns.* Unpublished doctoral dissertation, Ohio State University.

Kaplan, R. B., & Shaw, P. A. (1983). *Exploring academic discourse.* Rowley, MA: Newbury House.

Knoblauch, C. H., & Brannon, L. (1984). *Rhetorical tradition and the teaching of writing.* Upper Montclair, NJ: Boynton/Cook.

Krashen, S. D., & Terrell, T. D. (1983). *The natural approach: Language acquisition in the classroom.* Hayward, CA: Alemany.

Latorre, G. (1983). The binary structure of complex nominals in technical manuals. *English for Specific Purposes, 79,* 1-4.

Lozanov, G. (1979). *Suggestology and Outlines of Suggestopedia.* New York: Gordon & Brech Science.

Maldonado, P., & Guzman, A. (1984). Forms and functions of the noun phrases in EST. *English for Specific Purposes, 79,* 4-8.

Meyer, B.J.F. (1975a). Identification of the structure of prose and its implications for the study of reading and memory. *Journal of Reading Behavior, 7,* 7-47.

Meyer, B.J.F. (1975b). *The organization of prose and its effects on memory.* Amsterdam, The Netherlands: North Holland.

Meyer, B.J.F. (1977). The structure of prose: Effects on learning and memory and implications for educational practice. In R. C. Anderson, R. J. Spiro, & W. E. Montague (Eds.), *Schooling and the acquisition of knowledge* (pp. 179-200). Hillsdale, NJ: Lawrence Erlbaum.

Meyer, B.J.F. (1982). Reading research and the composition teacher: The importance of plans. *CCC, 33,* 37-49.

Mohan, B. A., & Lo, W.A.Y. (1985). Academic writing and Chinese students: Transfer and developmental factors. *TESOL Quarterly, 19*(3), 515-533.

Munby, J. (1978). *Communicative syllabus design.* Cambridge: Cambridge University Press.

Neu, J. (1985). *A multivariate linguistic analysis of business negotiations.* Unpublished doctoral dissertation, University of Southern California.

Ostler, S. E. (1987). English in parallels: A comparison of English and Arabic prose. In U. Connor & R. B. Kaplan (Eds.), *Writing across languages: Analysis of L2 text* (pp. 169-185). Reading, MA: Addison-Wesley.

Perelman, L. (1986). The context of classroom writing. *College English, 48*(5), 471-479.

Pike, K. L. (1982). *Linguistic concepts: An introduction to tagmemics.* Lincoln: University of Nebraska Press.

Pike, K. L. (1967). *Language in relation to a unified theory of structure of human behavior* (2nd ed.). The Hague: Mouton.

Pytlik, B. P. (1982). *Decision style, purpose of discourse, and direction of communication: The impact on writing styles of selected accountants in a big eight accounting firm.* Unpublished doctoral dissertation, University of Southern California.

Quinn, T. J. (1985). Functional approaches in language pedagogy. In R. B. Kaplan, R. L. Jones, & G. R. Tucker (Eds.), *Annual Review of Applied Linguistics* (Vol. V, pp. 60-80). New York: Cambridge University Press.

Rankin, D. S. (1985). *Coherence and cohesion: A discourse analysis comparing professional writing for adults, professional writing for children, and children's own writing at two grade levels.* Unpublished doctoral dissertation, University of Southern California.

Reichman-Adar, R. (1984). Technical discourse: The present progressive tense, the deitic "that" and pronominalizational. *Discourse Processes, 7,* 337-369.

Rottweiler, G. P. (1984). *Systematic cohesion in published general academic English: Analysis and register description.* Unpublished doctoral disseration, Rutgers University.

Santana-Seda, O., Sr. (1974). *A contrastive study in rhetoric: An analysis of the organization of English and Spanish paragraphs written by native speakers of each language.* Unpublished doctoral dissertation. New York University.

Santiago, R. (1968). *A contrastive analysis of some rhetorical aspects of writing in Spanish and English in Spanish-speaking college students in Puerto Rico.* Unpublished doctoral dissertation, Columbia University.

Searle, J. R. (1969). *Speech Acts.* Cambridge: Cambridge University Press.

Sellers, N. J. (1982). Modals and models in English for academic purposes: Science and technology. Unpublished doctoral dissertation, University of Florida.

Trimble, M. T., & Trimble, L. (1982). Rhetorical-grammatical features of scientific and technical texts as a major factor in written ESP communication. In J. Hoedt et al. (Eds.), *Proceedings of the third European symposium on LSP* (pp. 199-216). Copenhagen: School of Economics.

Trimble, M. T., & Trimble, L. (1985). Article use in reading scientific and technical English discourse. In J. M. Ulijin & A. K. Pugh (Eds.), *Reading for professional purposes: Methods and materials in teaching languages* (pp. 71-89). Leuwea: ACCO.

Trueba, H. T. (1986). Bilingualism and bilingual education (1984-1985). In R. B. Kaplan, R. L. Jones, & G. R. Tucker (Eds.), *Annual Review of Applied Linguistics, VI.* (pp. 47-64). New York: Cambridge University Press.

Tsao, F. F. (1983). Linguistics and written discourse in particular languages: Contrastive studies: English and Chinese (Mandarin). In R. B. Kaplan, R. L. Jones, & G. R. Tucker (Eds.), *Annual review of applied linguistics,* (Vol. III, pp. 99-117). Rowley, MA: Newbury House.

West, G. K. (1980). That-nominal constructions in traditional rhetorical divisions of scientific research papers. *TESOL Quarterly, 14*(4), 483-488.

Widdowson, H. G. (1984). *Explorations in Applied Linguistics* (Vol. 2). Oxford: Oxford University Press.

Wilkerson, B. M. (1986). On the principles of coherence in English academic, expository prose. Unpublished paper, Meiji University, Tokyo.

About the Authors

Robert Bickner first studied Thai as a U.S. Peace Corps volunteer in Thailand, where he taught ESL and related courses. He received an M.A. in Asian studies from the University of Michigan in 1977, and a Ph.D. in linguistics in 1981. He has since taught in and administered ESL programs in the United States, and now teaches Thai language and literature at the University of Wisconsin-Madison, where he is also Director of the college Year in Thailand program.

Sybil B. Carlson was an Associate Research Scientist in the Division of Educational Policy Research and Services, Educational Testing Service. She has directed, or codirected, the following writing assessment research projects: Survey of Academic Writing Tasks Required of Foreign Students in Undergraduate and Graduate U.S. Institutions, A Profile of Preparation in English—Part V, Relationships of Admissions Test Scores to Writing Performance of Native and Nonnative Speakers of English, an ETS development project on The Direct Assessment of Writing Abilities, the review of the Maryland Functional Writing Test, and Part I of the ETS creative writing component of a Rockefeller Foundation effort to design innovative approaches to assessment in the arts. She currently is directing a writing assessment research project, Relationships of Thinking and Writing Skills to GRE Analytical Ability Scores, recommendations for the design of a prototype for the computer delivery of open-ended items, and software development for her recent book, *Creative Classroom Testing*. She has published many reports and articles on the various projects. Her most recent publication is a coauthored chapter on "Testing ESL Student Writers" in the forthcoming book, *Writing Assessment: Issues and Strategies* (K. Greenberg, J. Wiener, & R. Donovan, Editors; Longman). She also consults with individuals and organizations on the design of writing assessment programs.

Ulla Connor is Associate Professor of English at Indiana University in Indianapolis where she teaches linguistics and writing and coordinates the ESL program. She is coeditor of a recent book (with Robert B. Kaplan) *Writing Across Languages: Analysis of L2 Text.* She serves on the Editorial Advisory Board of *TESOL Quarterly.* Her research on second-language reading and writing has been published in such journals as *Applied Linguistics, Language Learning, TESOL Quarterly,* and *Text.*

R. Elaine Degenhart, special researcher at the Institute for Educational Research, University of Jyväskylä, Finland, received her undergraduate education at DePauw University, Greencastle, Indiana, and her Ph.D. from the University of Illinois at Urbana-Champaign. Her research areas include foreign language education, bilingual/multilingual education, comparative education, and written composition in mother-tongue and language of instruction. Her publications include chapters in the recent national report (edited by W. Devahastin and P. Methakunavudhi), *Achievement in Written Composition in Thailand* (Bangkok, 1986). She is currently the International Coordinator of the IEA, International Study of Achievement in Written Composition.

Chantanee Indrasuta was born in Bangkok, Thailand. She graduated with a Bachelor of Arts degree and a Bachelor of Education degree from Chulalongkorn University, Thailand in 1964 and 1968, respectively. After that she was awarded a Master of Arts in TESOL from the University of New Mexico in 1977, and a Ph.D. in second language acquisition and teacher education from the University of Illinois, Urbana-Champaign in 1987. In addition, she was awarded a scholarship from Southeast Asia Ministers of Education Organization (SEAMEO) in 1976, and a scholarship from the Colombo Plan in 1981. She is now a Lecturer at Petchburiwittayalongkorn Teachers College, Pathumthani, Thailand.

Yamuna Kachru, Professor of Linguistics and Professor of English at the University of Illinois at Urbana-Champaign, has published several books and papers on the syntax, semantics, and discourse structure of Hindi. She has also published papers on writing conventions in nonnative varieties of English, second language acquisition research, stylistics, and bilingual lexicography. Currently, she is working on the topic of how the writing conventions of a first language influence the thetorical conventions of writing in a second or additional language in a multilingual community.

Judit Kádár-Fülop, Ph.D., is Senior Research Officer of the National Institute for Education, Budapest, Hungary. Her research interests include educational measurement, reading and writing education, text-linguistics, pragmatics, and the theory of education. She is Research Coordinator of the IEA Written Composition Study in Hungary. She has published in the area of measurement and teaching of reading comprehension and written composition.

Robert B. Kaplan, Ph.D., is Professor of Applied Linguistics at the University of Southern California. He has long been interested in contrastive rhetoric and in the pedagogical implications of text linguistics, particularly in ESL. He currently serves as Editor-in-Chief of the *Annual Review of Applied Linguistics* and has published widely in major journals in the United States, Asia, and Europe. He has also been interested in international educational exchanges and has served as President of the National Association for Foreign Student Affairs.

Janice Lauer is Professor of English and Director of the Graduate Program in Rhetoric and Composition at Purdue University. She is the author of *Four Worlds of Writing* and *Composition Research: Empirical Designs;* and essays in journals, such as *CCC, Rhetoric Review,* and *Rhetoric Society Quarterly.* She directs an annual two-week summer rhetoric seminar, Current Theories of Teaching Composition, is Chair of the College Section of NCTE, and a member of the executive committee of the MLA Discussion Group on the History and Theory of Rhetoric.

Young Mok Park received his Ph.D. in Educational Psychology from the University of Illinois with a specialization in measurement with a particular focus on language learning. His dissertation included a comprehensive analysis of the GRE-TOEFL data, and, in particular, the analysis of raters and tasks with different language groups. He has worked for the National Council of Korean Language and in the Office of Supervision of the Korean Ministry of Education.

Patcharin Peyasantiwong received her Ph.D. in Linguistics from the University of Michigan in 1981. She has taught both English and Thai in her native Thailand. She has taught ESL at the University of Michigan and, since 1981, for the public school system of Madison, Wisconsin. She has taught Thai at the University of Michigan and the University of Wisconsin-Madison, and has twice served as Field Director of the Advanced Summer Thai at Chiang Mai program.

Alan C. Purves is Professor of Education and Humanities at the State University of New York at Albany. Formerly, Chairman of IEA Study of Written Composition, he is now Chairman of IEA, which is undertaking a continuing series of assessment of learning in various subjects. His work on contrastive rhetoric follows his earlier work on the comparisons of responses to literature involving students from various countries.

Anna O. Söter received her Ph.D. in education from the University of Illinois at Urbana-Champaign in 1985. She is currently Assistant Professor of English Education at Ohio State University, Columbus, and is investigating rhetorical transfer in English students writing in Japanese, with with Dr. Keiko Koda at Ohio University, Athens, Ohio.

Sauli Takala, special researcher at the Institute for Educational Research, University of Jyväskylä, Finland, received his B.A. and M.A. degrees in English and education from the University of Jyväskylä, and his Ph.D. in education psychology at the University of Illinois at Urbana-Champaign. He is currently the Director of the Center for the Study of Language Teaching and Learning at the University of Jyvaskyla. During the academic year 1986-1987 he has been a visiting Associate Professor of Foreign Language pedagogy at the University of Helsinki. He has been the International Coordinator of the IEA Study of Achievement in Written Composition from its beginning in 1981 to 1986 and continues with the study as a senior technical advisor. Among his many publications are English language textbooks, technical research reports in the Institute's report series, and articles in major journals, such as the *Comparative*

Educational Review, Language Learning, and *Evaluation in Education.* He also serves as an Editor of *Kasvatus,* the Finnish journal of education. His special research interests include second language teaching and learning and he is actively involved in the organization and teaching of the in-service education of language teachers in Finland.

Anneli Vähäpassi, senior research officer at the Institute for Educational Research, University of Jyväskylä, Finland, has been in charge of the Mother-Tongue Teaching Evaluation Project since 1975. The project has developed national curricula for the comprehensive and senior academic secondary school on a theoretical and empirical basis and has undertaken research on student achievement in reading and writing. In addition to her scholarly writing and presentations, she is a workshop and convention leader in the in-service training of teachers across the country, and is involved in textbook writing. She chairs the International Steering Committee of the IEA Writing Study and has also participated in the international work of OECD, UNESCO, and Council of Europe in the area of writing and reading. Her publications in Finnish include reports of Mother-Tongue Teaching, reading and writing, and curriculum and evaluation research. Her main publications written in English are on the specification of the domain of school writing, *Written Communication as an Object of Comparative Research* (together with Sauli Takala), and *Providing Literacy Instruction to Young People: The Main Issues.*

NOTES

NOTES